BOOK SALE
Solano College Library

D1443257

FOCUSED EXPRESSIVE PSYCHOTHERAPY

Focused Expressive Psychotherapy

FREEING THE OVERCONTROLLED PATIENT

ROGER J. DALDRUP, PhD
LARRY E. BEUTLER, PhD
DAVID ENGLE, PhD
University of Arizona, Tucson

LESLIE S. GREENBERG, PhD
York University, Toronto

THE GUILFORD PRESS
New York   London

© 1988 The Guilford Press
A Division of Guilford Publications, Inc.
72 Spring Street, New York, NY 10012

Printed in the United States of America

The paper used in this publication meets the minimum requirements of
American National Standard for Information Sciences—Permanence of
Paper for Printed Library Materials, ANSI Z39.48-1984.   ∞

Last digit is print number: 9 8 7 6 5 4 3 2 1

Library of Congress Cataloging-in-Publication Data

Focused expressive psychotherapy : freeing the overcontrolled patient
  / Roger J. Daldrup . . . [et al.].
    p.   cm.
  Bibliography: p.
  Includes index.
  ISBN 0-89862-729-X
  1. Focused expressive psychotherapy. I. Daldrup, Roger J.
RC489.F62F63   1988
616.89′14—dc 19   88-21183
                                                        CIP

R. J. D.: To my parents, who blessed me with a full range of feelings

L. E. B.: To the memory of my father

D. E.: To my wife, Jeanne

L. S. G.: To my family

Preface

This manual represents a compilation of data and information obtained from more than 60 years of our accumulated clinical experience, as well as a decade of conducting training in focused expressive psychotherapy (FEP) at the university graduate level. In addition, we have been conducting research in medical settings on FEP for the past 7 years. Although the original development of the model predates the research efforts, refinements in principles, techniques, and process have been made as a result of research funded by the National Institute of Mental Health (Grant No. MH39859), for which Larry E. Beutler served as Principal Investigator, Roger J. Daldrup was Co-Principal Investigator, David Engle acted as Project Coordinator, and Leslie S. Greenberg provided consulting services.

After an initial pilot training workshop, a structure was developed for the training, from which this manual was then written. The research has focused on the effectiveness of the training program, as well as on the efficacy of FEP as a treatment modality for various patient populations. Instruments for monitoring compliance have been developed following the model for compliance rating devised by Beck, Rush, Shaw, and Emery (1979), using the principles of FEP as described in the present work. Although some data are still in the process of being analyzed, preliminary results indicate that significant training differences are obtained by following the manual for FEP.

The manual is designed to provide the therapist with the theoretical assumptions underlying FEP. These assumptions fit the purpose of assisting the patient in dealing with unfinished emotional business. This model of therapy is particularly appropriate for the overcontrolled patient who has difficulty in full expression of self, especially at the affective level. In FEP, there are defined roles and responsibilities for both the patient and the therapist.

A five-step process is followed in the implementation of FEP. First, the therapist assists the patient in identifying some unfinished business with a significant other that could be the focus of the session. Second, a commitment is elicited from the patient to work with the identified significant other.

Third, appropriate work experiments are developed to assist the patient in confronting the unfinished business. As each experiment proceeds, it is evaluated continuously so that changes can be made as appropriate to the patient's needs. At the end of the experiment, the patient assesses what has been accomplished or learned by doing the work. Finally, the therapist and patient develop plans for carrying on the work outside the session. This book is organized around these steps.

A working assumption in designing the manual is that the reader has a foundation in Gestalt theory and practice, so basic principles of Gestalt therapy are not emphasized in favor of depth of coverage in FEP. If the reader lacks this foundation, we recommend becoming familiar with Perls's (1973) *The Gestalt Approach and Eyewitness to Therapy* and the Polsters' (1973) *Gestalt Therapy Integrated.* An understanding of splits, unfinished business, and boundary disturbances is essential to the implementation of FEP.

In our research efforts, we are thankful to our medical consultants, Rebecca Potter, MD, and Arnold Nelson, MD; to our therapists, Marjorie Holiman, PhD, James Schelble, PhD, John Barbour, PhD, and Elizabeth Ziebell, PhD; and to our research assistants, Scott Collier, Trish Downer, Anne Corbishley, Glenn Stebbins III, Tina Glueck, Paul Guest, Paul Nussbaum, and Rick Hendrickson. During our international cross-cultural research on FEP training, we have depended upon the support and assistance of David Shapiro, PhD, of the University of Sheffield, England, and his associate, Ginny Firth; in Belgium, we received the cooperation of Winfrid Huber, PhD, Université Catholique de Louvain; and in Athens, Greece, Eugenia Nika-Vazakas has provided us with important data on the use of FEP there.

We are grateful to our patients for hours of sharing their innermost selves in trusting ways so that the principles and procedures included in this manual could be observed in actual practice. We are also indebted to the numerous trainees who challenged and helped refine our ideas about FEP. To the many people who have given us reports on how they have used FEP to enhance their therapeutic practice, and their lives in general, we are appreciative. A special appreciation is extended to David Wachter for his expertise with the word processor and for his ability to incorporate the editorial notes of four coauthors into a coherent manuscript.

R. J. D.

L. E. B.

D. E.

L. S. G.

Contents

FOCUSED EXPRESSIVE PSYCHOTHERAPY

1

Introduction

Focused expressive psychotherapy (FEP) is an experiential method for resolving suppressed, unfinished emotional reactions—emotions that are experienced but are not allowed to be expressed to the point of natural completion and resolution. In this therapeutic approach, primary attention is given to the range of emotions that relate to anger. The process includes the arousal of anger, its directed expression, and the natural recovery and relief that come after completed expression. The approach is based on principles of Gestalt psychotherapy, but many of the concepts and techniques can be seen as adjunctive to other theories and may serve the specific needs of patients with constricted affect.

Though FEP follows naturally from Gestalt theory, an acceptance of this theory is probably not necessary for effective practice of the techniques embodied in the procedure. Nonetheless, it may be advantageous for the practitioner who plans to use this method to acknowledge the view of development and change encapsulated by this theoretical perspective and to recognize the theoretical assumptions that follow from such a philosophy. In the current volume, this philosophy is described and the roles of therapist and patient are delineated. The processes of therapy dictated by FEP are outlined, along with appropriate methodologies for their implementation. In addition, the volume presents a set of procedures for clinically evaluating therapeutic movement.

A Position on Persons

FEP, like Gestalt therapy more generally, is based on a wholistic theory of personhood. This theory considers people to be fundamentally integrated organisms who interact in a continuous fashion with their environments. Other things being equal, interactions among the external environment and one's behavioral, cognitive, affective, and sensory experiences are smooth, unhampered, and balanced. Experiences are perceived realistically and smoothly integrated into a remembrance of past relationships. From these remembrances, workable expectancies are developed, and each new expe-

1

rience changes these expectancies without distorting the meaning or experiencing of events. Each experience is accepted, analyzed, and integrated completely within the existing set of expectancies. Cognitive, affective, sensory, and behavioral systems, in turn, are in constant interaction with the environment; through this interaction, people develop a conceptual view or integrated representation (i.e., a Gestalt) of the world and their position within it (Kaplan & Kaplan, 1985).

Unfortunately, all things are not equal, and individuals invariably come to "split" or defensively disown various of their experiences. For sundry reasons, sanctions are developed against acknowledging or taking responsibility for certain experiences, especially those related to sensing and feeling. Disowning occurs either because experiences are aborted and terminated before integration is possible or because rules exist against accepting certain types of experience. Because these experiences are not owned, they do not smoothly fit with either prior or present experiences, and thereafter intrude upon and distort new experiences.

Schemas

People's world views are composed of cognitive–affective schemas, which, when evoked by eliciting cues, govern conscious experience. A "schema," according to Leventhal and Everhart (1979), is the representation of a specific emotional experience that has taken place in the past, as well as the key perceptual features that have elicited the emotional responses to stimuli. Schemas link eliciting stimuli to emotional experience through a type of emotional learning, and result in automatic emotional responses. Schematic processing links specific expressive motor behaviors to an infinite variety of eliciting stimuli. To the degree that people are aware of current experiences, their world views or schemas can be appropriately modified with the accumulation of new experiences; to the degree that disowned past experiences color current perceptions, people's evolving schematic world views and cognitive representations are distorted and fragmented. When schematic representations of the world include injunctions against encountering certain types of experience, sensitivity to one's present internal and/or external environment is invariably reduced. Since the natural tendency of an integration-seeking organism is to retain a perception of congruence as applied to one's experience, disowned experiences are excluded from awareness. In order to preserve the illusion of constancy, incoming new and nonconfirmatory experiences are frequently made to appear consistent, but they do so at the expense of adaptable and controllable responses.

The way in which experience is distorted is governed by the internal representations or schemas that implement the injunctions against encountering certain kinds of cognitive, sensory, or affective stimuli. These internal representations or schemas, then, are the primary targets of therapeutic change. As schemas are modified in order to accommodate a wider variety of experience and sensory cues, an individual's reactions to the environment will change and the environment's reaction to the individual will also change, producing a reciprocating cycle (Greenberg & Safran, 1984).

Responsibility for Reactions

Since people are able to select from among a variety of responses for any given situation, they are considered, within the Gestalt framework, to be responsible for their interactions with the environment. To the degree that they increase their awareness of response alternatives, they also increase their "response-ability." The theory holds that people are competent organisms who are capable of governing and responding to the reactions they have to others, and in turn of coping with the ways that others respond to them. In this context, "coping" refers to the selection of a response alternative that seems most likely to retain constancy in one's perceptual representation of the world. One's coping responses are constrained, however, by the ways in which one's views of the environment are internally constricted and misrepresented.

Gestalt theory proposes that individuals' current actions are unknowingly influenced, through the medium of their schematic representations, by past experiences that have not been accepted and assimilated. This influence occurs when an individual does not integrate various sensory, cognitive, and affective experiences into a conscious view of the world. If these experiences have not been integrated into a consistent, perceptual Gestalt, they impede the individual's ability either to act in response to present events or to plan for future events.

Early Influences

It is a postulate of FEP that parental figures exert a strong influence on how a person views and acts in the present, as well as on how a person prepares for and looks towards the future. This viewpoint is comparable to Adler's (1930) position regarding the significance of parental influences early in life and their pervasiveness in later behavior. Likewise, the Gouldings (1979) take a position similar to the one taken here when they maintain, "Most clients are still repressing the emotions that were unacceptable in their childhood homes. They use, as substitutes for happiness, the emotions that were rewarded or allowed" (p. 113). Thus people learn to suppress the emotions that were not allowed and to express those that were encouraged in their families.

Range of Emotions

Gestalt therapy, and its derivative, FEP, more specifically, assume that people possess the capacity for the full range of opposite emotions, whether these are directed toward parents, siblings, or significant others in their lives. Emotions can be thought of a polarities of experience (Plutchick, 1980) in which different emotions represent opposite ends of continua—from love to hate, from sadness to joy, from fear to excitement. A dialectical perspective in which opposites are seen as being synthesized to form new solutions is helpful in understanding the process of change in FEP. Indeed, it is assumed that everyone actually experiences the full range of these feelings, although they may not be acknowledged or allowed awareness within some channels of experience (e.g., they may be experienced at the sensory but not at the cognitive level). Thus, failure to access the emotions at both ends of a continuum reflects an unwillingness to attend to certain aspects of current sensory or affective experiences. This unwillingness accrues from social fears (fantasies) and past histories (memories), which may be manifest as useless and unproductive value judgments. FEP directs itself to countermanding the value judgments that are made about emotions in order to prevent their expression, and to promoting an experience of the full range of emotions and their synthesis.

Theoretical Assumptions Regarding Emotions

In general, it is assumed that there are no "good" or "bad" emotions; emotions simply exist. Consequently, value can only be placed upon what is done with emotions, not upon the class or set of emotions that is being experienced. It is assumed that people choose to react in certain ways to their internalized representations of life, and, as such, that they are responsible for choosing those reactions. Moreover, it is assumed that individuals play an active role in determining their representations of the world by selecting, from among all possible events and stimuli, only those that best assist them to retain their pre-existing viewpoints and behaviors.

Parental Influence

Strategies for recognizing, blocking, or otherwise reconciling emotions, especially anger, hurt, and love, are learned early in childhood through the unquestioning adoption of the sanctions and representational systems of significant others. Usually, this training comes from parents (Rubin, 1969) and invariably locks present events under the control of past contracts or experiences. These early decisions about how one "ought to" deal with emotional events carry over into adult life, sometimes appropriately and many times inappropriately. "Appropriateness" is defined both in terms of the unrewarding consequences of one's actions and, more specifically, in terms of the degree to which these present decisions assist in integrating current with past experiences. The retention of past decisions typically serves the purpose of holding onto pre-existing viewpoints and of retaining (i.e., freezing) in memory valued or feared portions of past relationships, allowing these past influences to unduly determine current perceptions and abilities to change.

Whatever is not resolved in the relationship with parents as the child moves through the developmental stages of adulthood is often carried over to relationships with significant others in intimate, loving relationships (e.g., lovers, spouses) or with children and/or siblings.

Completion of the Emotional Cycle

Emotional intensity is assumed to coincide with the cyclical nature of biological systems. We take in, digest, use, and integrate experiences that are nurturing and nourishing, while at the same time expelling or disowning those that are judged to be inconsistent and threatening to our perceptual Gestalt. Emotional reactions can be left incomplete or unfinished through rationalization, intellectualized judgments, or denial. On the other hand, these reactions can be completed, finished, or resolved through intellectual, physical, and emotional expression directed at the source—for example, when a person is verbally expressing an emotional reaction within the context of a physical response to a significant other. Once a disowned feeling (e.g., anger) is aroused and expressed, there is a release of physical tension and the opportunity for reprocessing of experience. This reprocessing leads to a restructuring of schematic emotional memories and thereby to a change in the internal representations of an entire class of situations (Greenberg & Safran, 1987; Perls, Hefferline, & Goodman, 1951). For example, when the boss yells at a man who has restructured his schematic emotional memory, that situation does not evoke in the employee the old fearful responses experienced in response to his father's yelling.

Tendency toward Balance

The principle of homeostasis is assumed to apply to emotional systems in a similar way as it does to biological systems. For example, if certain injunctions permeate one's representational system they may allow only certain emotions into awareness, even when one is experiencing the excluded emotion. This denial of present experience represents an imbalance (i.e., a discrepancy between what is allowed into awareness and what is expressed) in one's Gestalt. Denied experiences have a natural tendency to strain toward becoming integrated into one's current Gestalt. If certain aspects of these experiences remain unrepresented and are driven out of consciousness, however, one's view of current experiences and situations is distorted. A prolonged period of such imbalance may cause both psychological and physical stress.

The Problem of Anger

Anger is a particularly problematic emotion in Western cultures, since many constraints are established against it. Gestalt therapy assumes that anger, like any other emotion, is an adaptive action tendency and as such pushes toward expression and conscious representation. Since anger is an aggressive emotion that increases adrenalin and promotes action (Megargee & Hokanson, 1979), it is inherent to our survival instinct and determines the degree of our potency, assertiveness, and vitality. The expression of potent anger, when consistent with current events, may help a person avoid being manipulated and allows him or her to become active and visible in a group. When anger is a characteristic of a past rather than a present event, however, it becomes disruptive and counterproductive. In Gestalt therapy, this disruption is referred to as "unfinished business," and is defined as a reaction or set of reactions that has not been allowed completion of response. Holding in or constraining angry feelings without resolution simply interrupts the action tendency. When the cognitive schema representing that unfinished situation is evoked, the interrupted action tendency pushes for completion and may intrude on a current event. For example, when a man who was afraid to raise his voice to his denigrating father now confronts a denigrating boss, his voice is likely to become constrained, and he is likely to struggle for expression. Constraint of impulse expression has the effect of suppressing the range of other accessible emotions. Therefore, as anger is constrained, the capacity for expressing an entire array of other emotions that may be appropriate in the current situation is also limited.

The action tendency associated with an experience of anger that was not satisfactorily completed at the time it was environmentally congruent becomes stored in schematic emotional memory and will be re-expressed when the schematic memory is reactivated by similar situations. However, because inhibited and disowned anger is frozen and appropriate to a past rather than a current situation, the re-evoked anger is likely to be both indirect and unproductive. Moreover, interruption of the action tendency that is associated with anger may also cause a direct loss of personal power in life. Expression of anger has been of great evolutionary significance, and the constraint of anger prevents people from assuming a visible, assertive, and dominant role on their own behalf. Suppression of anger counters survival. The socialized expression and completion of the action tendency, on the other hand, results in an increase of personal power by redirecting attention and action to current experiences and makes new actions available in response to current events. Arousal and completion of the anger also removes the need to distort present experience and permits the formation of a representational Gestalt that is harmonious with reality (Daldrup & Gust, 1988).

Relationship of Anger and Hurt

An important aspect of the human experience of anger is the awareness of "emotional hurt." Indeed, anger and hurt may be considered to represent two sides of the same emotional coin. Anger, however, is an externally directed feeling, whereas hurt is internally directed. Because of their dialectic relationship, when anger is denied direct expression, it is often expressed as hurt, and vice versa. Since it is assumed that only one emotion at any given time can achieve a state of completion or integration, it is important for the organismic system to experience different emotions distinctly and separately. When dialectic emotions (e.g., hurt and anger) vie for attention simultaneously, the emotions intrude upon and compete with each other so that completion cannot be achieved.

When hurt and anger are pitted against each other, one feeling must come to the fore, but may vacillate from moment to moment with the other. For example, complaining may be a form of expressing anger and hurt at the same time; blaming is a similar expression, but one in which anger takes the form of revenge seeking; a whiny voice and/or a persistent quest for "why" may also indicate vacillation between anger and hurt. This type of expression is neither clearly hurt nor authentically anger, so these mixed communications have an ambivalent impact on others who receive them: They are affected by both emotions at once.

Forms of Anger

Because of its unacceptability and easy attachment to dialectic emotions of hurt, love, and dependence, anger appears in a number of different forms in the process of therapy. It is important for purposes of intervention to distinguish among the many different configurations of anger. The major manifestations of anger are described below.

CONFLUENT ANGER

Confluent anger exists when anger and hurt flow together to create an experience in which the person feels wronged, victimized, and helpless. Complaining is a sign of confluent anger, and signals the need for these emotions to be differentiated and given the opportunity for separate expression. Once a clear expression of hurt is achieved, the anger often flows naturally out of this experience as an adaptive biological emotional response. On other occasions, the anger needs to be clearly expressed before the person feels sufficiently safe to express the hurt, sadness, and longing often associated with the sources of the confluent emotions.

DEFLECTIVE ANGER

Deflection is another means of interrupting the direct expression of unwanted anger. Deflection and minimization are observed when topics and targets of emotion are changed while intense emotional experience is directly denied. These maneuvers represent efforts to attain conceptual or attentional control of anger. The patient takes the "heat" off emotional expression by one of two forms of deflection: (1) indiscriminately expressing the emotion (e.g., "I hate everyone in my life"), or (2) changing the focus away from the emotional expression (e.g., "talking about" rather than experiencing the emotion). An example of the former is a patient who is continually angry, scattering the anger on a hit-or-miss basis across situations. An example of the latter is a patient who changes the subject, who only "talks about" the anger, or who intellectualizes it away. The therapeutic task is to get the patient to stay with the focus of the anger as it arises from the organism or to learn to refocus on the emotion after a deflection. Once a clear focus and awareness develop, the task is to help the patient to stay with the emotion until the arousal level builds and expression is complete. The best means of dealing with this interruption is by focusing attention on the sensory and behavioral manifestations of anger and by intensifying the experience and expression of the anger through directed activity so that it cannot be avoided.

DEFENSIVE ANGER

Defensive anger is a specific form of deflection in which people appear to express anger, but the expression is actually a mask for another inhibited or unfinished emotion, such as fear or hurt. For example, each time a patient begins to cry, anger is generated to overcome the tears. Sometimes a brusque facade of anger serves to keep a distance between the patient and others. In this situation, the task of the therapist is to learn to recognize the signs of the masked emotion and to encourage the person to focus on the sensory and behavioral aspects of the emotion being masked by the anger until it comes fully into experience and can be integrated.

INSTRUMENTAL ANGER

Instrumental anger is observed when people express their anger, but the intent is not to finish unfinished emotional expression as much as to manipulate, change, or punish someone else. The therapeutic task is to encourage such people to give up the manipulative stance and to move toward ownership of the motivational underpinnings of the angry expression. Anger-directed behaviors may then be redirected to complete unfinished emotions and to bring such persons to a state of balance.

The Manifestation of Splits

In addition to the multiple manifestations of anger, the therapist must also be aware of the several ways in which uncompleted experiences fragment an individual. These fragmenting experiences are represented as "splits" between and among various components of the individual's perceptual or representational field. Awareness of these splits allows the therapist first to separate the components of the split cleanly and then to move the patient toward closure of the conflictual elements. The following types of splits (Greenberg, 1979) are particularly representative of issues related to anger management.

CONFLICT SPLITS

Conflict splits are defined by introjections about anger. The person manifesting such splits is angry but believes he or she should not be. A conflict split is created (Greenberg, 1979) in which one tendency or part of the self is angry and the other part opposes the anger. A struggle between these two tendencies ensues. The therapeutic task here is to resolve the split that is interrupting the expression of the adaptive anger.

SUBJECT–OBJECT SPLITS

Subject–object split occurs when people are angry at themselves and become intropunitive rather than expressing their anger outwardly. The Gestalt boundary disturbance representing this split is called "retroflection." In this state, people alternate between feeling strong and powerful as agents of their anger toward themselves, and weak and helpless as passive victims of that same anger. The therapeutic task, under these conditions, is to enhance such patients' awareness that it is they who are angry at themselves. The split can be resolved if the patients will delineate and differentiate what they are doing to themselves (e.g., persecuting or demolishing) from what others are doing to them. When patients appropriately recognize retroflexive patterns, they can then take responsibility for them. This process is sometimes facilitated by externalizing the retroflexive activity and paradoxically directing the patients in the act of controlling and enacting the angry activity at themselves. When patients take control of the self-condemnation and direct it explicitly, actually doing it to themselves in the therapeutic situation, the dialectic underpinnings of the experience often emerge. This can be done in an experiment of putting patients in the empty chair and having them use the encounter bat on themselves. Counterbalancing positive statements can replace negative ones and anger can be redirected toward the offending environment, by which means the anger may be expressed and completed.

ATTRIBUTION SPLITS

Attribution splits are reflected in the Gestalt boundary disturbance of "projection." When individuals either are hypersensitive to anger in other people or believe that their responses are inordinately righteous, to the point of disallowing others' expressions of anger, the therapist should be alert to the probability of misattribution of personal anger. Such individuals disown the independence of their own anger by making it a "justified reaction" to the anger of others. The task of the therapist is to encourage the reowning of the projected anger and its expression. In this process, the schemas associated with and through which these experiences are filtered are restructured.

Suppression of Anger

Anger is centrally involved in many forms of distress. Perls (1969) observed a cardinal role of anger when he stated, "We see guilt as projected resentment" (pp. 47–48). A corollary proposition can be stated for the role of anger in depression. Rubin (1969) concluded that "Sustained depression equals sustained self-hatred" (p. 53). Suicide, then, becomes the ultimate angry act expressed as a self-destructive behavior, revealing the two portions of self struggling for dominance. A principal assumption in focusing on the emotion of anger in therapy is that the capacity for hostility and its urge for expression are never lost, even though the overt expression of hostility may be interrupted.

Reformulation of Assumptive Stances

It follows from the foregoing principles that magnification of splits can be accomplished by "experiments" that are designed to focus upon, confront, and engage the patient with the denied experiences. The use of both physical and imagery-based release and magnification experiments (e.g., Beutler, 1983) is thereby justified. It is further assumed that once such magnification has taken place, the patient will be forced to incorporate new awareness into current conceptual and perceptual systems, such that there will be a schematic restructuring and an overall reformulation of the assumptive stance toward the world. This reformulation is described as a "new Gestalt." It is anticipated that this new Gestalt will be more sensitive than its predecessor to current environmental cues, having both discharged and integrated "unfinished business" from the past. A final assumption is that the therapist may then direct the patient toward a more realistic and fulfilling method of communicating anger.

Summary

The experience and expression of unwanted and unsanctioned emotions may be interrupted in a variety of ways and for a variety of reasons. Since anger is a central component of these troublesome emotional experiences, it is therapeutically important to be able to assess when and how anger has been interrupted and to intervene so as to allow it to be expressed to completion.

A number of critical assumptions inherent to the therapeutic process and fundamental to the work of FEP have been discussed. These are summarized in somewhat different language below:

1. Awareness of anger, or of other denied and disowned emotions, can be facilitated by magnifying current emotional sensory, or cognitive experiences.
2. It is assumed that disowned sensory and emotional experiences are the appropriate targets of interventions, and that magnification of the split between anger and its internal constraining forces will maximize therapeutic benefit.
3. It is assumed that patients' discovery of aspects of their emotional experience can be best facilitated by their active involvement in the relearning process.

2

Selecting the Appropriate Patient

Thoughtful clinicians are faced daily with the dilemma of selecting and defining what they believe will be the most appropriate treatment for a given patient. With the acute and often painful awareness that no one is equally effective with all individuals, clinicians have sought to broaden their repertoire of effective therapeutic procedures and to expand the range of their theories in order to gain greater understanding of human functioning. In a social climate that has become increasingly accepting of mental health treatments generally and psychotherapy specifically, clinicians have begun to see an ever-expanding array of patient presentations. No longer are we constrained either to treating the seriously distressed and disturbed or to working within the confines of a closely monitored office. Treatment procedures that were developed in past times to deal with what were then the most frequent presentations and problems may not be applicable to those who currently seek professional mental health services.

In response to the demands of changing times, some clinicians have attempted to incorporate a wide array of therapeutic procedures and methods into their armamentaria. Others, including ourselves, have attempted to become more specific and selective in the application of therapeutic methods. The former group of clinicians is composed of those who have moved away from parochial adherences to narrow models of change and increasingly identify themselves as "eclectics" (Garfield & Kurtz, 1977; Prochaska & Norcross, 1983). By this term, however, clinicians mean a variety of things, ranging from the unsystematic and intuitive use of procedures drawn from various approaches, to the systematic integration of theoretical concepts independent of the technologies deriving from them, to the systematic application of techniques and procedures without regard to theories that have generated them.

Norcross (1986) has clearly defined the array of philosophical viewpoints and stances that are uncomfortably melded together under the term "eclecticism." Conveniently, eclectic approaches can be defined as falling within one of three general camps. "Common-factors" eclecticism (e.g.,

Garfield, 1980) assumes that all effective therapy derives from the establishment of a caring and warm relationship, confrontation of the patient with new knowledge and experience, the development of a healing bond, and providing a corrective emotional experience.

"Theoretical" eclecticism, in contrast, represents an effort to integrate the theoretical concepts and principles from different points of view into an understanding both of change processes and of psychopathology (e.g., Arkowitz & Messer, 1984; Wachtel, 1977). Most commonly, behavioral and psychoanalytic viewpoints are integrated or merged following the tradition of Dollard and Miller (1950), and represent a retranslation of the separate theories into a single framework.

Finally, "technical" eclecticism considers theories of psychopathology and change to be of minor importance when contrasted with the pragmatics and empirical observations of the relationships that exist between technical applications and outcomes. The technical eclectic (e.g., Lazarus, 1981) emphasizes that all psychotherapies employ unique as well as shared procedures and that each of the unique procedures may have specific outcomes.

All of these eclectic models have certain limitations. Common-factors eclecticism, for example, fails to account for the intriguing paradox that specific psychotherapy procedures or theoretical orientations are associated with dramatically and identifiably different therapeutic processes, even though many of the outcomes appear to be similar. Hence, common-factors theorists present a model of therapeutic change that frequently disagrees with the clinical wisdom and belief systems of practicing therapists who emphasize that specific procedures have specific effects.

Similarly, the theoretical eclectic must ultimately select which theories are most relevant or "real" and in need of integration. With the number of theoretical schools, as applied to psychotherapy, now numbering close to 300 (Corsini, 1981), an integration of all theoretical formulations seems to be impractical. Moreover, certain theoretical constructs are adamantly at odds with one another and defy integration. For example, the humanistic theorists' emphasis upon inherent self-actualization and growth-facilitating potentials is not easily integrated with the psychoanalytic theorists' emphasis upon destructive urges. The technical eclectic also is faced with a problem of integration when faced with an ever-expanding range of treatment procedures and technologies, but with comparatively little research to demonstrate the differential effectiveness of most. Even if research were available, the technical eclectic could not hope to keep abreast of, proficient at, and skilled in the use of all procedures that have been advocated, because of their sheer number.

Since it seems impossible either to retain skill in a broad range of therapeutic procedures or to adequately grasp the intricacies of numerous theories, an alternative to eclecticism is to define the types of patients and types of problems that best fit one's own theory, technical armamentarium, and philosophical view. In confronting the many dilemmas of selecting appropriate strategies, most clinicians retain general agreement on two fundamental principles: (1) Not all people respond equally well to the same therapy or therapist, and (2) traditional diagnostic dimensions are poor indicators for determining what types of psychotherapy should be applied to a given patient. With these bases of agreement, all therapists struggle with the same fundamental questions when they approach each new patient. These questions have been summarized by Beutler (1986):

1. Is this patient a suitable candidate for treatment?
2. What should the focus of treatment be?
3. How tolerant will this patient be of my efforts to influence him or her?
4. What types of interventions are likely to yield the greatest gains?
5. How should the interventions be altered as the patient changes or resists change?

The decision to work within a given theoretical framework and with a given array of treatment procedures does not alter the need to address the five questions enumerated above. However, such a decision does emphasize an additional question: "What patients can I most effectively treat with the knowledge and procedures available to me?"

The current volume is an effort to describe a group-based approach to treatment, utilizing Gestalt principles and theories. Identification of appropriate candidates for this treatment is a multistep process. Our search for the answers to the questions enumerated above reflects this process. Rather than attempting to derive an exhaustive range of theories and technical procedures, we intend to remain theoretically consistent and to explore the alternative approach of selecting the right patient for the therapeutic procedures encompassed by a Gestalt-oriented treatment. We do this in the context of addressing three lockstep, sequential questions:

1. Who should be treated?
2. For whom is psychotherapy an option?
3. For whom is experiential group psychotherapy a reasonable alternative?

It is our hope to emphasize that not all who seek our services are candidates for psychotherapy and that not all who seek psychotherapy are candidates for group therapy. By the same token, not all those who enter group therapy may be candidates for experiential psychotherapy or for the specific variant of this therapy that we have called FEP. We hope to make the therapist's job somewhat easier by identifying the indicators and enabling factors that will allow the patient to take advantage of the type of learning represented in this particular model of treatment.

The Decision to Treat

Upon the first contact, the therapist begins struggling with what appears to be the most fundamental of all issues—whether or not to treat the patient. Intuitively, it would seem that this question is easy to answer, and in fact most mental health practitioners treat everyone with sufficient motivation to present themselves at the door. In part, this latter decision is an economic one, as reflected in a recent experience one of us (L.E.B.) had. A newly graduated psychologist was anticipating taking the state licensing exam, which consisted of both a written and an oral presentation. In discussing the oral presentation, this recent graduate reported that he had heard that during the oral exam one should be careful to avoid indicating any desire or plan to enter private practice. To do so, it was rumored, would result in a host of "impossible" questions being posed. When asked for an example of an "impossible" question, the fledgling's immediate response was "Whom would you elect not to treat?" He then continued somewhat jestingly with his imagined answer: "Those who can't pay."

Although it was tendered in jest, the foregoing response, coupled with the perception that this was an "impossible" question and one to be avoided by a fledgling practitioner, suggests that our training programs have not yet adequately addressed such an important issue as who to treat. Hence, even before one decides whether group therapy, FEP, or some other type of therapy modality is appropriate to the client, an initial decision as to whether or not the presenting client or patient is a candidate for *any* form of mental health treatment (and especially for psychotherapy) must be addressed.

To us, the question of whether or not to provide mental health treatment reflects a combination of (1) the patient's needs for safety, (2) available support systems, and (3) potential treatment resources. With this in mind, the clinician's first task is to determine whether the patient presents with sufficient distress as to represent a significant threat to self or others. As this issue becomes clear, the clinician must assess the available resources for treatment and the strength of the patient's own social support systems.

In their effort to address the issue of whom to treat, Frances, Clarkin, and Perry (1984) suggest that there are certain patients for whom a recommendation against treatment is reasonable. These patients include those who are at risk for incurring negative response; those who are at risk for no response; those who are likely to improve spontaneously without treatment; and those for whom such a recommendation may be considered a therapeutic intervention in its own right.

Patients who are considered to be at risk for becoming worse with the application of treatment and for whom treatment rightly may be withheld to prevent their deterioration may include those who have severe masochistic tendencies; severely oppositional patients; borderline patients with a history of repeated treatment failure; and patients who enter treatment primarily because of external pressures or financial gain. In the last category are those who present no observable psychological disorder but who are forced into treatment by disgruntled parents, spouses, or significant others who have unspoken agendas, as well as individuals who enter treatment in order to support or justify a claim for compensation or disability. Individuals with antisocial or criminal backgrounds; those who are malingering or have factitious illnesses; those whose treatment response has previously been characterized by infantilized behaviors; and poorly motivated patients who do not have incapacitating symptoms may also be risks for treatment. An additional group for whom Frances *et al.* (1984) propose that a no-treatment option is feasible includes individuals who are oppositional and refuse treatment, as well as those for whom the clinician expects that circumstances require a delay before treatment is initiated. There may even be prospective patients for whom the act of denying treatment may convey an important message about their adequacy and well-being, such as to support adaptive defenses already in place.

For each of the foregoing groups of individuals, however, there may be exceptions to the no-treatment rule. Exceptions include individuals whose psychopathology, though appearing intractable and negatively responsive to treatment, may represent sufficient danger to self and to others as to suggest that even the risk of a negative outcome may be a lesser evil than the danger posed by the patient's pathology. Likewise, certain borderline patients who have a history of treatment failures may still be responsive to treatments that focus upon circumscribed problems and that are applied in order to prevent immediate danger. Patients who have treatable psychiatric disorders, irrespective of their antisocial or criminal history, malingering, or low motivation, should also be offered treatment. For example, the infantilized patient may be responsive to a medication regimen, though psychotherapy may iatrogenically foster the immature response.

More obvious to most therapists is the awareness that some people simply do not need treatment, either because their condition is transitory and likely to undergo spontaneous improvement, or because they have little subjective distress on which to base an intervention. This is not to say that such individuals should not be provided with some assistance with a present crisis; reassurance that the crisis will pass and that they will cope satisfactorily should be considered as a reasonable option to active treatment. Those who have a history of clearly pathological responses to crisis, even though otherwise healthy, may be given special consideration for treatment in spite of the transitory nature of their distress. For example, those who are in mourning and are experiencing severe consequences of loss may need some supportive assistance, even though the symptoms of loss are likely to pass. To these basically healthy individuals who have transitory problems, external resources such as family, friends, and religious organizations should be considered as adjunctive options or substitutes for direct treatment. In the absence of such external support systems, treatment may be indicated even for individuals whose condition would not otherwise require treatment.

Selecting Candidates for Psychotherapy

Nearly as important as the decision to treat, the question of whether or not a given individual is a candidate for psychotherapy emerges as central in the clinician's decisional process. It is appropriate at this point to emphasize that we do not make a distinction between behavior therapy and psychotherapy, as many would do. In our discussion, the term "psychotherapy" subsumes those interventions that rely upon psychological means, persuasion, support, and interpersonal influence to alleviate emotional suffering and/or distress. This viewpoint implies that behavior therapies, psychoanalytic therapies, Gestalt and other experiential therapies, interpersonal therapies, cognitive therapies, and the many permutations and variations of these "schools" are all part of a common body of treatments whose appropriateness is indicated by a common set of patient variables and characteristics. The characteristics that are common to the many brands of psychotherapy and that contribute to the healing process serve as a focus for the current question of "appropriateness" (e.g., Garfield, 1978, 1980).

By collapsing numerous psychological interventions under the general heading of "psychotherapy," we do not mean to imply that psychotherapy is only appropriate for individuals who suffer. There are times, particularly in the context of family and institutional interactions, when the person directly treated often suffers relatively less than the person who arranges for, sponsors, encourages, or enforces treatment. Although the absence of personal suffering may be a contraindication for psychotherapy, it is not uniformly so. Indeed, external resources, support systems, and influence powers may be brought to bear to encourage and sponsor treatment for the unsuffering behaviorally disordered, both within institutional settings and in outpatient environments. In the context of these treatments, benefit to an individual may partially be indexed through the change of suffering level in those around the targeted "patient."

Having said the foregoing, we must now confront the problem of defining the patient characteristics that contribute to much of successful psychological intervention (e.g., Lambert & DeJulio, 1978). This task requires that one know something about the role of personal motivation and social support systems, as well as those factors that work against change. The task also requires an awareness both of social systems that are conducive to treatment effects and of the nature of pharmacological interventions.

The relative enabling or indicating variables for employing psychotherapy, within the broad context by which we have defined it, center around the dynamic concept of "ego resources." Although definitions of this term have emanated from numerous theoretical orientations, the basic attributes that lend themselves to enhancing the success of psychotherapy are relatively constant. Garfield (1978, 1986) has suggested that the young, attractive, verbal, intelligent, and socially mobile client is the one most often accepted into psychotherapy and also the one most likely to benefit from it. Certainly, in our culture, it appears that there is some advantage accorded to the individual who is described by these characteristics. If it is taken literally, however, restricting treatment to this group leaves us in the uncomfortable position of encouraging treatment only for those who need it the least.

Lest readers prematurely take the foregoing as a rationale for rejecting the value of psychotherapy, let us introduce a broader perspective. Although youth, attractiveness, verbal facility, interpersonal skill, and social ascendance seem to be characteristics of successful psychotherapy patients, the procedures and opportunities of psychotherapy are sufficiently broad to be applicable to wider populations as well. Indeed, just as it is ill conceived to argue that psychotherapy *should* be the treatment of choice for all individuals, it is equally short-sighted to argue that the procedures of psychotherapy are immutable and cannot be adjusted to the unique needs of an increasingly diverse but receptive population. However, irrespective of how one might modify the procedures, there are probably basic ego resources that enhance the value of all the forms of interpersonal persuasion and influence we call "psychotherapy." Strupp and Binder (1984) have suggested that such variables as a positive history of attachment patterns, willingness to make a commitment, and the presence of a changeable and identifiable problem are necessary ingredients before psychological interventions can be implemented. Indeed, we believe that the central ingredient that establishes the patient's ability to benefit from psychotherapy is a history of having benefited from prior interpersonal relationships.

We do not concede that internal motivation is a necessary requirement for benefit, nor are youth and insightfulness. Although intellectual resources and the capacity to evaluate one's behavior, its consequences, and its interpersonal significance are probably cardinal to making self-induced change, perhaps more important to the maintenance of change (e.g., Schramski,

Feldman, Harvey, & Holiman, 1984) is the availability of a suitable social support system to encourage and reinforce improved functioning. Hence, within the current framework, a psychological intervention is appropriate under the following circumstances:

1. The patient's history suggests that he or she can anticipate and understand social cause-and-effect relationships, and that he or she places sufficient value upon interpersonal contacts as to control and modify behavior. Such value is often indicated by a history of controlling behavior in response to the expressed wishes and needs of others.

2. The patient's environment presents a sufficient number of interpersonal and social contacts to serve as a resource and controlling influence for the support of behavior change. Family members, significant others, or valued friends serve as such resources. At the very least, the therapist should be assured that the patient has social contacts and desires for establishing or maintaining relationships with identified others in his or her environment.

These minimal qualifications for psychological interventions should not mislead one into believing that the decision to employ psychotherapy rules out the implementation of concomitant interventions. Pharmacological treatments are indicated in the presence of severely dysphoric moods that render patients incapacitated in social relationships or place them at danger for self-injury. Vegetative signs of disturbances in appetite, sleep, sexual activity, social involvements, and the experience of pleasure are all indirect indices of a magnitude of withdrawal from the social world that warrants pharmacological intervention. Individuals with such disturbances of basic functions often are sufficiently impaired that external social resources are not available or cannot adequately be implemented through psychological means alone. Hence, the use of antidepressant medication may facilitate or enhance the enabling social factors, person contacts, and interpersonal or self-interest that support long-term change (e.g., Weissman, Prusoff, Thompson, Harding, & Myers, 1978).

Similarly, disturbances of perception, social withdrawal, reversion to autistic stimulation, and inability to judge social cause-and-effect relationships accurately and adequately may also be indicators for concomitant medical management. Schizoid qualities reflect detachment from social systems, inability to evaluate and appropriately construct responses to external events, and lack of investment in social support systems. As such, restoration of requisite interpersonal interest and activity may require medical and chemical management as a prerequisite to psychotherapeutic change. Certainly, recent research with young schizophrenic subjects suggests that psychological interventions, principally family modalities, can be a potent resource in reducing morbidity and recidivism rates (Falloon, 1985). As such information accumulates, the criteria for applying psychotherapeutic procedures may broaden even further.

The Specific Requirements of Group FEP

Empirical literature has failed to define many specific indicators for experiential psychotherapies, let alone the particular variant of such psychotherapies presented here. However, the need for specific indicators is clearly seen in research literature suggesting that the effectiveness of experiential and Gestalt interventions may be highly dependent upon both the therapist who employs them and the patient who receives them. For example, in their classic study, Lieberman, Yalom, and Miles (1973) observed that group therapists who evoked both the best and the worst improvement rates practiced experiential procedures. In our own studies, even therapists who are highly effective, selectively trained, and closely monitored in the application of experiential treatments vary considerably in the implementation and effectiveness of these procedures (Beutler & Mitchell, 1981; Hill, 1986).

Similarly, whereas early variants of our experiential procedures have been found to be very effective among outpatient groups when compared to other models of intervention (Beutler & Mitchell, 1981), acutely disturbed psychiatric populations and individuals with seriously impaired interpersonal resources may be at risk for negative effects when treated with such procedures (Beutler, Frank, Scheiber, Calvert, & Gaines, 1984). This observation requires careful exploration of the types of patients who are best suited to FEP.

Because FEP is applied in groups, the thoughtful therapist must first be aware of the indicating and enabling factors that facilitate the effects of group interventions. Lazarus (1981) emphasizes that groups may be particularly helpful when interpersonal deficits are present or when myths about social needs and social values inordinately constrain the exercise of personal responsibility. He observes that the group process offers a wider latitude for learning, modeling, and observation than does individual therapy. Lazarus emphasizes that the lonely and isolated person may particularly benefit from group interventions, by virtue of the practice that this modality affords in establishing close contact. Likewise, the hostile, disruptive, and impulsive patient may utilize group resources to assist in the inhibition of behavior and the assessment of its appropriateness.

Frances et al. (1984) have also emphasized that group therapy may be more beneficial than individual therapy when patients' pressing problems occur in the context of impaired interpersonal relationships, and when change requires some degree of external reinforcement and control. Patients whose weak social support systems render them lonely, dependent, hostile, or impulsive may be particular candidates for the constraining and educative influences that characterize group therapy programs. For example, patients whose capacity for intimacy is impaired by the absence of an external support system may be benefited by a group process that brings to bear social support, encouragement, and external behavioral controls. Likewise, a severely inhibited patient who tends to become excessively dependent upon others may benefit from group therapy because such an environment provides an external support system that is maintained by several group members, rather than embodied in a single therapist. When such a patient interacts with several group members rather than focusing solely upon the therapist, both the capacity for attachment and the capacity for differentiating interpersonal boundaries may be enhanced.

Frances *et al.* (1984) suggest that identifiable and overt symptomatic problems may also be particularly amenable to group interventions. Alcoholism, smoking, and eating disorders, for instance, may yield to the constraining influences of group pressure. Similarly, both those with stress-related disorders and elderly patients may benefit from the restoration of social contacts (Yost, Beutler, Corbishley, & Allender, 1986).

Yalom (1975) emphasizes that a stable group therapy process relies upon the selection of individuals who perceive the group as having potential for meeting their interpersonal needs; who either are able to desire to derive satisfaction through interpersonal contact; who are willing to commit themselves to participation in group tasks; and who derive reference appeal through associations with valued social systems. All of these factors suggest that group therapy may be particularly advantageous for individuals who have an investment in social systems. Although these individuals may be impaired in social ability and contact, the successful group member values interpersonal relationships and sees them as opportunities for deriving gratification and furthering personal goals.

However, Frances *et al.* (1984) also observe that there are contraindications for group interventions. These include the presence of an acute psychiatric emergency or crisis that requires urgent, intensive, or specialized individual attention; refusal to participate in group intervention; easy access to brief and focused individual therapy; and the presence of psychiatric conditions that disrupt group processes (e.g., manic disorder, organic brain syndrome, severe impairment of reality testing, or a pattern of interpersonal manipulation). In these last conditions, it may not be so much that the group itself will not be helpful to the patient as that the patient's presence may be disruptive and thus lessen the benefit to be achieved by other group members. In such situations, the therapist must balance the needs of the individual patient with those of the other group members when deciding who should be included in a group.

Once a decision about group appropriateness has been made, one must then consider the options of homogeneous versus heterogeneous groups, time-limited versus non-time-limited groups, and open versus closed groups. Rather than considering these options and their permutations in detail, let us simply state that, for most intents and purposes and within the constraints mentioned in the foregoing paragraphs, there is no great need to homogenize group membership. If a therapist works with populations that include large groups of individuals characterized by an extreme position in the distribution of social relatedness (severe withdrawal, impulsivity, lack of attachment, etc.), homogenizing the group composition toward one end of the distribution may be warranted. In the absence of such extremes, however, a certain degree of heterogeneity among group members is advantageous; the therapist should insure only that all are willing and able to make interpersonal attachments, have problems of interpersonal significance, and are willing to engage in the process of group sharing and review. The current volume presents a model of group therapy that emphasizes closed groups of limited duration. More specific characteristics of patients relative to this particular model must be considered in the context of defining the specific aspects, foci, and objectives of FEP.

Aside from the general recommendations that we have explored for the implementation of psychotherapy (and particularly group psychotherapy), there are also a few clinical guidelines that we employ in deciding to implement FEP. These guidelines can best be understood if one understands the rationale of the intervention itself. Chapter 1 has emphasized that experiential therapies and FEP in particular are designed to enhance emotional arousal and to focus energy upon anger resolution. This understanding embodies two central concepts that are relevant to patient selection.

First, we believe that FEP may be most advantageous for individuals who have problems because of excessive emotional constraint as manifested in restricted emotional expression and focus. Since an objective of the treatment is to enhance emotional arousal, it is logical that this treatment is less appropriate when applied to individuals who undercontrol the expression of their feelings, especially if they exist in a hyperaroused state. At present, the evidence indicates that FEP can have a significantly positive effect on prisoners' self-rating of change in a penal setting (Schramski et al., 1984); however, it has also been found that as patients feel better as a result of experiential therapy, their acting-out behavior may increase (Calvert, Beutler, & Crago, in press). Therefore, it is our position that the use of FEP with emotionally undercontrolled patients should be viewed with caution until such time as more supportive data are available.

Second, the emphasis of FEP is upon the failure to resolve interpersonal anger. Hence, the intervention is most appropriate when applied with those who are able to identify specific interpersonal relationships in which hurt, resentment, and fear (all potential variants of unfinished anger) are or were historically significant. Patients who can identify significant others with whom they have aborted interpersonal relationships, or with whom they have failed to complete interpersonal experiences because of intimidation, fear, hurt, anger, and so on, constitute the target group of FEP.

To summarize the foregoing, we anticipate that FEP will be least effective among individuals who tend to undercontrol impulses and who are diffusively and unselectively aroused or agitated, and who cannot focus upon the lingering elements of interpersonal relationships. Conversely, we anticipate that those whose depression and unhappiness reflect aborted anger and a sense of interpersonal helplessness; those who are able to identify important but troubled relationships in their lives; and those who tend to deal with interpersonal conflict through emotional constraint, inhibitive self-injunctions, and emotional overcontrol are appropriate treatment responders.

Summary and Implementation

Having presented a general outline of the appropriate candidate for psychotherapy, group psychotherapy, and FEP, the question arises as to how to identify the relevant parameters in a systematic and reliable way. In response to this concern, we offer the following guidelines.

Ego Resources and Social Support Systems

Ego resources and social support systems can best be evaluated through a combination of historical review and formal evaluation. In reviewing the patient's history, one looks for evidence of a continuing commitment to interpersonal relationships, of prior group support, and of some stable family attachments. One also looks for prior evidence of the ability to resolve problems and for prior successes in carrying out activities requiring planning, impulse control, and an accurate perception of social contingencies. An exploration of job achievements, school activities, marital relationships, and friendships is helpful. Encouraging patients to describe significant relationships in their lives—how these relationships were initiated, maintained, and terminated—may provide important clues to how they utilize social systems as support and as objects of reference.

In addition, paper-and-pencil screening procedures such as the Minnesota Multiphasic Personality Inventory (MMPI; Dahlstrom, Welsh, & Dahlstrom, 1972) may be particularly useful for defining ego resources among those who have adequate reading and educational levels to complete the procedures. Patients who reveal on such instruments severe disorganization, chaotic emotional experiences, and few stable social or intellectual attachments and interests are likely to be poor candidates for psychotherapy. Such instruments provide information about patients' capacity for insight or self-inspection, impulse control, and tolerance of intimacy.

Patient Motivation and Group Centeredness

A patient's motivation and group centeredness can be assessed by reviewing the patient's history of group memberships and contacts with legal systems. Individuals whose histories show disregard for social conventions, rules, and others' needs either should be considered for a homogeneous group in which attendance is externally enforced or should be excluded from psychotherapy. One should be particularly sensitive to cases of alcoholism, substance abuse, traumatic injury, medical conditions, and other contraindicating factors as one reviews patients' histories. Patients who have a history of alcoholism and/or substance abuse should be referred for an addiction evaluation and chemical detoxification before FEP is initiated. Referral for medical evaluation, as well as ready access to the consultation services of a neuropsychologist and neurologist, may help one to make difficult treatment decisions.

While reviewing a patient's history, one should be particularly attentive to what changes have occurred from premorbid levels of social functioning. Such changes provide important information for differentiating individuals who are environmentally reactive and those whose conditions may be organic or medical. The appropriate patient for FEP is one whose change in functional level has been coincidental with the advent of social stresses and interpersonal pressures, suggesting a socially responsive individual. The acceptable candidate is also one whose medical condition is stable and in whom medical causes of behavioral change have been appropriately ruled out. Whenever the patient's moods and feelings seem not to have occurred coincidentally with and in responce to environmental changes, and do not coincidentally respond to positive corrections in the environment, the role of nonpsychological factors should be considered with greater seriousness.

Since many aspects of depression, impulse disorder, and major functional psychiatric disturbance may be mirrored by organic disorders, careful medical evaluation is often required. Medical referral is particularly required for the patient who does not obtain regular medical evaluations and for whom a medical history is not readily available. Explosive disorders should be routinely evaluated for neurological correlates, and both insidiously developing and nonreactive depressive disorders may suggest the onset of dementia. Specific psychological and neuropsychological procedures, as well as medical diagnostic procedures, have been developed and employed to assist in the differentiation of functional from nonfunctional disorders (Kaszniak & Allender, 1985). Such evaluation procedures provide important information about current functional levels, as distinguished from subjective levels of dysfunction. Individuals in psychological distress are particularly likely to overestimate the degree of impairment they experience and to be acutely sensitive to change in functional levels. This pattern of response contrasts with that of individuals who are neurologically impaired. The latter individuals often are unable to acknowledge their reduced functioning levels, and they demonstrate substantially less distress in the face of dysfunction then their nonorganic peers (Kaszniak, Sadeh, & Stern, 1985).

Patient Overcontrol and Possible Responsivity to FEP

There are no currently available sensitive and accurate instruments for assessing patient overcontrol and for predicting responsivity to FEP. Although numerous instruments have been designed to assess level of anger, methods of controlling and dealing with anger, and tendency to overcontrol impulses, these instruments have not been found to have strongly predictive relationships with outcome in psychotherapy. For example, the most used instrument, the Overcontrolled Hostility Scale (Megargee, Cook, & Mendelsohn, 1967), was standardized on incarcerated individuals with a history of assaultive behavior. Whereas the instrument has been found to be useful in differentiating the uninhibited assaultive person from the overinhibited but explosive one, it is not sensitive to the milder forms of emotional constraint that characterize most psychotherapy patients.

In our own research programs, we have explored the utility of certain scale compositions constructed from the MMPI in differentiating patient coping styles. Within some limits, these indicators of defensive styles have been found to be predictive of differential response (Beutler & Mitchell, 1981; Calvert et al., 1988). Drawing from the early work of Welsh (1952), we have found that individuals who adopt internalizing defensive styles, characterized by compartmentalization, internal hypersensitivity, and anxiety as opposed to acting out, projection, and behavioral activity, tend to respond well to Gestalt and FEP procedures. Once again, however, derived scores from available instruments, however constructed, are not sufficiently sensitive at present to provide individual prediction. Hence, the determination of the patient's emotional control level relies upon a clinical judgment of constraint and withholding. In our programs, we augment these clinical judgments with in-therapy observations. We find that such direct observations of response to the stresses that are created within the context of the group process provide direct and relevant indicators of patient constraint. Since these latter indicators are not available before treatment, however, they are currently used to modify the use of various treatment procedures rather than to make decisions about whether to treat with FEP.

Figure 2.1 presents the Emotional Arousal Scale, which we use in our psychotherapy research programs to explore patients' emotional arousal in FEP. In addition to providing information about patient constraint, this

FIGURE 2.1. Emotional Arousal Scale.

A Rating of Patient's Expression of Emotion during the Therapy Session

Rater: _____

Date: _____

Therapist: _____

Patient: _____

Session No.: _____

Date: _____

Directions: The form uses the word "anger," but you are to rate whatever emotion the patient presents.

For each item, give two ratings: Decide on the average or mode (most of the time) and put an "M" above the number from 1 to 7. This is the "mode" rating.

For the highest level reached during the portion being rated, put a "p" above the number from 1 to 7. This is the "peak" rating.

Do not use half numbers.

Do not leave any item blank.

A. Intensity:

This is a measure of the intensity or strength of the emotional arousal. At one end, the rater can detect no emotional arousal in the voice, body cues, or verbal cues. At the other end of the scale, the voice, body, and language are intensely involved.

1	2	3	4	5	6	7
Patient does not admit to any feelings of anger. Voice, gestures, and posture do not disclose any arousal.	Patient may admit to feelings of anger, but there is no overt emotional expression of anger or other emotion.	Patient expresses the anger but very little emotional arousal in voice or body or words.	Patient verbalizes the anger and sometimes allows the voice, body, and gestures to be involved.	Patient expresses the anger so that the voice, body, and words are involved. Level of emotional arousal is moderately intense.	Patient expresses the anger with a fairly full arousal level. Still has a line that he or she will not cross. Will allow voice to be only so loud, or body to move only so much.	Arousal is full and intense. No sense of restriction. The person is focused, freely releasing, with voice, words, and physical movement at intense state of arousal.

B. Focus:

This is a measure of how specifically the patient is willing to identify unfinished emotional business with a significant other, and a measure of how well the patient engages the significant other in a two-chair dialogue.

1	2	3	4	5	6	7
Patient remains unfocused and general. Unaware of unfinished business with significant others.	Patient expresses unfinished business toward a number of people, but will not identify a significant other as the focus.	Patient identifies a specific significant other with whom there is unfinished business, but will not engage that person in the here-and-now of the session.	Patient identifies a specific significant other and is willing to engage that person in the here-and-now of the session, but the issues remain vague and ill-defined.	Patient identifies and engages a specific significant other. Begins to express specific unfinished issues with that person in dialogue.	Patient identifies and engages a specific significant other. Clear about the specific issues that provoke anger toward that person in dialogue.	Patient establishes especially solid and full engagement with the significant other. Extremely clear and direct about personal reactions toward the significant other.

scale allows us to obtain objective information about the effectiveness of the procedures in enhancing emotional expression. For the latter purpose, the Emotional Arousal Scale is coupled with an assessment of emotional response patterns.

Gestalt therapy details a number of configural patterns that patients employ when confronting emotion. These styles of boundary disturbance range from retroflection, to introjection, to confluence and deflection. These patterns have been described briefly in Chapter 1 and are discussed at greater length in subsequent chapters. At present, it is sufficient to emphasize that observations of changes in patients' response patterns during the therapy process are utilized to identify preferred patterns and to identify those patients in whom a pattern of emotional inhibition is most dominant. These latter patients are the ones who may respond best to FEP.

Through a process of initial selection coupled with in-therapy observations, we believe that the likely value of FEP can be predetermined and that the procedures to be employed within the group setting can be tailored and modified to fit most needs and circumstances. With this in mind, we now turn our attention to the specific procedures that constitute FEP. We begin this process by contrasting therapist and patient roles, and follow with more specific descriptions of the methods of FEP.

3

Therapeutic Roles

Lambert, Shapiro, and Bergin (1986) observe that most therapeutic change can be attributed to general therapist and patient variables. Many of these important characteristics are inherent to the therapist or patient and remain relatively constant from one relationship to another (Beutler, Crago, & Arizmendi, 1986). Such things as the therapist's ability and willingness to provide a caring and supportive atmosphere, the patient's ability to enter into a collaborative alliance, shared belief systems and backgrounds, and a general capacity for the therapist to cope with environmental changes in healthy and adaptable ways foster a substantial therapeutic environment. Under the best of circumstances, the willing and committed patient, the healthy and caring therapist, and the mutual expectation for positive change will produce benefit, aside from any particular therapeutic procedures or philosophical orientation the therapist may employ.

Unfortunately, the best of circumstances do not always prevail. The patient is not always endowed with a history of establishing collaborative relationships. The therapist is not always attuned to the patient's expectations and wants. The patient does not always have favorable expectations of the treatment relationship or outcome. And the procedures used by the therapist are not always able to accommodate discrepanices in patient and therapist backgrounds and belief systems. Because of this, the therapist must do all that is possible to create the atmosphere that will facilitate or accommodate the existing circumstances in order to create the maximal therapeutic effect.

The Role of the Therapist

We have already stated that the goal of FEP is reintegration of disowned anger. This goal is conceptually distinct from the role adopted (e.g., authoritative, informal, directive, etc.) and from the intermediate tasks that aid in the accomplishment of this objective. The role of the therapist in FEP is flexible and multifaceted. However, the major tasks of the therapist are finite and include the following:

1. To facilitate the establishment of a focus for the session based on awareness of here-and-now thoughts, feelings, and behavior.
2. To develop appropriate experiments.
3. To facilitate integration of disowned material.
4. To focus on emotions and information processing.
5. To facilitate a therapeutic alliance.
6. To be aware of the therapist's own emotional states.
7. To facilitate assessment, evaluation, and homework phases of the session.

Although there is variability among therapists in the way these tasks are accomplished, there are guidelines to their implementation that are designed to facilitate the process. We review these guidelines briefly in this chapter as we contrast therapist and patient roles. We also return to them in later chapters as we define the strategies of FEP in more detail. The reader may find it helpful to refer to Appendix 1, however, which presents an anchored scale and criteria for assessing how well the therapist is able to comply with the tasks of FEP. We refer to this appendix periodically, as we treat each step in the FEP process in greater detail.

Establishment of a Treatment Focus

The therapist is responsible for helping the emotionally blocked patient to identify occluded and distorted experiences. This task is best accomplished by focusing on the "here-and-now," and on the "what" and "how" rather than upon the "why" of one's experiences (Fagan & Shepherd, 1970). It is the therapist's role, therefore, to direct the patient's attention to an exploration of anger (i.e., the "what" and "how" of being blocked). This process consists of focusing upon current experiences, including primary sensory and affective cues. Special attention is given to significant others with whom the patient has "unfinished business."

Development of Experiments

In the service of clarifying, uncovering, exploring, enhancing, owning, and controlling anger, the therapist creates "experiments." The overall aim of these experiments is to encourage the patient to contact and express denied and disowned feelings. In these experiments, the therapist enters into the relationship as a collaborator who assumes the responsibility of guide, but not the responsibility for dictating the outcome of the experience. As a guide, the therapist provides a focus and direction to the process and relies upon the strength of the therapeutic bond and the patient's pain to provide the impetus for change. Within the general guidelines provided by the therapeutic mandate to track and follow the patient's anger, the therapy experience is one of moving from moment to moment as awarenesses ebb and flow.

Integration of Disowned Material

The process of the Gestalt therapy experiment is to promote identification with, and to facilitate the integration of, disowned parts of self. This is accomplished within the context of the general assumption that magnifying the separateness of parts of the self that are in conflict (i.e., the "split") will result in all of these parts being acknowledged, owned, and accommodated within the more fundamental constructs composing self-identity. This process emphasizes the patient's responsibility for his or her experience as each part is expressed and as the patient's attention is directed to the sensory, behavioral, and cognitive cues that identify each side of the split. This process is consistent with the general tenets of experiential psychotherapy (e.g., Gendlin, 1978; Mahrer, 1983, 1986). Namely, by focusing on current, sensory cues, the patient's awareness is heightened and affect is magnified to an extent that is difficult to deny. This heightening of awareness then often allows the patient to connect previous and current experience. In FEP and other Gestalt therapies (Goulding & Goulding, 1979; Polster & Polster, 1976; Daldrup & Gust, 1988), as distinct from less directive forms of experiential therapy (e.g., Mahrer, 1986), patients are also given guidance in, practice in, and suggestions for the expression of the emotions to which their awareness is directed.

Focus on Emotions and Information Processing

The guiding focus for the therapist in FEP is upon that range of emotions centering around anger and hurt. These emotions may take the form of resentment, irritation, frustration, or even depression. Greenberg and Safran (1981) have suggested that experiments promote a change in faulty encoding functions and in information processing, resulting in the formation of a new representational system or Gestalt. That is, those aspects of self that the patient attends to are changed through the process of focusing upon aspects that are at the edge of his or her awareness. One moves, in FEP, from a focus on the sensory to the affective to the cognitive realms of experience, rather than vice versa, as one might do in more cognitively oriented therapies. At all times, the therapist provides acknowledgment rather than approval of the patient and attempts to frustrate the "games" or maneuvers that symbolize the patient's struggle to avoid the negatively connoted emotion.

The Therapeutic Alliance

Understanding the role of acknowledgment necessitates that the therapist be aware of and facilitate the influence power of the therapeutic alliance. Although some forms of experiential therapy, most notably that advocated by Mahrer (1983, 1986), disavow interest in the quality and nature of the therapeutic relationship, FEP accepts the importance of therapist warmth, empathic ability, integrity, respect, credibility, trustworthiness, and caring. FEP also emphasizes the therapist's responsibility for facilitating and creating an atmosphere in which these qualities become apparent. Acceptance of these characteristics reflects the kinship of FEP to traditional client-centered-therapy, and also acknowledges a respect for empirical findings on the importance of the therapist's qualities and perceived qualities for therapeutic effectiveness (Beutler, Crago, & Arizmendi, 1986; Orlinsky & Howard, 1986).

Awareness of Therapist's Own Emotional State

Emanating from the general concern with the quality of the therapeutic relationship, it also is important that the therapist be aware of his or her own emotional states during the therapeutic process and share this awareness with the patient appropriately. If the therapist is not aware of or denies his or her emotional state, it may contaminate the work that is being done with the patient, both by distorting the therapist's viewpoint and by misdirecting the therapeutic focus.

First, there are emotions that are unrelated to what is going on in the therapy session. In this case, the therapist is not able to be present to the person in front of him or her:

> "I am preoccupied and I need your indulgence for a moment. I just received a call that my mother-in-law is undergoing surgery. I feel very uneasy because she has a very weak heart and there is some question that she may not tolerate the surgery. I am scared for her, and worried about my wife, who feels very close to her mother. When this session is over, I will call my wife and talk

with her. (*Pause*) Having decided to talk with her, I now find myself interested in what you want for you today."

Second, there are emotions that are related to what is taking place in the present therapy hour:

"I feel sad as you talk about being abused as a child. I am sorry that those things happened to you."

or

"I am embarrassed. I feel that I ought to know what to do right now, and I don't. Perhaps we need to talk a little longer and I will be more clear about what we need to do next."

Such genuine responses as these are much more appropriate than a neutral response that ignores the fact that the therapist is a part of the therapeutic dialogue.

Assessment, Evaluation, and Homework

Finally, the therapist is responsible for assisting the patient in the assessment, evaluation, and homework phases of the therapy. Characteristically, Gestalt therapy is conducted in a group setting, and this is true of FEP as well. The group setting provides a unique opportunity for patients to explore their feelings with ample input and feedback. Moreover, the group provides a laboratory for practicing the effects of new perceptions and developing new expectancies. Nonetheless, the therapeutic "work" experiences themselves are conducted as transactions do not rely upon group processes in the same way that they do in other types of group treatment. The focus is upon each patient's unfinished business, and in the pursuit of this focus, the therapist assumes a patient-oriented dialogue just as would be done in individual therapy. As each experiment is developed, proceeds through its stages, and arrives at a satisfactory conclusion, the therapist and patient typically then turn to the group to obtain additional feedback and practice to support the patient's altered view of his or her dilemma.

The therapist's role, therefore, is both to serve as guide through the individual work and to moderate between the patient and the other group members during the task of soliciting feedback and obtaining practice experience (Feder & Ronall, 1980; Harman & Tarleton, 1983). In addition, however, other group members can be utilized in developing experiments; and it is the joint function of patient and therapist to define which individuals will be utilized and in what way, so that the experiment can work most effectively and completely with the unfinished business at hand. Assessment of the work done and planning for integration of that work outside of the session are essential parts of the therapist's responsibilities. This integration can be accomplished through mutually agreed-upon homework assignments.

The Role of the Patient

The role of the patient is to be fully present in the relationship. This role is facilitated by attendance to the following tasks:

1. To acknowledge behavior, thoughts, and feelings.
2. To trust one's own organism.
3. To make a definite commitment to work or not to work.
4. To assess the work that has been done in the session.
5. To carry out the homework assignments.

Agreement to enter FEP includes agreement to engage in these tasks. As "guide," the therapist helps the patient comply with the designated tasks. Collectively, the therapist's and patient's tasks constitute the treatment contract.

Acknowledgment of Behavior, Thoughts, and Feelings

Uniformly, through Gestalt therapy, patients are assumed to be responsible for their own behavior, thoughts, and feelings. They are also responsible for their own change and have a right to decide whether in fact they are willing to change. As we discuss in more detail later, the importance of an initial contract at the beginning of each major transaction or work experiment becomes critical in defining this responsibility. If the patient is to experience maximal benefits, the contract must be extended to the entire therapy process as well as to individual pieces of work. In this more general contract, the patient must be willing to attend to present sensations, thoughts, and feelings (i.e., to stay in the here-and-now), and then to share his or her awareness of these experiences with the therapist and with other group members. Yet this process of focusing on the present requires little effort on the part of the therapist or patient. Paradoxically, focusing on the present implies exerting less effort than that expended to prevent awareness.

Trust in One's Organism

To achieve awareness, one must let go of the bounds and limits placed upon experience. Awareness of present events is assumed to be the natural state of an organism and can only be impeded by the binding of and sanctions against certain current experiences. Again, paradoxically, the inhibition of an emotion (not necessarily of its behavioral impulses) preserves rather than prevents the influence of that emotion (Seltzer, 1984). Since emotions are assumed to be always present and to be straining toward resolution, the very act of denying them prevents them from being resolved or integrated, and thereby preserves their influence. Therefore, it is important that during the therapy process, the patient comes to trust his or her organism's inherent sense. Acceptance of an inherent growth or actualizing potential assumes the organism's willing struggle to bring unfinished experiences into the present so that they can be resolved, assimilated, and released. If the patient trusts this internal sense, he or she will allow these experiences to emerge into the foreground, providing the opportunity for past experiences to be integrated with the present.

Commitment to Work

In the beginning of the therapy session, patients are asked to make a commitment to work. Work implies an activity designed to confront fears and to release the rules that have frozen certain angry emotions in the past. Any resistance to work and subsequent change becomes the full responsibility of the patient and is seen by the therapist as a right that all possess. Although exercise of this right is questioned, explored, and challenged, it is also respected as a reflection of a patient's internal struggle for self and constancy preservation. Rather than being conceived as a resistance to the therapist, such patterns are considered to reflect internal dialogues with aspects of self.

Evaluation of the Work

At the end of each work experiment, the patient is responsible for an evaluation and assessment of the session. The patient is asked to report on changes in the benchmarks identified at the beginning of the work phase as a primary form of indications of movement or lack of it. If there has been no movement, the patient is encouraged to identify how progress in the session may have been sabotaged. At the end of the work, the patient reports present thoughts, feelings, and physical awarenesses as a means of acknowledging self.

Homework Assignments

After the patient and therapist have mutually agreed to a homework assignment, it is the responsibility of the patient to follow through on the contract. If the patient chooses not to do the homework, the responsibility for such a decision lies with the patient, and the purposes of such a decision are explored in the subsequent session.

Role Induction

Since patients enter therapy with varying experiences and expectations, the nature of the therapy contract and the roles and tasks required of each patient must be made explicit. The first task of treatment is to clarify the nature of the required patient and therapist roles.

Preparation for FEP

Beginning in the early 1960s, a persuasive body of research has accumulated to suggest that pretherapy training in patient roles (i.e., "role induction") can facilitate the development of treatment-appropriate expectations and behaviors. These roles, in turn, enhance group cohesion and group process (Yalom, Houts, Newell, & Rank, 1967), reduce dropout rates (Hoehn-Saric et al., 1964), and improve rates of beneficial therapeutic outcome (Childress & Gillis, 1977; Strupp & Bloxon, 1973). These findings have led to consistent conclusions among reviewers of this literature that pretherapy role induction procedures can attenuate some of the negative and countertherapeutic effects of poor patient motivation, incompatibility between patient and therapist expectations, and unsupportive social environments (Beutler et al., 1986; Orlinsky & Howard, 1986). This literature has also led us to develop a procedure for preparing patients for group FEP.

Steps in Role Induction

Role induction occurs at several stages: as people are screened for the group; during the initial group meeting; and during the early group meetings when preparing patients for therapeutic work.

ROLE INDUCTION PROCESSES PRIOR TO INITIAL SESSION

Before the first group session, prospective patients are given the theoretical rationale both for group treatment and for FEP. For example, they are told that group therapy provides them the opportunity not only to discuss issues, but to "work through" issues with the benefit of others' experience. They are also told that they will have time in the group devoted specifically to them. Through simple illustrations and explanations, they are taught the concept of "unfinished business." They are also told that the focus of the group will be on attending to the unfinished expression of emotions that are problematic to them, and they are asked to specify an unfinished issue they may want to bring to group sessions.

The various tasks and roles of patient and therapist are described, and the interviewer seeks the prospective patient's verbal agreement to comply. This induction process can be accomplished either in a group preview session or in individual interviews. In either case, it is best if this induction is presented by the leader(s) of the group.

ROLE INDUCTION PROCEDURES DURING THE FIRST SESSION

In the initial session, after people in the group are introduced to one another, a round is begun in which each person states his or her goals and reasons for being in the group. In order to introduce the concept of "present" experience, participants are asked to express their current feelings about being in the group (nervous, scared, excited, etc.).

To help patients understand the difference between "talking about" and "working through" an issue, the first session includes the presentation of a videotape of a previous FEP session, selected on the basis of FEP concepts and willingness of the patients to have the tape used for demonstration purposes. Members are told to attend to their reactions and to notice what they experience in their bodies as they view the tape.

After the videotape, group members are reminded that the purpose is not to discuss the persons in the video, but to stay focused on their own experience as they viewed the tape. They are prompted to observe and disclose any difficulty experienced in maintaining focus on the tape, the type of emotions experienced, and their ability to imagine working through issues in a similar manner as that observed. Each patient is then asked to identify an "unfinished issue," preferably an issue involving someone significant in his or her present or past life. If patients are willing, they are asked to disclose their issues to the group, although their right to privacy if they choose is emphasized. They are also asked to think about how ready they might be to work on such issues in the next weekly meeting.

If a group member is unable to identify unfinished business, exercises are introduced to assist in the identification. In one exercise, an empty chair is set in front of each person, one at a time; the person is asked to imagine that someone from his or her life sits in the chair. Each is asked to identify that person and to say something to him or her. This procedure prompts the expression of a range of unfinished issues, often reacting to others in the group, and extending from unexpressed love or gratitude to unresolved, deep-seated anger or hate. This exercise begins to establish the focus for future work. At the end of this exercise, patients are told that an extra chair will remain in the group. This is the "working chair"; when a patient wants to work on a personal issue, he or she is asked to take the chair.

ROLE INDUCTION PROCEDURES AFTER THE INITIAL SESSION

Even after the general induction presented in the first session, group members usually need some specific help to get into their therapy work during the early meetings. The following transcript is from the first session of a group, after the general induction outlined above had taken place.

In the opening round, a patient was visibly upset about a recent interaction with her brother. She said she wanted the issue to be resolved. When the round was complete, the therapist returned to her and verified that she still wanted to work in the group. She said "Yes," and moved to the working chair.

THERAPIST: What I am going to ask you to do is to make your brother present to you in the chair across from you, and, as much as possible, to talk to him. You might begin by telling him what is going on in your body as you sit down face to face with him.

PATIENT: I'm getting tired of it. This time I wouldn't talk with him. I mean I have tried to confront him. [In dialogue with the therapist, not her brother.]

T: Yeah. Often we're stuck with "unfinished business" because we try to take it to a person and work it out. And sometimes that person doesn't cooperate. It takes two people to work things out that way.

P: That's exactly where I am right now.

T: OK. What this process can help you to do is to bring him in here today where he can't cut you off, you know? You can make him sit here and hear you out, so that you can take care of *you*. You can't change *him*, but you can take care of *you* today. What's going on in your body right now? I want to know.

P: My stomach's shaking.

T: OK.

P: I just want to cry.

T: All right. Fighting back some tears, huh?

P: Yeah.

T: Just let the tears be there and tell your brother about them.

This dialogue demonstrates both how the therapist helped the patient to keep her contract to acknowledge, trust, and commit to work, and how

the patient was introduced to the possibility of resolving unfinished situations in the therapy group, even without the cooperation of the significant other. This latter is an especially important concept when the other person is dead, absent, unwilling, or otherwise unavailable. At this time, it can also be pointed out that the purpose of emotional arousal and expression is not to blame, manipulate, or change the other person, but simply to attend to the needs of the patient and to enable him or her to come to a state of completion and balance. From the beginning, the therapist makes it clear that the patient is to speak *to* the significant other, not *about* him or her.

After the first piece of work in the group, the therapist again clarifies the roles of group members. The therapist follows up by making it clear to all group members that the group is not to keep the work going; instead, members are asked to focus on and to express how the work of the focal individual has affected them. They are asked to speak directly to the person who has just completed some work. Some examples might be as follows:

PATIENT 2 TO PATIENT 1: I did not come tonight with my stepfather in mind, but as you worked out your anger about being raped, I was feeling very angry also. I realized how upset I still am at my stepfather for molesting me. Right now my head aches and I feel sick at my stomach.

or

P2 TO P1: Seeing you express your anger toward your mother helped me a lot. I've never allowed myself to do that. I hear a big voice inside that says, "You're awful if you resent your mother." I'm closer to being able to look at my anger now.

Because FEP is process-oriented, it is important to teach group members how to attend to their own inner processes and how to work through their own issues. Therapy is facilitated when the induction of roles initially is presented before the person comes to the group, and is reinforced both during the first session, which is given specifically to role induction, and during the first examples of individual work in the group.

Summary

Although the roles and tasks of the therapist sometimes overlap with those of the patient, each has specific functions to perform. Agreement to perform these tasks and functions constitutes the therapy contract. It is the therapist's responsibility to make the patient aware of what each participant's roles and responsibilities are in this contract and how they may affect the

treatment process. This task is accomplished through instruction, example, and systematic role induction procedures. These procedures, as well as careful selection of appropriate patients, are designed to establish the basis for both parties to join together and become collaborators—the patient as focus and the therapist as guide.

The development of "experiments" in psychotherapy can be applied equally well to role induction and to in-therapy activities of the therapeutic union. The very term "experiment" implies that the outcomes of various activities are not known in advance. The therapy process that occurs between patient and therapist becomes one of observing consequences of experiments and constructing new experiments in order to move the therapy forward. A more specific delineation of this process and descriptions of the steps required to accomplish it are included in later chapters of this volume.

4

Working in the Session

The processes of FEP are interwoven with the healing forces of the group experience. Although relevant, the development of a healing and supportive group process is taken for granted in FEP and is not targeted for direct attention, unless the need for such attention unfolds. These healing group processes assume the role of background on which a series of individual, patient-to-therapist transactions (i.e., work experienes) are superimposed. In turn, each step in the patient-to-therapist process dictates the next step and is inextricably bound to and inherent in the collective group experience. Hence, no clear formula can be derived for deciding what procedure or procedures to utilize in advance of these moment-to-moment work experiences. Nonetheless, it is possible to define the tasks and processes of work experiences, along with the general nature of the procedures that are appropriate to each.

Five steps or tasks can be defined and are designed to evoke a gradual increase of emotional intensity, followed by diminution of affective level, and finally by reconceptualization or reframing of past experiences. At each step, procedures are developed and introduced as "experiments." Their results are observed and assessed. If they serve to facilitate this expected flow of emotion, they are retained. If they interrupt the emotional level or reintegration process, they are terminated and replaced.

The tasks of each work experience are as follows:

1. Establishment of a focus for work.
2. Elicitation of a commitment to work.
3. Development of the work process itself to the point at which affective intensity peaks and then gradually begins to decline.
4. Assessment or review of the work conducted, during which the patient reformulates the experience.
5. Development of plans and homework for the future.

In any given therapy session, a series of such work processes will be initiated. In the group setting, each piece of work should be followed by allowing group members to assess their own experiences with the process before proceeding to the next piece of work. The five steps, along with both their goals and the associated therapist action, are outlined in Table 4.1. As indicated earlier, Appendix 1 contains a scaling procedure that we have developed for assessing the adequacy with which each step is applied. The interested reader may find it helpful to refer to this scale periodically throughout this and the next five chapters as we discuss the implementation of treatment procedures.

Identifying a Focus for Work

In the first step of therapeutic work, a focal point is identified with the patient. This focal point is usually identified by a feeling or behavior that the patient desires to change. In individual sessions, this exploration of a focal point is accomplished by a review of how the patient has been conditioned regarding emotions and how the various models in the early years have influenced the patient's ideas about expression of emotion. In group sessions, the identification of a focus for work can be part of a "tailgate"

TABLE 4.1. Steps in FEP Sessions

Step	Purpose	Action
1. Focus	To identify a focal point for work.	Pinpoint problem; note benchmarks; assess significant other's influence.
2. Commitment	To obtain a commitment to work on chosen focal point.	Change tentativeness to definiteness; provide encouragement and assurance.
3. Experiment	To engage the significant other in a piece of unfinished business; to increase affective and sensory experience.	Use appropriate experiential techniques to intensify experience to the point of expression and release.
4. Assessment	To assess and evaluate the work done; to begin the process of recognizing perceptual Gestalts.	Attend to here-and-now awareness; acknowledge sensory, affective, and cognitive sensations; assess benchmarks of Step 1; specify results of the work.
5. Plans, homework	To plan future use of knowledge, insights, and awareness obtained from the work; to complete the process of reorganizing the internal schemas.	Rehearsal; role playing; plan of action; homework.

process, in which the work just completed by a member of the group can stimulate the definition of another member's focal point, as in this excerpt from a session:

THERAPIST: (*To Patient 1*) Take a minute to check out how you're doing right now. You can sit and rest for a while—you've been working really hard. Do you remember what you said about emotional pain? Well, you've been looking at that for the last few minutes and it's not—it takes energy, and I appreciate what you've been doing.

PATIENT 1: Well, I keep thinking, "Won't it ever stop?"

T: Yeah, if you come back next week and say, "No, it hasn't stopped yet," then we'll do some more work. OK? That's what we're here for. We can't know that until after the time passes. (*Pause*) Are you willing to hear something from Margaret [Patient 2] and Karen [Patient 3] about how things are going with them?

PATIENT 2: I'd like (*unintelligible—masked by cough*)

T: (*Turning to Patient 2*) What I'd like for you to do is talk about anything that you thought about in your own life while Dorothy [Patient 1] was doing her work. If there's something in her work that's true for you. What were you thinking about your life as she was—

P2: Well, it was kind of fascinating, because I have a 3½-year-old son who was abducted by my husband for the second time in August. He'd taken him for a year before, but he's over in Europe somewhere now and so—essentialy, half of his life I've already had to say goodbye to him several times, and I know that letting go is extremely painful.

T: OK. Make one statement about how you feel, OK?

P2: About how my—

T: How you feel about your son.

P2: OK, how I feel about my son? Oh, I adore him. He's my little pumpkin. He brings sunshine into my life, and aggravation and (*laughing*) uh, hard work and worry, and, you know, all those good things. Yeah.

T: And you've had to say goodbye.

P2: And I've had to say goodbye to him, in a sense, but I always look at it like, as long as he's alive, that I'll still have the opportunity to see him again, and meanwhile I've got a chance to do something for myself that I wouldn't have had the chance to do otherwise. What really upsets me is that I don't get to be with him when he's just a little baby, and I want to watch that growing-up period, I want to be a part of it. I want to be able to—to teach him and to guide him, and I'm being robbed of that, um, that—that responsibility and that—that, uh, right to be his mother, and I'm very mad about that.

T: Who are you mad at?

P2: His father and his grandparents and—I worry about him. I worry

about his mental health and whether he misses me or not. I worry about his
physical health because his mental health affects his physical health—his
health isn't much better than mine—

T: OK. That sounds like a focus for some work to me. Can we come
back and work on that?

P2: Yes, I'd like to.

T: OK. I'm going to stop you at this point, then, and check in with
Karen, and we can come back to talk some more about what you're talking
about if you want to.

Clinical experience has demonstrated the important impact of significant others in setting up unfinished business for patients. Therefore, the
therapist explores with patients their memories of how their parents dealt
with various emotions and what decisions patients may have made about
responding emotionally as a result of watching parents' reactions. This
decision is usually the basis for the trouble they are having with emotional
issues in their lives. It is also productive to explore with patients the
possibilities of unfinished business with past and present intimate relationships (i.e., lovers, ex-lovers, spouses, ex-spouses). Another area conducive
to the development of unfinished business is that of relationships with
children and siblings, where appropriate. In discussing any of these areas,
the therapist is alert to indicators of unfinished business as discussed below.

Indicators of Unfinished Business

The therapist identifies an appropriate piece of work by the presence of
indicators of unfinished business. From an inspection of a number of
samples of in-therapy process, patients' experiences of unfinished business
in therapy appear to be identifiable by a number of visible indicators
(Greenberg & Safran, 1987). We have identified four of these performance
indicators, which, when they occur together, constitute a marker of unfinished business for FEP.

1. The patient has a lively experience of a feeling of anger, sadness,
   hurt, or grief.
2. The expression of this feeling is related to a significant other, such as
   a parent, spouse, or lover.
3. The experience and expression is being currently interrupted and/or
   restricted.
4. The experience of the feeling and of its interruption is problematic
   for the patient, as indicated by direct verbal acknowledgments,

indirect verbal signs of the difficulty (e.g., verbal statements of hopelessness, cynicism, and despair), or nonverbal signs of inter-rupted expression (e.g., lip biting, swallowing of tears, or tightened jaw or fist).

Often an identification of a split preventing expression and completion of unfinished business is facilitated by observing the presence of ritualized and repetitive methods for avoiding confrontation with a troublesome feel-ing. There are a number of such habitual methods of interrupting anger; these are not characteristically within a person's awareness, and therefore are not immediately visible in the patient's performance. These methods of anger control become visible as the patient discusses important relation-ships. Later the therapist will attempt to undermine their use, but at this stage they simply serve as indicators of the presence of important unfinished business.

Interruption of emotional expression by confluence and deflection, as well as by introjection, retroflection, and projection, can be addressed through Gestalt methods for clarifying emotional responses (Levitsky & Perls, 1970; Polster & Polster, 1973). These methods of accessing unfinished business and encouraging unexpressed anger are illustrated throughout this chapter. Before we do this, however, it is important to emphasize how these patterns can be recognized, especially as manifested in their more subtle forms. Often the only visible signs of unfinished business are verbal reports of disturbances in sensory or expressive motor systems. These disturbances are observed in such complaints as headaches, pain, tensions, and other aversive body experiences. In these cases, the interpersonal splits that are reflected in these bodily sensations need to be identified and addressed through experiments designed to magnify their presence.

Introjections Related to Expression of Anger

In FEP, it is most important to identify those splits that emanate from introjections related to anger expression. In defining the poles of an inter-personal split, it is most efficient and effective for the therapist to explore parental and family influences on, and attitudes toward the expression of, emotional reactions. An early decision about the unacceptability of anger is often derived from a parental model's denial of feeling or from parental reinforcements of an emotional rule against sensory or behavioral expe-rience. These rules, even when not explicitly stated, convey an attitude about the place of emotions in one's life and should be explored in order to define relevant anger-laden splits, as in the following excerpt:

PATIENT: (*To therapist*) I'm so enraged with her I could kill her [her daughter].

THERAPIST: Yet you say that to me, but not to her. [The patient has been imagining her daughter in the empty chair.]

P: I just have a sick feeling that I'm some kind of monster if I'm angry with her.

T: So you feel the struggle of two parts of yourself: the angry part, and the part that has rules about anger.

P: Yeah. (*Pause*) I just keep feeling how awful I am to be this angry as a mother. A voice inside keeps saying, "Just what kind of mother are you? You're unnatural!"

T: I'm going to put another chair beside you. When you feel angry, talk from the chair where you're sitting. When you hear the voice condemning your anger, come and speak from this chair.

P: (*In angry chair*) Kathy, I'm really furious that you went off with those boys without my knowing it!

T: Now switch to the other chair.

P: (*In antianger chair*) But if I'd say that to you, I'm sure you'd hate me.

T: Tell her what you experience as you say that.

P: I feel all stopped up inside, and the pain in my chest is stronger.

T: Want to move back to the other chair?

P: Yeah, I can't live with this pain any more. (*Switches back to angry chair*)

T: Speak from here.

P: I'm furious that you won't talk with me when we've got problems to solve. I hate your defiance! (*Her face changes*)

T: What just happened?

P: I'm back in the other chair telling myself how *unnatural* I am to be so angry.

T: Move back to the other chair and say that.

[The patient moves back and forth a few more times and then speaks from the angry chair.]

P: It's not unnatural. I love you and I'm angry. In fact, I'm furious and you're going to hear it from me! And I'm sick and tired—no, I'm making myself sick and tired by keeping these feelings in.

T: What do you experience saying that?

P: Relief that I'm allowing myself to express what's been inside for so long.

T: OK. If you're ready, let your body be your guide and express what you need to do.

P: Oh. . . . I feel like punching something right now.

T: OK, you can do that. Just use the cushion and move into your anger.

Identification of Benchmarks for Change

It is helpful, when working on unfinished business, to establish initial "benchmarks" in the patient's current sensory system (i.e., physical symptoms such as headaches, tensions, backaches, etc.) that the patient is experiencing at the beginning of the work. These are often the only initial signs of unfinished business. At other times, when the patient is aware of the role that unfinished business plays in evoking a specific and uncomfortable psychological state (i.e., anxiety or fear), the identification of physical benchmarks in the form of sensory experiences that accompany uncomfortable emotions is frequently used as an indication of benefit received from the therapeutic procedure (Mahrer, 1986).

Obtaining a Commitment to Work

Once a focal marker of unfinished business has been established, the second step is to obtain a commitment from the patient to work on the feeling and to move toward change. A simple question as to the patient's willingness to change, or a query about the interest he or she has in changing the feeling or behavior that has been identified, is frequently sufficient.

THERAPIST: Richard, I want to come back to you—to what you said you wanted to work on before.

PATIENT: Well, I don't know. I don't feel right now that there is anything really going on that I need help with, other than maybe trying to sleep at night.

T: OK—I can hear your uncertainty. What about the sleep problem?

P: Well, that—I just don't know what to do about it. I've tried everything. I just feel helpless.

T: Helpless?

P: Yeah! It's like—I don't feel capable of doing anything about it.

T: Does that helpless feeling remind you of anything?

P: Well—hmmm, yeah, I guess. Maybe. Maybe it's like when I feel like Paula is getting to me. I can't make things turn around.

T: OK. Is that something that you're willing to work on for the next few minutes—how those two feelings of being helpless are alike?

P: I guess so.

T: Are you sure you want to work? I hear you being very tentative. You can stop the work any time you want, you know.

P: Yes, that's good. I'm ready.

It is important to be aware of any hesitancy or lack of commitment on the part of the patient. Noncommitment can be noticed in tentative language and such nonverbal cues as the patient's tone of voice or posture. When such tentativeness is observed, it should be pointed out and perhaps discussed or elucidated. At this point, it may be helpful to give any needed assurances to the patient, so that a fuller commitment to the process can be made. These assurances can include permission to stop the work whenever the patient wishes and the expression of acceptance toward the patient's ambivalance. Exploration of the patient's hesitancy to make a commitment may itself reveal a split that may supplant the first focus of therapeutic work. Until the patient is able to make a willful commitment to engaging in work on a focused issue, the unfinished business initially presented as a point of focus is unlikely to be satisfactorily settled. The therapist should be aware that focus can change among segments of the session or may change from one session to another. If the patient's focus changes often within a session, it may be a sign of the patient's fear of staying with one focal issue long enough to experience confrontation and completion. In this case, the therapist should renegotiate a specific single focus and encourage the patient to stay with that focus until completion has been reached or a decision is made to stop the action on that focus.

The act of obtaining a commitment serves another purpose as well. The patient's sense of truly participating in the treatment process is especially critical in FEP and other therapies that emphasize the therapist's directive activity. Establishing the therapy process as a collaborative activity is critical to the ultimate outcome (Beutler, Crago, & Arizmendi, 1986; Orlinsky & Howard, 1986). When the therapist ensures that all therapist-directed activities are preceded by the patient's expression of agreement and willingness to work, collaboration is likely to be enhanced. Collaboration can also be clarified by designating a special chair as the working chair. Patients commit themselves to work and signify to others their readiness to work by physically moving from their usual seats to the working chair.

Doing the Experiment

The third step in the therapy process is the experiment itself. In this step, the goal is to develop a series of experiments with the patient, in order to assist the patient to encounter the unfinished business that has been targeted and to magnify the emotional and sensory components associated with that experience. Zinker (1977) has described this process succinctly:

> The experiment is a cornerstone of experiential learning. It transforms talking about into doing, stale reminiscing and theorizing into being fully here with all one's imagination, energy, and excitement. For example, by acting out an old, unfinished situation, the patient is able to comprehend it in its richest context

and to complete the experience using the resources of his present wisdom and understanding of life. (p. 123)

This quotation underlines a cardinal assumption of Gestalt psychotherapy that has been adopted in FEP—namely, that experiential learning is more valuable and long-lasting than either externally directed or passive learning (Orlinsky & Howard, 1986).

Working with What and How

In entering the working or experimental phase of the session, two self-directed questions center the therapist's selection of tasks: (1) What is the patient avoiding? (2) How is the patient avoiding it? Simply, the therapeutic experiment is designed in order to confront the patient with the "what" and to remove the "how" of avoidance. In FEP, the question of "what" is sought most frequently, though not exclusively, in some experience of anger. That is, the therapist assumes that patients are avoiding either some expression of or some awareness of anger. They may be symbolizing and internally representing anger in an alternative, nonangry way, or they may be discharging past anger in an inappropriate present environment. The task of the therapist, therefore, becomes that of moving such patients closer to both the source and the experience of angry emotions. Sometimes this can be accomplished by disarming the current method (i.e., the "how") of avoiding that emotion.

Methods of Experimenting

Some of the major categories of experiments that can be used to facilitate emotional arousal and awareness are listed in Table 4.2. While the list is neither detailed nor exhaustive, it does capture some of the diversity of techniques and objectives available to the therapist. The procedures are readily adapted to different expressive systems or contact boundaries and are suitable to different purposes within the session.

As noted in Table 4.2, the therapist has at his or her disposal a variety of procedures to utilize as experiments to help the patient confront avoided experience. Some of these intervention methods are decribed in detail within traditional Gestalt therapy literature (e.g., Perls, 1969; Polster & Polster, 1973), and others are illustrated and described more completely throughout this book. It should be noted that the experiments that can be employed cover the entire range of behavior, including verbal dialogue, nonverbal behavior, and both imagery and sensory experiences. However, it is usually

TABLE 4.2. Methodology in FEP: Experiments

Type	Purpose	Techniques
1. Dialogue	To confront suppressed, stored emotions.	Empty chair; fantasy; rehearsal; refinishing; role playing; puppetry.
2. Motoric	To involve the body's sensory system in release of suppressed emotion.	Acting out (e.g., hitting, kicking, etc.); writing, drawing, coloring; use of bataca (encounter bat).
3. Verbal	To reorganize the cognitive system so that it no longer blocks ownership of, and allows a release of, feelings.	Changes in language: from tentative to definite; from disowning to owning; from "about"-ism to "is"-ism; from "can't" to "won't"; from questions to statements; incomplete to complete sentences; from qualified to unqualified; from "you" to "I". Feeding of "try-on" statements. Use of language of anger.
4. Nonverbal	To put patient in heightened contact with bodily reactions.	Breathing; clenched hands/teeth; voice energy; screams vs. whining; facial reactions.
5. Closure	To provide closure for patient in the work to this point and to facilitate a move to the next step.	Goodbye; burial scene; quiet time.

convenient to begin with the process of sensory awareness (Mahrer, 1986) and dialogue methods when initially constructing experiments that are designed to magnify the emotions associated with unfinished business. These procedures are illustrated in the following example.

PATIENT: But it's still—it's very tight in here. Very tight.

THERAPIST: OK. If you were gonna give a voice to that tightness, what would it say?

P: I'm being squeezed (*laughing*).

T: I'm being squeezed? All right, who squeezes?

P: I'm being smothered.

T: I'm being smothered? What's the rest of you saying back? Like maybe your head? What's your head saying back?

P: It wants to open up, in that area. The rest of my body feels pretty open, to me anyway. I'm sure I'm very tense.

T: Uh-huh? OK.

P: I've gone in to the doctor a hundred times, and he says, "Boy, are you tense!" and I'm going, "Really, I didn't know that."

T: OK, so this part's saying, "I'm being squeezed," and the rest of you is saying, "I'm feeling open."

P: Mmm-hmm.

T: Close your eyes again and go back and forth between those two parts, the squeezed part and the open part. Just move your attention from one to the other (*Pause*) You're doing a real good job of staying focused right now, so just keep it up, just focus on that tense part, squeezed part and then focus on the rest of you. (*Pause*) Do those two parts like each other?

P: I don't know (*laughing*) what you mean by "like." They're pretty independent.

T: Oh, OK, they don't know each other much, huh? Why don't you introduce them? (*Laughing*) I know, I do weird things sometimes, I mean, do it! Squeezed part, this is the open part. Open part, this is the squeezed part. See if they'll shake hands, like at a cocktail party (*laughing*).

P: It just seems like the lower part, it wants to dominate this part.

T: OK.

P: But it's not having much success. I kind of relate it to myself.

T: OK, and what would—

P: I'm this part.

T: OK. And what about the part down here?

P: That's somebody else.

T: Are we talking about the new me and the old me, or not?

P: No.

T: No? It's something else? OK.

P: It's somebody exterior to me.

T: OK. Close your eyes again and check that out, see what that exterior part is.

P: It's male, whatever it is, it's a male.

T: It's a male? OK, and the squeezed part is—

P: Is me.

T: OK. Female, OK. Let the female part have a voice and say something to the male part.

P: Shut up! (*Laughing*)

T: What does the male part say back?

As one can see from the foregoing example, the process of sensory focus can readily lead to a verbal dialogue between the person and a significant other. The use of an empty chair facilitates this latter exchange. Experiments such as this are among the unique characteristics of Gestalt therapy that also apply to its more circumscribed offspring, FEP. Engaging the patient in a dialogue with a significant other creates the opportunity for the patient to experience new concepts as they arise in awareness. As the dialogue evolves, other Gestalt techniques, including observations made by the therapist, suggestions, repetition of sentences, and sensory focus, may all be acceptable; the guiding principle is to increase or magnify the patient's current emotional state. As more communication systems (e.g., motoric, nonverbal, sensory) are invoked, the likelihood of successfully escalating feelings and awareness also increases. This process can be traced in the following extended example of a therapeutic exchange.

THERAPIST: Go back and pay attention to your breathing right now. What's going on?

PATIENT: Well, I'm spitting up mucus.

T: OK. OK. You need more Kleenex next to you?

P: I'm wheezing. I just took my medication, so I don't know why I'm having this.

T: OK. Part of that may be because of the feelings that you're having, too, so let's just kind of monitor what's going on with that. If you need to change your physical position or something, then just tell me, "I need to pay attention to what's going on with my breathing."

P: Mmm-hmm.

T: The scene that I get in my mind with that sense of choking is the one that you described one night when your husband was choking you and your son was there, because that's the most graphic scene that I know about where you were the victim. I don't know whether that's a focus for you or not at this point. Is it?

P: Not particularly.

T: OK. Is there another situation that is?

P: Well, it's hard to say, there are so many incidents that . . .

T: OK, what we need is something specific. OK, a particular time.

P: Well, the other—it was him or with my first husband too.

T: You pick which one to start with; you may need to work on both of them.

P: Well, one with my first husband—

T: OK.

P: —that I remember real well—

T: OK.

P: —and that was the last one. He—(*coughing*) I was in bed and sleeping. He had followed me all over town for 24 hours that day and said, "If you don't come home then I'm gonna"—you know—"things are gonna be worse." I had these high heels on and I was exhausted. I tried to escape him and he'd find me and I was running through the streets, he'd come in the other direction. I screamed. So finally, I was so exhausted I went home. We both—we were both tired so we went to bed and then first thing in the morning he got up really early, pulled the covers off me, and said "Get up!" You know? And I was naked, and he started looking, he says, "I want to know where your passports are and your money." And he started looking all over the place for it. I had the address of some friends I left it with, in my purse, and I didn't want him having that stuff, you know. That was mine. I said, "You're never going to find them!" because I had figured out a week before that, when I sort of sensed things were not right here, that I better give my passport to a friend and my money too—for safekeeping; just in case it blows up. And sure enough, you know. So we fought over the purse and he grabbed me by the hair and threw me against the wall, and threw me all over the place and punched me in the eye and the stomach and all over. I managed to get my clothes on, just barely, but he grabbed my keys and that's when I ran out of the house. I just ran and ran to the police station. And I was hysterical for 4 days. I had to sit there for 12 hours in the police station and they said, "Well, we need a doctor's report and we need your documents," and so on. I said—after 12 hours of sitting there, I said, "I don't have them with me." And they said, "Well, that's what you need." So I went to the doctor and all he did, he just asked me one question, "Does your neck hurt?" And I said, "Yeah! How do *you* know?" And he just said, "Well, honey," and he just wrote down something—"you go take this to the police." And so I got my passport from my friend and went back to the police, presented it to them, and they said, "Well, what do you expect us to do?" You know, "What do you want us to do?"

T: So there's more than one person that's a focus for your anger in this situation. One's your first husband and the others are the police, who didn't help the way you needed help.

P: Well, they don't have the facilities there, but I finally said, "Well, either you file a report or you can shoot me right now." You know, "I'm not gonna leave until you file it." So they finally did.

T: OK.

P: And even though I was laughing, they said, "Why are you laughing?" I said, "Well, I'd rather laugh than cry, wouldn't you?" (*Laughing*) You know, I—

T: Check out what's happening with your breathing right now as you're talking about this particular incident. Is it changing, or is it staying the same?

P: It's better. It's a little better.

T: OK. I'm going to ask you to take a snapshot of that scene, you know, like the one thing that is most vivid to you in this scene with your husband—

P: It's when he's pulling my hair and throws me against the wall.

T: OK. Close your eyes for a minute, please, and if you're willing to, go back and experience him doing that again. Only this time, I want you to say something to him, not from your laughing place, but from your scared place.

P: I just can't feel scared.

T: What would happen if you did?

P: I'd feel sick.

T: OK. I'm asking you to do that because I've got a hunch that part of what you need to understand and finish what happened is to know that you were scared. OK? And if you feel sick, we'll get something for you to throw up in. I believe that it makes sense to be scared when you've got somebody grabbing you by the hair—

P: I was angry.

T: —and throwing you, that too. That too. OK.

P: I was just angry. And I couldn't—I really wasn't feeling emotion so much as trying to figure out what to do next.

T: But we're not in this situation now, OK? We're dealing with feelings from that situation now, 'cause he's not really here. Close your eyes again and just check out what's happening with your body, and just report to me what you're aware of in your body.

P: As usual, my stomach always tightens up.

T: OK, what else?

P: And my throat kind of tightens up.

T: OK.

P: Chest.

T: OK.

P: And I feel—I can feel the tension, like my whole body's just curled up.

T: OK. All right. Go ahead and do that. Just do it more, in fact. Tighten up your stomach more and tighten up your chin and your throat more and just tighten up.

P: I can't do it, not naturally.

T: OK. What happened just then as you let go?

P: I feel sick. I feel sick to my stomach.

T: OK.

P: I'm not gonna throw up, though, I don't think.

T: Just stay with what's going on with your body. What's happening right now?

P: I'm hot, but cold at the same time.

T: OK. Just experience those two things going on at the same time. I'm going to ask you to visualize him in front of you getting ready to grab your hair.

P: Oh, Jesus, it turns my stomach!

T: OK, just stay with what's going on. OK? Say something to him.

P: You bastard. (*Laughs*)

T: OK. Do it without laughing.

P: (*In Spanish*) Son of a bitch.

T: OK, that's fine. If you do it in Spanish, it'll be OK. OK. Say it again.

P: (*In Spanish*) Miserable bastard. (*Laughs*)

T: And I laugh. Say that to him too in Spanish.

P: What?

T: I laugh.

P: (*In Spanish*) I laugh. (*Pause*) What's wrong with you? (*Pause*) I don't understand why you do these things. (*To therapist, in English*) It doesn't help you, does it, to hear it in Spanish? (*Laughing*)

T: Don't worry about that, 'cause that's what you would have done in the situation, so just keep using Spanish.

P: Well, he doesn't speak English, so there's no way I could have talked to him—

T: Yeah, right, just keep going.

P: (*In Spanish*)Why don't you leave me alone? Why do you torment me so? Why do you treat me this way? What have I done to deserve your treating me this way? I don't understand.

T: And right now I'm feeling—

P: (*In Spanish*) And now I'm feeling—(*In English*) I'm feeling just, there's no meaning to this, you know, if there's—I don't see the rhyme or reason—

T: And he's grabbing you by the hair and he's throwing you up against the wall—

P: And I give him a kick to release myself.

T: OK. Do it. Again. Again. Again. What do you want to do?

P: You know, give some, you know, hit him like that. And then I'd run off or something, you know.

T: What's happening in your body right now?

P: I feel tired.

T: Tired. OK. Why don't you go back and sit over there? Close your eyes again and just rest for a little bit if you're feeling tired.

P: I just want him to leave me alone.

T: OK. And he's still coming at you.

P: I just would keep kicking him.

T: What are you going to do right now?

P: Now? I don't feel like moving. (*Laughing*)

T: OK. So one way to survive in that situation is for you to be real still like you are now, OK?

P: Mmm-hmm.

T: That's one choice you have. Another choice is to kick. I'm just asking you to make that choice right now and do what you need to do.

P: Well, for some reason I just see myself as being free of that situation.

T: OK. Say goodbye to him then.

P: (*Laughing*) *Adios*. (*In Spanish*) If I see you, I won't remember. (*Laughing*)

Notice, in this example, how the therapist moved the patient from a sensory awareness (wheezing) to a past experience (being choked by her husband) that indicated the possibility of unfinished business. The therapist allowed the patient to retell her experience of a traumatic event of abuse, while at the same time tying together the reliving of the event and her present physiological responses (i.e., nausea, tight throat, etc.). Finally, the therapist moved the patient to a strong physical reaction (kicking the imagined husband), enabling the patient to release herself from the helpless stance left over from the actual experience of the abuse in the past.

Escalation of Experience

In escalating the intensity of the patient's experiences, the therapist does well to attend to the patient's process as it unfolds. The patient moves from moment to moment to increase the intensity of an experience and to remove the constraining influences of defenses. Hence, the therapist may ask the patient to focus on a nonverbal behavior that either may be a sign of an interruption preventing experience or may symbolize the presence of experience not yet within the patient's awareness. By exaggerating statements, voice inflections, and bodily movements, and by polarizing the patient's verbal statements, the therapist escalates affect and forces features of these emotions into the patient's awareness. The therapist, however, must remain sensitive to indications of both the completion and lack of completion of this work process. Typically, completion is indexed by the achievement of a plateau in the level of intensity, and subsequently by a spontaneous diminution of emotional intensity in the absence of defensive maneuvers. This latter process may be accompanied by a spontaneous reformulation or insight about how the patient has organized his or her world.

Indexing Completion Experiences

Some of the characteristic behaviors that index completion are an increased freedom of emotional expression, a shift from negative to positive awareness, and an expanded breadth of affective display. Figure 4.1 is a scale that defines completion in terms of these characteristics. This scale has been used in our research programs to help therapist and other clinical raters learn to identify completion states. The reader will note that completion is rated both from the patient's report of emotional acknowledgment and from behavioral indices of emotional change, of an increased range of acceptable feelings, and of unhalting expression of intense feelings. An ideal completion experience exists when the patient can identify and congruently express

FIGURE 4.1. Emotional Completion Scale.

Completion:

This is a measure of how much the patient allows emotions to come to the surface and to be expressed in the here-and-now of the counseling session. It assesses to what extent the patient permits the complete expression of emotion.

1	2	3	4	5	6	7
Denial: Although the patient presents as having lingering, persistent ill feelings, there is denial of unfinished business with people and/or denial of anger.	No acknowledgment. Unaware expression. Signs of unfinished business are available (foot tapping, restricted breathing, clenched fists, etc.). Patient is unaware.	Acknowledgment—blocked expression. Patient will acknowledge the presence of unfinished anger or other emotion, but will only "talk about" it.	Acknowledgment—immediate interruption. Emotional arousal begins in the patient, but then the patient interrupts and will not stay with the physical sensation (moist eyes, etc.).	Acknowledgment—early interruption. Emotion begins to be expressed, but the patient interrupts the natural flow (e.g., may have angry voice for a moment and then moves away from further expression).	Acknowledgment—incomplete release. The patient allows extended expression of emotions, but completion is not achieved. No full shift of emotional experience. Still some signs of lingering unfinished feelings.	Acknowledgment—free expression, emotional shift. Patient allows free and full expression of emotion, complete with bodily changes, a sense of completion, and a shift in emotional experience of self and of significant other.

57

an array of positive and negative feelings and has moved from a negative feeling to a positive sense of freedom and release.

In the following excerpt from a session, one can observe the ebb and flow as the patient neared, then blocked completion. One can also perceive change in the patient's experience from one of negativity—confusion—to one of pleasure.

PATIENT: Now, at night if some—I have some question in my mind, um, I have to allow my brain to function so it can find a solution and until I find the solution I'm not gonna sleep. You know, that's what it boils down to—I have to find a solution or—until I find the solution I'm gonna be awake, and I'm gonna find it.

THERAPIST: OK. So you're gonna go looking for it.

P: Right. Even if it's at one o'clock at night (*laughing*).

T: Then you might look for a solution in the green chair, and you might look for a solution in the orange chair, and then you might move over to the turquoise chair over there, back to the couch—

P: Right, right.

T: —and that's the way your brain's working, you're looking for an answer. You want to do that, see how it feels to act it out, kind of?

P: Act it out?

T: Yeah.

P: You mean just from chair to chair?

T: Yeah.

P: Usually I go into a book (*laughing*).

T: Well, let's just use the chairs to represent it, if that's OK. It's just a way to get it out, kind of, so we can understand what's going on. Like, what is something you might be thinking about at night before you go to sleep that you want a solution for?

P: (*Sighing*) How to handle a relationship.

T: OK. OK. So you sit in that chair, what might you say? What's the way to handle it?

P: This is the way I handle it. Um, disappear for about 3 weeks (*laughing*).

T: OK, move over to this one. You just kind of go like that?

P: Yeah.

T: How about this one?

P: This one? What do I do—about the same relationship?

T: Yeah, what else might you say?

P: Call him up (*laughing*).

T: OK. Go over there and think of something else.

P: Over there?

T: Yeah. This is a little more far out, this is more fun (*laughing*).

P: Um, let's see. Hmmm—what can I do?

T: OK, OK. There's no answer, it's a little like, what's the che—what do I do, what do I do?

P: No, no, let me see, no, um, go out with somebody else! (*laughing*)

T: OK, all right. Move to that one. See what you get.

P: OK. Write a letter.

T: How about that chair?

P: Forget him (*laughing*).

T: Uh-huh? Ok, come back to this one. Keep moving now, 'cause you can't go to sleep. We gotta stay awake (*laughing*).

P: That's right (*laughing*). I'm gonna get rid of him altogether (*laughing*).

ANOTHER PATIENT: Maybe you can sleep better then. (*General laughter*)

T: Somebody's being practical over here. What do we want somebody being practical for?

P: Now, now in this chair I'm waiting for him to call me.

T: Oh, OK. All right, move again.

P: Shucks, he hasn't called me, so now I've gotta go looking for him, at one o'clock (*laughing*). No, no, no, that's not me, that's not my style.

T: OK, so you think about that one or reject it. Now, OK (*laughing*).

P: That's what I do (*laughing*).

T: How are you doing?

P: Fine! I think it's funny!

T: I remember you said last week that you thought laughing was real healthy sometimes. I think that's right.

P: Well, like you said when I came in, you were concerned that I was laughing, that maybe it was inappropriate, but I was really having fun with myself too.

T: But it can be—

P: I tell jokes to myself and people don't know it, you know it?

T: I liked laughing just then. It was fun, I think it was fun for all of us.

The Impasse

When the therapist becomes aware that the patient is no longer increasing the level of arousal, is employing a previously observed defense, and does not appear to be spontaneously reformulating or integrating the experience, an impasse has been defined. Frequently, the increased use of physical expressiveness at these points can move the patient through the impasse by engaging more of his or her sensory and cognitive systems in the experiment. In the following segment, this occurred at the point when the therapist asked the patient to stand up and continue the dialogue.

THERAPIST: "I'm hurt by"—say it to her [the patient's mother].

PATIENT: I'm hurt by—(*Pause*)

T: What's your objection to telling her?

P: (*To empty chair*) Because you think I am—you rely on me to be the strong one in the family, but at the same time you belittle me.

T: OK. Take some time to hear what you just said. OK? Don't move on, just stay with it for a while.

P: And that's a contradictory message.

T: What are you feeling right now?

P: I'm observing.

T: So you moved away. OK. Just be conscious of what you're doing and what you want to do right now. You can observe, or you can feel the hurt, or you can express your anger. Just make a choice about what you're going to do.

P: Hmmm—I think I want to express some anger.

T: OK. Just try standing up again. Start some sentences with "I resent . . ."

P: I resent the fact that you expected me for so long to watch over Christine.

T: OK. "I resent *you* for . . ."

P: I resent the fact that you relied on me to—to take care of everything, and I resent the fact that you tell me I can't have my son, that I'm not well enough to take care of him.

T: OK. Change "I resent the fact . . ." to "I resent *you* for . . ."

P: I resent you when you tell me that I need to move from my place. I don't want to move any more, and I feel like you don't understand that I just don't want to move any more. I like it where I'm at and I don't want to be running away from this impossible man all my life. I'm gonna stand and fight back, you know, and you keep telling me to run all the time. Well, I'm not a coward and I have to have some self-respect (*sighing*).

T: Just feel that sigh? What's that about?

P: Sort of a release.

T: OK. I noticed you moved your feet, too, like you're standing there. What else do you need to say to her?

P: Well, I wish you would stop criticizing men all the time. It's almost like you hate them, and that's been another source of conflict for me, and, you know—I see people as human beings with good sides and bad sides and weak points and strong points, not as being bad and good, but as being human. And every time you put somebody down it's like a knife inside of me, you know. Sure, I'm dealing with a crazy man, that's true (*sighing*).

T: What's happening right now, Sally? What are you aware of?

P: Just I sighed. I feel—

T: Helpless?

P: Helpless.

T: OK. Where do you want to be right now? Do you want to express anger, do you want to feel the hurt, or do you want to move away?

P: I'm moving away.

T: OK. What do you want to do right now? Just be conscious of what's happening.

P: I just want to tell her a few things.

T: Do you want to do it from the standing place or the sitting place?

P: This is fine.

T: OK. Go ahead.

P: (Sighing) It's really hard for me to say that I love you. I don't think I've ever said it.

T: Can you say it right now?

P: No, I can say, "I care a lot about you," but saying, "I love you" is really hard.

T: OK. Take your time and just decide whether or not you're willing to try that out, and see how it sounds if you say it directly to her.

P: No, I can't say it.

T: What do you think would happen if you did?

P: It wouldn't be true—

T: OK.

P: —and it—it's sort of true, it's—I don't love her the way I love my son.

T: OK.

P: And to me, when you say—love to me is a big word, it's not a small word.

T: Is there something that you need to do with her before you can say "I love you" to her?

P: I think so.

T: What is it?

P: (Sighs)

T: Not meaning that your love for her would be the same as for your son—I think they're different, too. But what would you need to do with her before you can say "I love you" to her?

P: Feel that she really appreciates and respects me as an adult, that she doesn't see me as an uncapable or helpless child any more, but doesn't rely on me to solve all her problems and be the mother to her. I've had to be the mother to you so many times and you're not aware of that.

T: Tell her what you're willing to do about that and what you're not willing to do.

P: Well, you know, I'm willing to listen to things that upset you 'cause I don't want you to be upset, but I'm not willing to listen to things you complain about over and over again and do nothing about. That you're not willing to do something about. I don't want to hear it at all, and I don't want to hear any arguments between you and your husband. Not in front of me. If you're going to argue, don't argue in front of me. Just go away. Don't come back until you've grown up.

T: Do you feel like that?

P: Yes. I hate arguments and I hate that condescending tone in your voice where you go, "Oh, honey, why don't you realize—" you know, you just have this tone of voice that just puts people down, and I also think you need to give your husband more space and other people a little more space.

T: OK. You're moving over to telling her what she should do right now. Come back and tell her what you're gonna do and what you're not, or tell her what you feel, but stay in your place, don't come over to hers.

P: I don't want to tell you what you should do, I just—

T: Tell her what you're feeling.

Time Limits

Sometimes, when an impasse is reached, establishing time limits for the patient can help him or her to mobilize unused sources of energy in the service of pushing through the blockage. It is appropriate, however, to end the experiment with a promise to return, if the work is not completed. At the end of the experiment phase, the therapist elicits from the patient a "good-bye"—a process that keeps the door open to further work on the unfinished business, and also facilitates a sense of hopeful resolution.

THERAPIST: OK! Are you ready to stop there for a while?

PATIENT: Yes, I am. I feel really good about what I said to her.

T: Good! Now say goodbye to your mother. We may want to come back to her later.

P: I don't know what to say.

T: How about just saying "Goodbye" and telling her you may be back when you have more to say?

P: OK! Mom, I'm going to leave you now for a while. I'll be back and we can finish this later. Goodbye.

Assessing the Impact of Work

The fourth step immediately follows the "goodbye" process of the experi-ment in the preceding phase. This fourth step is an assessment phase, in which the goal is to integrate and assess the results of the work accomp-lished in the third step. This assessment establishes the emotional changes at a cognitive level and reinforces a cognitive reformulation of experience.

Evaluation is accomplished by soliciting here-and-now awareness of changes in physical benchmarks, as well as in emotional and cognitive reactions, and by applying a new formulation to these reactions, thereby allowing a reintegration of new awareness to occur. Frequently, input from other group members is appropriate and solicited for this task. Nonetheless, the therapist continues to encourage the patient to focus upon current experience in the process of reintegration. For example, a statement that encourages the patient to notice current feelings, current sensations, or changes from previous sensations and experiences is helpful.

THERAPIST: How are you feeling right now?

PATIENT: My chest is a little looser and my breathing is a bit easier.

T: How does it compare to when you started today?

P: Well, it's a lot better, actually. The pain in my legs is gone, too. That's funny, I'm not even aware of when they quit hurting.

And an evaluation such as the following goes beyond assessment of the physical benchmarks.

THERAPIST: OK. Anything else you need to say to him right now?

PATIENT: I'm glad you're gone.

T: Tell him what you did for you this morning and then say goodbye.

P: Jeff, I made myself more of a whole person. I don't have to walk around worrying about you, about how I'm going to react to you, or what you are going to do to me. You're physically in my life, but emotionally and mentally, goodbye. I don't need you any more. (*Silence*)

T: What's going on right now?

P: It's really strange. You know . . .

T: Notice the difference between what you felt when you sat down in the chair and what you feel now.

P: It's different—really different, you know?

T: Just stay with it and notice what it is. Be aware of what those differences are, and as you're in touch with them say what they are.

P: Control. I mean it's like I'm—he's not controlling me any more. You know, I feel free. I feel—I feel like I can talk about him and not cry. And, you know, you could ask questions about him and I wouldn't fall apart.

Developing Plans and Homework

The fifth step in the therapy process is devoted to making plans for the immediate future. This step is similar to what is described as the "working agreement" by Woollams and Brown (1978):

From time to time throughout the course of therapy, a client may be asked to do a specific task. These requests are made by the therapists and/or group members, and are intended to help the client reach their treatment goals. On other occasions, the client herself may suggest subcontracts which she thinks will help her reach her goals or provide her with some extra protection while she is trying out new behaviors. These working agreements are frequently referred to colloquially as contracts, or subcontracts. When these agreements call for behaviors to be performed outside of the treatment session, they are called homework assignments. (p. 255)

Utilization of the Work

The patient is given assistance in making use of the information and awareness gained from the work completed. This help may include needed rehearsal with other group members within the group or contact with significant others outside of the group. Homework contracts for the immediate future are also made; these are pursued in subsequent sessions, and often develop into separate integrative experiments.

THERAPIST: Perhaps it would be helpful if you would keep track of your pain over the next week. Each time you experience the feeling in your back, maybe notice what else is going on.

PATIENT: OK! I can do that. I'm not sure what you want me to do, though.

T: Well, I guess I look at this as an experiment. You've seen today how your pain changes when you begin to really let some of that rage loose. The question that comes to me is whether or not your pain gets worse as you find yourself in new situations in which anger would be an appropriate experience.

P: Oh, yeah! Maybe when I experience pain in my back, I'm wanting someone to get off of it. Yeah, I can keep track of what is happening when I get that back pain.

T: Good! Some people find it helpful to carry a little pad of paper around and to mark down whenever they are having pain, how strong it is, and what else is happening.

Here is an example of reversing the introjection (in this case, changing guilt to resentment):

THERAPIST: Today you turned your guilt around and expressed your resentment.

PATIENT: Yeah. (*Pause*) I didn't see the connection before.

T: I'd like to have you continue to work with that idea. Would you be willing?

P: Yes.

T: OK. Each time you find yourself feeling guilty this week, ask yourself what you might be resenting—and not expressing. Make some notes of what happens.

P: OK.

To assist the patient in keeping the work done in the session in the foreground, so that it will not get lost during the intervening week, an assignment can be given of daily putting the significant other in the "empty chair" (or on the floor mat) at home and carrying out a 20- to 30-minute dialogue. Patients who are consistent in carrying out the assignment often report resolution of the issue as a result of the homework.

Sometimes group members who have not worked in the session will develop homework with the assistance and encouragement of the leader, as a result of the discussion and feedback in the closing round that concludes each session.

Homework possibilities include the following:

1. "For the next 24 hours, be very self-observant so you will be aware of changes in your thinking, feeling, and behaving."
2. "Sit down once a day for 10 minutes, put your significant other in a facing chair, and tell that person how you are feeling toward him or her that day."
3. (If work is not completed or is blocked in the session:) "This week make a list of all the resentments (appreciations) you did not mention to your significant other in today's session, and bring the list to next session."
4. (For patients who tend to deny or sabotage their work:) "When you get home, call up two people of your choosing to tell them about the feelings you are experiencing as a result of today's session."
5. "Take the rest of the evening to be quietly with yourself so that digestion of the results of your work can take place—put 'on hold' the commencement of any new or additional activities until tomorrow."
6. "This week tabulate the times you use tentative language. Make notes as to when, where, with whom, about what, and so on, this tentative language takes place."
7. For couples:
   a. "Give each other one resentment a day for the next week, using the 'I resent you for . . .' sentence, *and also* two appreciations, using the 'I appreciate you for . . .' statement—no 'you' language allowed!"

b. "Ask your significant other to catch you when you qualify or discount yourself."

Summary

Although there are no absolute rules for conducting a session, the process of FEP can be distilled to five major tasks:

1. Identification of a focus for the work of the session.
2. Commitment from the patient to risk exploration and confrontation of that focal point.
3. Doing a work experiment, in which the patient allows himself or herself to become totally involved in the confrontation and possible resolution of the unfinished business.
4. Assessment of the impact the work has upon the patient.
5. Development of ways to further the work beyond the therapeutic session.

We have identified markers for unfinished business that we find useful in establishing a focal point for the session. Therapists also need to be aware of common methods for interruption and control of anger, so that they can help identify the presence of significant areas of unfinished business. There are at least four classes of significant others with whom unfinished business is often associated: (1) parents, (2) intimate partners, (3) children, and (4) siblings. Patterns of avoidance should be particularly observed when patients discuss members of these relationship categories.

Benchmarks are important for both therapist and patient as a means of assessing the impact of the work as it proceeds. Physical benchmarks are most impactful, since physiological changes have a tendency to be concrete rather than abstract.

The therapist has available an endless supply of techniques to use for the benefit of the patient; these are limited only by appropriateness to the situation and by the therapist's creativity. There is, however, a common group of procedures that originate from traditional Gestalt methodology as well as from other sources. Dialogue and sensory awareness are foundations from which procedures can be derived to extend and escalate disowned experience.

The assessment and homework phases of the process are critical to the reorganization of the perceptual system through integration of the new world view achieved as a result of the work. It is important to assure ways of carrying the work outside the session into everyday living.

5

Phases of Patient Experience

While the therapist follows his or her "road map" through the stages of the session, the successful patient concomitantly goes through various layers of experience to achieve an ever-increasing sense of awareness and purity of experience. The process of traversing these layers requires sequentially giving up what Perls (1973) has described as "neurotic mechanisms." This process usually takes place in five experiential phases defined by the apparent struggle of the patient. These phases usually follow the sequence outlined below, but the flow and particularly the intensity vary with which any given patient experiences these phases. One patient may experience strongly the process of implosion, whereas another may react more intensely to the phase of explosion; one may experience the phases in one order, and another may experience them in a slightly different sequence. Regardless of order or intensity, each phase usually requires several sessions of direct or vicarious therapeutic work. The phases are as follows:

1. Disownment
2. Phobia
3. Implosion
4. Explosion
5. Completion

Disownment

Psychological problems are defined by experience disownment. Angry and irritable feelings are the most frequently disowned, and, concomitantly, are the ones that produce the greatest difficulty in social interactions. People deny their experiences of anger directly; they may indirectly attribute these feelings externally; or they may otherwise distance themselves from the experience and expected consequences of anger. By definition, however, all who sense themselves in need of emotional assistance are disowning aspects of their emotional existence and are engaging in self-deception. Concomitantly, they experience disturbance in differentiating emotional experience, in discriminating associated introjections, and in maintaining authenticity.

When the patient is disowning emotional reactions, it is often beneficial to start by calling attention to physical sensations.

THERAPIST: As you talk with your father, I'm taken by what your hand is doing.

PATIENT: I wasn't noticing.

T: OK, continue to talk with him and be aware of your hand—notice how it continues to clench into a fist.

P: (*To father*) I really don't understand why you say those hurtful things to me.

T: There—don't change what your hand is doing—just move your focus to your hand.

P: Yeah, I guess it is a fist.

T: Just let your hand continue to tighten. You might stop talking for a moment and let your hand move. That's it. Now, shake your fist at your father and say something.

P: Ooh—I'm beginning to feel my face get hot.

T: Tell your father that.

The process of emotional disownment may be partial or complete. Complete disownment is accomplished either through simple denial of one's own inner state (e.g., "I'm not angry") or through the added process of attributing one's anger to others as projection (e.g., "I'm not angry, *you're* angry"). This process is easily observed and recognized by even the novice therapist. On the other hand, partial disownment is more difficult to recognize than complete disownment, and the skilled patient may seduce the therapist into believing that he or she is actually accepting anger while in the very process of disowning it.

The therapist should be aware that even though the patient may express an appreciation for the introjected values regarding anger that are represented by the process of disowning, both the process of justifying this experience and that of externally attributing it are forms of self-deception and disownment. This self-deception is exemplified by the patient who rejects the therapist's offers to work on identified unfinished business. This refusal may be justified with the suggestion that any anger there is has evolved from insignificant, past behaviors, and therefore the anger is either unjustified or insignificant in the present. One observes in this pattern a paradoxical relationship between the patient's presentation of anger as a significant experience and either the concomitant denial of its significance or its justification as a means of avoiding further conflict. Hence, work is often resisted through intellectualizing, making judgments on feelings or behavior, changing the topic, and lapsing into helplessness (e.g., "I can't express my anger"). The therapist should pay attention to these commitment struggles and think of them as "splits" that characterize the patient's pattern of moving toward and simultaneously away from the experience of his or her own anger.

When the patient is not aware of suppressed anger or is denying it in some way, it can be helpful to elicit statements of motivation for coming to therapy. Sometimes these statements contain the signs of suppressed anger. A patient who is feeling depressed may be willing to admit to that feeling, but often will not be aware of anger, since depression is characteristically the result of failing to own and express angry responses to events in the patient's life. This type of disowning is often manifested by a patient who says, "I just feel hurt, I don't feel angry." In this type of situation, the therapist has an opportunity to help the patient distinguish between a feeling that is within one's self and a feeling one has toward the other person.

THERAPIST: How do you feel about your dad never having confidence in you?

PATIENT: I just feel terribly hurt—I want to cry as I think about that (*eyes tearing up*).

T: Right—that's the feeling you have *inside* of you. And how do you feel *toward* Dad for his lack of confidence in you?

P: Well, I'm mad at him, I guess.

T: Take the "I guess" out of that statement and see if you will own that sentence.

Likewise, for patients who are aware of feeling guilty but are not in touch with their resentment, it is often productive to explore resentment as though it is an expression of guilt. Mahrer (1983, 1986) has conceptualized the patient's struggle as one between dialectic feelings, only one of which is allowed expression. Indeed, the therapist does well to assume that expressed feelings of discomfort represent conflicts between the voice of the "operating domain" (the realm of current and conscious experience) and the opposing forces of the "deeper potential." To expand upon the suggestions of Gendlin (1968), the therapist is encouraged to focus on and magnify feeling states, and from there to initiate a dialogue with the patient that represents the two sides of this struggle. In Mahrer's procedure, the therapist takes the voice of the inaccessible deeper potential and confronts the patient's conscious experience with argument, insult, demand, and plea.

In more traditional Gestalt therapy procedures, the patient is asked to take the voice of both sides of the struggle—to engage in a dialogue in which each side represents an aspect of the patient's internal issue with anger. Often, however, dialogues that start as expressions of different parts of one's self rapidly become recognized as representations of interpersonal rather than intrapsychic splits; the two sides of the internal dialogue represent a struggle between one's self and a significant other earlier in the patient's life.

PATIENT: (*In first chair*) You never get off my back. I'm doing the best I can.

THERAPIST: Switch chairs.

P: (*In second chair*) If I left you alone, you'd never get anywhere. I always have to push you to follow through on things. (*Gets up and switches chairs*)

P: (*In first chair*) But I feel awful, when you never let up on me. I'm tired of you always pushing me to go faster—do more.

T: Who else in your life did you need to say that to?

P: Oh . . . my father. Yeah, my father. I could never do enough for him. I never was able to relax—there was always more.

T: I suggest we change the experiment. Bring you father in and see what happens as you say what you just said, but say it to him.

P: (*To father*) I could never do enough for you. You never let up on me. You just pushed and pushed and pushed.

T: Tell him how you feel as you say that.

P: I feel like I did as a kid. My gut hurts right now as I talk to you.

T: Tell him what you resent.

P: (*To therapist*) I could never do that—he'd hand me my head.

T: And here is a place for you to experiment with saying what is unsaid. Willing to see what happens?

P: I feel nervous, but OK.

T: Tell your father what you resent.

As the foregoing suggests, at the point at which the dialogue is recognized as an interpersonal conflict, the therapy process may be reconstructed as a direct dialogue between the patient and significant other. If the dialogue has evolved from the patient's initial resistance to work, for example, the dialogue is then encouraged to continue, with sequential magnifications of the dialectic messages until both the patient and the therapist can recognize that the original inability to commit to work is simply a re-enactment in the therapy environment of earlier struggles with objects of anger and love.

THERAPIST: So, your goal is to stop scaring yourself so much.

PATIENT: I believe that. And the constant—I worry so much about something happening to my husband.

T: Mmm-Hmm.

P: Now I'm worried about, and I'm worried about him working in Yuma. The depth of fear. The fear is if I—I think to myself if I was a "normal" 34-year-old woman and my husband had to go out of town to work, well, that's life. You know, he has to work, he has to pay the bills, and that's it. But no, I have to—I bring up all these things. Who's gonna, you know, do the pool?

T: Well, if you get normal, how will you be?

P: Normal? (*Speaking rapidly*) "OK, honey, just mail the check home. Mail the check home, I'll take care of everything. Don't worry. I'll mow the grass, and I'll—and I'll clean the swimming pool." I'm not cleaning the swimming pool, I don't even swim. If I fell in, I'd be dead. And who can take care of the yard?

T: Wait a minute, now (*laughing*). Wait a minute. This is going too fast for me.

(*General laughter.*)

P: I followed that perfectly (*laughing*).

(*General laughter.*)

T: That's a normal person? You just rushed from being very understanding to predicting death.

P: No, no, that one wasn't normal—then I flew back to, you know, me. No, I can't do it. The normal person is "Go ahead, I understand. I'll take care of things." It's not—and not fearful. He told me at first he was gonna sleep in a tent. I went like, I went crazy. "You know, they kill people," I said, "in the desert. You're not sleeping in a tent." And then I saw myself that I was saying, he's gonna do this. Even though this may not happen, I mean, he may not have to go to Yuma. But he may, and I'm of course worrying about it.

T: Willing to experiment with this?

P: Yeah, OK.

T: OK? I'm gonna have you—I need another chair.

P: (*Laughing*) Playing musical chairs?

(*General laughter.*)

T: I'm gonna have you divide yourself in half.

P: (*Indicating vertical or horizontal*) This way or this way?

(*General laughter.*)

T: Well, I hear two parts of you going on, two parts that are there. One part of you is that part that would like to be able to let him go if he needs to go because his job takes him there. And then there's the other part of you that just scares the hell out of yourself about it.

P: Mmm-hmm.

T: So let's divide those two parts out, and what I would suggest that you do is get those two parts of you talking to each other. Kind of slow it down, because sometimes, I think, we talk to ourselves that way, but in high gear up here (*pointing to head*). It's kind of like, I say "X" to myself, and then I say "Y" to myself and it's going so fast and I get to the point where it doesn't get solved, I just go around in circles.

P: OK.

T: So, come over here and be the part of you that's real fearful and talk to her.

P: Talk to me?

T: Yeah. Talk to the part of you that would like to be normal. You know, would like to—

P: Well, should I say it as "I'm scared," like that, or—how do you want me to—

T: Yeah, well, let's try it out this way: "You should be scared because . . ."

P: Oh. OK. You should be scared because he'll be living alone and maybe somebody will come in and kill him in a motel room. You should be scared because if something happens at the job, you won't be able to get there fast. You should be scared because he'll have to eat all his meals himself. What if, God forbid, something happens to him and he should choke on his food? You should be scared—what if he gets sick in the middle of the night and something's wrong with him? You won't be there. You should be scared because you don't want to be alone. What if something happens to you? What if something happens to the dogs? You should be scared if you wake up in the middle of the night and you're fearful and there's no one home. You should be scared because he could get a heat-stroke and it's really hot there. You should be scared because you don't want him by himself.

T: Switch chairs, OK? The part of you that wants to get rid of all that fear and live without it is in this other chair.

P: Should I say it that—

T: Say something back to her. She's just telling you a thousand and one reasons. We interrupted her, 'cause she was just getting started. Say something back to her.

P: What are you always so worried about? You constantly worry. That's all you do is worry. You spend most of your day worrying about all kinds of crazy things that don't even happen. You make yourself sick.

T: Try it out as "I'm sick of you."

P: I'm sick of you. You make me feel ill. You make me worry need-lessly. You make me very nervous. You make me yell a lot.

T: Switch back.

P: I make you yell because I'm scared. You should be scared. There's enough wrong in your life that something more will probably happen, something terrible. Things aren't done with you yet. You should have fears 'cause you're still young and there will probably be a lot more happening to you, a lot more terrible things.

T: Who do you remind you of, like that? Who in your life would talk to you that way?

P: My grandmother. She would talk to me that way. She was a terribly fearful person.

T: Mmm-hmm. Switch back over here. Continue to see that part of yourself that scares you, and right behind her, see Grandma.

P: She's so scary to me.

T: OK, now, as you see Grandma there, pay attention to what you experience inside your body.

P: I'm just scared (*voice becomes frightened*).

T: Yeah. Do you hear your voice right now? Your voice sounds shaky.

P: Mmm-hmm. She was very scary.

T: And your face looks as if you're a little girl right now. Do you feel young?

P: No.

T: OK. And your face and your voice look young to me.

P: Well, I—I kind of see myself, yeah, I kind of do see myself as a little girl with her.

T: Uh-huh. OK.

P: And she's terrifying me, constantly.

T: OK, what else do you notice about your body?

P: Just that I feel kind of sick, like—

T: Where?

P: Just, my head, and nervousness in here (*pointing to chest*).

T: Uh-huh, OK.

P: And a frightened feeling, like I want to get away. But I never can. I'm always—I never can run away from her.

T: OK, what would happen if you tried to run away?

P: Oh, oh boy—when she'd get hold of me, she'd hit the hell out of me. I'd be too scared.

T: OK. All right. I'm going to suggest a change in the experiment. Say goodbye to this scared part of you right now and let Grandmother move down and be here.

P: OK.

T: Now, what I'm gonna invite you to do right now is to say to Grandma what you didn't dare say as a kid.

P: (*To grandmother, in chair*) You are so mean. I hate you. I do love you, but I hate you. You embarrass me. You're a dirty old woman. You remind me of death. I don't want to live with you. You scare me.

T: Try out, "I'm *angry* at you for scaring me."

P: I'm angry at you for scaring me. I'm afraid enough.

T: Whoa, your voice does not sound angry. Do you feel any anger about it?

P: No, I feel scared.

T: Yeah, you're feeling more scared than angry, huh?

P: Mmm-hmm.

T: OK. Feel the fear.

P: (*To grandmother, in chair*) I hate being here with you. You constantly talk about dying and death—death, that's it, every day, every day (*voice begins to sound resentful*).

T: "I *resent* your talking about death every day."

P: I resent you talking about death every day. Every day! You talk about my mother died, and my father died, and this one died. You constantly talk about dying yourself. I don't want to talk about dying. I'm a little girl! I want to live! I want to be like a child, not like somebody just waiting to die.

T: OK. How are you doing right now?

P: I'm all right, just nauseous, like, you know, just—

T: Mmm-hmm. Do you want to get past this fear?

P: Yes.

T: I'm gonna ask you to experiment with getting really angry with your grandmother, with you giving your anger back to her, all of the anger that you couldn't express as a kid.

P: OK.

Phobia

The phase of disownment transcends all other phases, but as the patient begins to recognize the availability and significance of leftover anger, the second phase of working through becomes ascendant. Usually this second phase is experienced as a phobic reaction to the emerging intensity of experienced anger and hurt. In this phase, the patient predicts that catastrophic results will occur if he or she fully owns that new found anger or expresses it. The patient may become preoccupied with his or her slightest expression of unwanted emotions for fear that once the defenses are removed, the result will be uncontrollable.

The predictions of catastophic results are often reflective of introjections against anger in early life. "Introjections" are ways of acting, feeling, or evaluating that have been taken into the system of behavior but that have not been assimilated. That is, they have not become a genuine part of the organism. Van de Riet, Korb, and Gorrell (1980) describe introjected material as resembling a sandwich that has been swallowed with the plastic sandwich bag left on. The "bag" is treated as something valuable, but it actually is something foreign and perhaps toxic. This point is exemplified by the patient who incorporates and retains, unchanged, rules accepted in early life experiences.

THERAPIST: Do you remember when you stopped allowing yourself to feel your anger?

PATIENT: You know, I really can. It's very clear. I remember being 10 years old and I was crouching under the dining room table.

T: Why were you there?

P: My father was angry again and he was tearing up the living room. He was smashing up things and looking wild.

T: Be in that scene for a moment. Be under the table. Allow yourself to know what you are feeling and what you are saying to yourself in your head. Say it to your father.

P: I am terrified and I'm saying that I'll never allow myself to get that way. I'll never be like you.

T: Now say that directly to your father.

P: I'll *never* allow myself to rant and rave. I'll never be like *you*!

T: It sounds as if you believe that to get angry is to get crazy.

P: Yeah. (*pause*) If I get angry I'm convinced I'll go crazy. I'll be like my father!

T: Are you willing to experiment by letting out a small piece of anger and seeing what happens?

P: That's scary!

T: I know. You might start by dealing with something about which you have only moderate anger.

The phase of phobia is treated paradoxically. That is, the patient is encouraged to move toward instead of away from the anxiety and to become more rather than less sensitive to the anger. This paradoxical strategy should not be confused, either in its form or in its objectives, with the defiance-based paradoxical interventions usually associated with strategic family therapy and other systems theories (e.g., Weeks & L'Abate, 1982). Seltzer (1986) has succinctly distinguished between the assumptions underlying complicance-based and defiance-based paradoxical interventions. In FEP and other Gestalt/experiential therapies, the interventions at this phase of experience are based upon a belief that compliance with the injunction to intensify experience is necessary to achieve integration of denied experience (Polster & Polster, 1976). This assumptive faith contrasts with the beliefs that underlie definance-based approaches, such as symptom prescription. These latter procedures capitalize upon the patient's resistance to external directives. In FEP, no effort is made to mislead, coerce, or outguess the patient. In fact, the therapist may point out that patients have the right to choose to use fear to stop themelves. That right is respected; it is the therapist's task to encourage the *conscious* choice, whatever it may be. Simply, such compliance-based injunctions encourage patients to do what they will do anyway—to experience anxiety as their anger becomes more clearly symbolized. This is done both with an awareness that phobia of feelings will only pass as a patient does face anxiety and with an implied confidence in the patient's ability and willingness to control destructive behaviors.

The therapist may assist further in this phobic phase of therapy by asking the patient to list and magnify all the catastrophic predictions, so that they are fully owned and acknowledged. Then, one by one, the therapist helps the patient to face or confront each expectation in order to allow reality testing or resolution in some form.

In order to insure that the patient maintains the willingness to control destructive behaviors, the process of moving from the phase of disownment to the phase of phobia should be set to the patient's pace. The therapist initially confronts gently and with support. Although the intensity of confrontation may increase substantially (Zinker, 1977), care should be taken to insure that the alienating force of confrontation never exceeds the affiliative strength of the patient–therapist bond. In Gestalt terms, this has been referred to as the "safe emergency" (Swanson, 1982). The following dialogue demonstrates how a therapist can continually check on the level of self-support experienced by the patient, while continuing to suggest ways in which the patient can move forward a step at a time.

THERAPIST: Do you sit more to one side to kind of relieve your pain? Is that it?

PATIENT: Yeah.

T: OK. All right. That would be a good area, then, to pay attention to, and we'll see if anything changes there. Any other areas that you want to note right now before we go farther?

P: I feel like I'm vibrating from my hair down to my feet.

T: OK.

P: I really feel like I'm coming apart.

P: All right. If you're willing to, if you feel safe enough to do that, I'd like for you to just stay with the vibrations and just let yourself vibrate as much as possible.

P: That scares me.

T: All right. What do you say to yourself that gets scary? What do you see as going to happen? "If I let myself vibrate, I'll what?"

P: I'll lose control of myself (*quietly*).

T: I didn't hear the tail end of that.

P: I'll lose control of myself.

T: "Of myself." yeah. OK—

P: —And everything around me (*gulping breath*).

T: That meant something there. Could you feel the sucking in on that one? Yeah. OK. All right. (*Patient is nodding agreement*) What does it mean in terms of what will happen, losing control? What will you do? Will you cry or will you yell or what would you do if you lost control here?

P: I don't know. Maybe yell and scream and carry on—

T: OK. All right.

P: —Be irrational.

T: Right. Are you ever irrational?

P: No, not totally. I'm always—you know, I do get some irrational, but not completely. I always have some kind of control on it. A leash, like.

T: Right, like a string that you can always pull yourself back, right.

P: Mmm-hmm.

T: To center or something like that. OK. One of the things that I hope to be able to do is to provide some kind of safe place here for you to go even past that string if you want to. You're not gonna have to, but it's all right to. Nothing bad will happen is what I'm saying. OK? And that you can go past that string and then you can still come back and get in touch with your rational self. You won't be letting go of it that way.

P: OK (*tentativeness in voice*).

T: What happened to you as I said that just now about going past the string?

P: It's hard to explain. I got frightened, very frightened, but then when you said it would be safe, then that felt like a warm wave.

As the therapist encourages the patient to confront the fear and to remove methods of disowning it, the phobic reaction usually diminishes, and the third phase of the work experience emerges.

Implosion

The phobic reaction to angry feelings is often followed by an implosive phase, wherein the patient begins to feel dead or numb and has no awareness of anger. This feeling state characterizes an impasse and signals the patient's effort to avoid the discomfort by retrenching himself or herself in the earlier pattern of disownment and self-deception.

The therapeutic task at the juncture of the impasse is to reactivate arousal. A multitude of methods have been developed to assist in this process and are detailed in Chapter 6. Much depends, however, on how successful the therapist has been in establishing a collaborative and "safe" environment for the patient. Within this safe context, an effort is made to intensify affect and to work against the patient's withdrawal. Setting time limits within the session for moving through the impasse, and assuming the voice of the avoidant and resistant deeper potential, are both useful tools.

At this stage as well, defiance-based paradoxical strategies may be indicated, where they were not in the stage of phobia. Prescribing the resistance
("Try not to feel any anger at all!"), and encouraging even stronger resistance ("it's important that you don't feel anything at all right now, and even
if you do, don't let me know—that will help you be in control again"), are
examples of this type of strategy. These and other procedures described by
Beutler (1983) for magnifying resistive symptoms may rob the patient of
the interpersonal force that maintains the impasse—a need for personal
control. At the point when the therapist encourages a behavior that is
designed and maintained by those forces that mandate against that behavior
(e.g., "Be a good girl and do what you're told"), the power behind such
behaviors dissipates. Thereafter, the therapist may ask the patient to give
voice to the numbness or deadness that often accompanies the implosion
phase, and to develop an intradialogue following the style of split work in
Gestalt therapy.

The major point here is for the therapist to persist in keeping the
patient in his or her implosive stance until resolution occurs. To allow the
patient to withdraw from the impasse too quickly can be discouraging to
the patient and adds one more failure to the list. The following excerpt from
a session provides an example of staying with the patient at the impasse.

THERAPIST: What do you need to do right now?

PATIENT: I need to let out my anger. I've had it with feeling this way.

T: There is the bataca. When you are ready, stand and say what you
need to say.

P: (*Picks up bataca, stands, and faces the significant other. She stands
for an extended period without saying anything and holds the bataca behind
her back as if hidden.*) I suddenly don't feel anything.

T: That is OK. Tell your friend what you are experiencing right now.

P: It's as if someone turned a switch when I stood up. I was so mad a
moment ago. But as soon as I stood up I felt blank.

T: Tell her what you notice about your body right this moment.

P: I'm standing very still. I'm almost not breathing. There is a pain in
my neck—no, more in my throat.

T: Just move into the pain in your throat. See what is is like for you to
have that pain.

P: (*Pause*) It's like I want to scream.

T: And you don't.

P: No, I don't (*smiling slightly*).

T: Try this out: "I want to scream at you and I won't. I'll be in pain
instead."

P: I want to scream at you and I won't. I'll be in pain. Yeah, that seems
to be what is happening.

T: Just be aware of what it is like for you to have that scream and to not express it.

P: I don't like this. Part of me just wants to run out of the room.

T: And the other part?

P: Wants to face up to what I'm angry about.

T: Try out: "I want to face up to you."

P: I do—I want to face up to you and (*voice drops off*) I find it so damned difficult.

T: Where's the scream?

P: It's still here—right here in my throat.

T: Continue to pay attention to what your body is doing.

P: I just feel immobilized.

T: It's OK, don't talk for a moment. Just be with yourself and see what happens.

P: (*Silence. Patient's body continues to tighten. Her jaw is very set, and her eyes get very intense and focused.*)

T: There is a lot going on in your body right now. Feel it and allow yourself to do what you need to do.

P: (*Silence continues for a short period of time. Then the patient takes a deep breath, brings the bataca up, and hits the cushion very hard*) DAMN YOU! (*She is mobilized, but looks surprised.*)

T: That's fine; say it again.

Notice that the therapist accepted the patient's emotional expression and encouraged her to "lean into" it even more, creating safety for her "surprising" experience.

It also can be facilitative to give homework to the patient who is stuck in the impasse. If this is done at the end of the session, the task will keep the patient attending to the stuck place over the intervening period. For the woman who leaves the session with a "knot" in her stomach that she did not let go of, for example, it may be appropriately symbolic for her to carry a rock around in her purse until the next session. Often this kind of attention to and exaggeration of the impasse increases ownership to a point at which the patient is ready to move. When patients successfully negotiate the impasse, they frequently enter a phase that is best described as "explosive."

Explosion

Emergence from the implosive phase is usually accompanied by renewed feelings of anger. Often, the expression of these feelings represents a level of intensity at the opposite extreme from the overconstraint of affect observed at the beginning of the implosion phase. Re-entry is often sudden, anger-laden, and directed at the therapist or at a significant other. Though sudden and somewhat frightening to other group members, the shift represents a reawakening of emotion and an acceptance of denied and disowned anger.

The intensity with which the patient's affect explodes at this point may at once reflect the degree of prior suppressive control and signal the patient's decision either to give up or reorganize constraining defenses. Nonetheless, because it is a volatile phase and one in which new behaviors and perceptions are being born, it is a critical period. It is important that the therapist see it through with support and care. Confrontive interventions are to be avoided, and the therapist becomes an advocate and referent for the patient. The novice therapist is to be comforted in the knowledge that such intensity always runs its course if it is not impeded by acts of therapist placating, ignoring, avoiding, or discounting.

The therapist's main and most difficult task during this phase of the patient's experience is remaining stable and constant as a support and guide. The therapist observes intensity, directs the patient's rage toward objects of significance, encourages the continuance of emotion to natural completion, and accepts whatever is there. For example, consider the following situation: A patient had experienced a brutal rape. Initially, she reacted with unusually intense emotion to the work of another individual in the group who had reported being sexually abused. In the subsequent work, she moved into her anger, using a bataca on a cushioned block. Her sudden eruption of anger provoked other members to move closer to the walls.

THERAPIST: Good, you are doing fine. You don't have to lock those feelings away anymore. Just direct your energy to the cushion.

PATIENT: (*Hitting cushion violently*) I'm furious! I'm furious! You disgust me. I still feel you standing on my arms while your partner raped me! I hate you both!

T: You're doing fine. Continue to say what you resent, what you hate. Let the energy come.

P: (*Continuing to hit*) I've waited so long to beat the shit out of you. I'd love to cut your balls off! (*Hitting*)

T: Right now you can act on those feelings in a safe way.

P: I'm just boiling up inside—like I might explode.

T: It's OK for you to explode right here. Just direct your energy onto the cushion and use the bataca so you don't hurt yourself.

P: (*To cushion*) I waited a long time for this. You bastards! (*Hitting*) I hate you! (*Stops to catch her breath*)

T: When you catch your breath, tell them how it feels for you to be fighting back and expressing your anger instead of being helpless to react.

P: That feels good—*I* feel good—I feel strong—I feel OK—I *can* take care of myself.

As a safe and accepting atmosphere is provided, patients typically explore (and are encouraged to explore) a wide range of feelings in the anger spectrum and a wide range of objects toward whom these feelings could be directed. It is this exploration, coupled with the sanity and reasonableness of the therapist's own attitudes toward anger and anger expression, that allows a patient to begin to express spontaneously, in a more integrated fashion, the constellation of feelings, thoughts, and behaviors associated with the previously interrupted experience.

The therapist should encourage the patient to note the physiological changes that occur simultaneously with the explosion, when it occurs. In this way the patient is immediately reinforced at cognitive and sensory levels for the progress he or she is making. To supplement this reinforcement further, the patient is often asked to tell the imagined significant other or "target" of the outrage the results of his or her explosive behavior.

THERAPIST: Tell your mother how you feel right now after telling her about your anger rather than choking on it inside yourself.

PATIENT: That feels good, dammit! I've spent enough years beating myself with this anger—it's yours and now you've got it. (*Turns to therapist, surprised*) You know, my headache is gone!

T: Tell your mother about your headache.

P: Mother, since I just expressed my anger to you, my headache has gone. I feel stronger. I *can* stand on my own. (*Her spine straightens and lengthens, and she shows a confident smile*)

Completion

As the patient's emotional intensity spontaneously decreases, the process of completion begins. This phase is one of cognitive reprocessing of both the therapy work and the evoking experiences. It is a balancing of the swing from implosion to explosion. Hence, therapist feedback, discussion with group members, and feedback from group members become of central and critical importance. Although it is perfectly legitimate for the work of one patient to provoke "tailgating" work by others, the therapist should take care to complete the experience with the working patient before proceeding to a new therapeutic encounter. Before the patient terminates the discussion with the imagined significant other, it is important that a statement of accomplishment from the work be given to the other. This procedure enhances the cognitive reprocessing and allows the patient to acknowledge, in a public way, success in the confrontation. The "goodbye" procedure described in Chapter 6 is designed, in part, to insure that the process is complete and that the working patient is ready to move on with his or her life.

The completion stage is indexed by the spontaneous experience of integrated and increasingly complex affective states (see Figure 4.1). One particularly observes a change in those feelings, thoughts, and behaviors related to the self. Greenberg (1979) has observed spontaneous changes in self-reflective language at this stage, during intrapersonal dialogues using a two-chair procedure. Spontaneous language characteristically changes from "you" to "I" or "me," and indicates the increasing ownership and reintegration of previously disowned feeling states. At the same time as these verbal changes occur, the patient's physical reactions may begin to become more consistent with vocal expressions. At this point, the patient may feel a renewed sense of *aliveness*. This heightened energy is experienced as a new source of energy devoted to the process of living, breathing, and interacting. These feelings are self-reinforcing. Moreover, as practice makes the processes more consistent and less halting, the patient often observes a significant diminution of hostile feelings. The patient is encouraged to stay with the feelings generated by completion of the work so that integration can occur at a significant level. Homework assignments can be developed to assist this process. An example of such an assignment is self-monitoring to keep patients aware of how they are handling the new feelings. When this is done, the patients can identify and acknowledge ways in which they can sabotage their growth. Often, feedback from others can be reinforcing for a patient. Sometimes patients receive spontaneous responses from others, such as "You seem (look) different; what's happened to you?" The patient often feels taller, straighter, stronger, or more competent and less fearful.

Dynamics of Change

The dynamics that facilitate therapeutic and affective change through the directed expression of anger are not clearly known. Research has suggested, however, that both physically and verbally symbolized expression of anger relieves bodily tension and may have a direct influence upon physiological functioning (Beutler, Engle, Oró-Beutler, Daldrup, & Meredith, 1986; Mahrer, 1980). Nonetheless, many of the dynamics through which experiential therapy exerts its impact are left to speculation.

Movement to Fuller Experience

FEP assumes that through magnifying and intensifying current feelings and sensory states, patients will move from a restricted range of affective reaction to a full range and awareness of human emotions (e.g., Mahrer, 1986). Concomitantly, it is assumed that confrontation with denied experience will force patients to intergrate past and present experiences. Instead of being suppressors and repressors of feeling states, patients who come to face feared emotions are thought to become more fully expressive of their feelings or reactions, to become more spontaneous and flexible in their behavior, and to assume a more open posture in dealing with the changing world (Daldrup & Gust, 1988).

Movement to Spontaneity

As past feelings become unfrozen, patients may lose many of their anxiety-producing preoccupations with the past and future, and begin living in a less encumbered present. A more fluid interplay of emotions should be observed as the emotional system changes from a state of imbalance to one of homeostasis. Concomitantly, many patients experience a heightened sense of energy, reinforcing the belief that constraint against anger works to capture potential that then is no longer available to deal with present experiences. Once the unbound feelings are allowed to alter a patient's view of the world, symbols of past experience may reveal their hidden meanings, and the patient may express the sense of completing "unfinished business" and moving on to living life in the present.

Movement to Schematic Restructuring

Greenberg and Safran (1987) suggest that the completion of unfinished business leads to emotional restructuring. Not only is the interrupted action tendency allowed to complete itself, thereby providing a release of tension and an experience of cathartic relief, but also the schematic emotional memories involved in the experience are restructured in consciousness and perceived with new meaning. Once the anger-generating schema is evoked in the present by the arousal of anger, it is unpacked into expressive-motor, memorial, stimulus, and conceptual components. These are then reinspected and reprocessed, and the person's current processing capacities are used to create new experientially derived schemas. These new schemas incorporate new features of environment, behavior, and awareness. These new features, which now assume the role of a figure rather than background, may include such things as an awareness of abilities to assert oneself, not heretofore sensed; a feeling of potency to replace one of impotency; and a new, therapeutically encouraged belief in the legitimacy of angry feelings.

Schematic restructuring is achieved by providing new experiences that focus on and attend to the present, so that old features are reinspected, new aspects of them are brought forward, and these latter features can then be represented in the schema that influences current behavior. This repacking of an emotionally laden schema with both old and new perceptual features of experience modifies the schema and provides a new view of self and situation. If successful, patients who emotionally restructure themselves in this fashion will cease to deny and distort their experience, and will begin to make full use of their emotions and behaviors.

Movement to Health

Patients are not infrequently observed to give up aches, pains, and even physical illnesses as they learn to unravel and to "own" the symbolized messages these symptoms represent, and as they finish their unfinished business (e.g., Beutler, Engle, *et al.*, 1986; Mahrer, 1986, in press). Therapy procedures and experiments are designed to help patients move from a pattern in which they deny what is happening to them to an acknowledgment of how they choose their social roles, thereby increasing their ownership of and responsibility for behavior and feelings. It is believed that aches, pains, and even many illnesses may be efforts of the denied aspects of one's self to communicate and integrate with current experiences (Simonton, Simonton, & Creighton, 1978). Hence, the therapist may encourage interpersonal contact or confrontation in order to combat a patient's avoidance of interactions with the environment. Patients are encouraged to give up a view of themselves as passive participants in life and to experience themselves as active creators of their own experiences.

Movement to Realism

It is assumed that improvement will be reflected in a movement from a "phony" to an "authentic" stance. When patients are behaving as victims both of past experiences and of unsymbolized feelings such as anger, they may feel that they are role-playing or "acting" while interacting with others. When past experiences no longer serve as filters through which present experiences are drawn, more realistic interpersonal actions are possible, and patients may note a complementry sense that they are more involved with and capable of contact in these interactions than they have been previously. This latter state is defined as "congruency."

Movement to Potency

As patients move from a position in which they are controlled by fear to a posture of facing fear, they acquire increasing confidence and trust in themselves and in others. concomitantly, there is a change from a sense of impotency or incompetence to one of potency and competence in dealing with life. Low self-concepts often change to allow increased self-acceptance. At the same time, patients come to see even their own negatively viewed emotions as being sources of important energy with which to combat feelings of "deadness." The unavailability of energy, by virtue of its investment in constraining emotional experience, is frequently experienced as depression and a lack of vitality. Paradoxically, as a patient moves with the experience of anger, he or she is inclined to give up blaming and complaining in favor of doing. Rather than choosing a stance of guilt, patients may choose to assume responsibility for their behavior, feelings, and experiences. With increased awareness of positive feelings, there is often a change from being self-deprecatory to being more caring and sharing, both with one's self and with others.

Summary

The patient goes through various phases of experience while the therapist is directing the session. This becomes a process of giving up layers of "neurotic mechanisms." The sequence of these phases follows a similar pattern; however, the level of experience in any one phase varies among patients. The phases are listed in their usual sequence:

1. Disownment: Denial of emotional experience or attribution of the feelings to outside sources.
2. Phobia: Fear of the consequences of ownership of emotional reactions.
3. Implosion: The impasse characterized by lack of awareness, deadness, or numbness.
4. Explosion: Acceptance of and expression of previously disowned emotion.
5. Completion: Process characterized by decrease of emotional intensity cognitive reprocessing, and a feeling of aliveness. Homework is often used to assist the completion phase in reaching its highest level of integration and usefulness.

Although some research indicates that both physical and symbolized expression of anger may have an influence on bodily tension and physiological functioning, many of the dynamics that facilitate change in FEP must be left to speculation. It can be expected that the patient who uses the intervention successfully will experience movement to a fuller experience of life, to more spontaneous responses to living, to a more realistic posture to the present world, and to potency to deal with things as they are. These changes are exhibited in a schematic restructuring of a patient's world view.

6

Implementing the Experiment

Up to this point, our discussion has primarily centered upon the psychother-apeutic process and the technical procedures that distinguish Gestalt ther-apy and FEP from other therapeutic interventions. In implementing these methodologies, however, one must be aware that there is also a great deal of similarity among various effective therapeutic approaches.

Common Ingredients

Establishing Safety

Fundamental to an FEP viewpoint is the awareness that no psychotherapy procedure can have a consistent psychotherapeutic effect if the therapy relationship itself is nonfacilitative and perceived as "unsafe." The effective therapist, of whatever persuasion, is one who holds a high level of regard and respect for the patient (Strupp, 1981). The ability to establish a safe environment in which the actions of the patient will be respected and trusted is cardinal to the successful implementation of therapeutic procedures. This observation may be especially true in the implementation of such highly directed procedures as those embodied in the psychotherapeutic approach described here. A therapist must be careful to establish a sense of confidence and trust. Therapists must convey to patients that they are able to receive and accept whatever negative expressions or behaviors occur, that they respect patients' abilities to decide their own fate, that they are able to receive patients' communications warmly, and that they will provide sup-port through times of crisis and struggle.

Collaboration between Therapist and Patient

Central to conveying the foregoing attitudes is the development of a sense of collaboration and mutuality in the treatment process. Orlinsky and Howard (1986) conclude that the more patients and therapists collaborate in sharing initiative and responsibility, the more favorable the outcome of the psychotherapy is likely to be. A therapist should emphasize the concept of "we" in developing therapeutic procedures and experiments. Likewise, the therapist should seek the patient's permission before beginning and ending experiences, and should be careful to engage the patient in the process of designing these experiments wherever this appears possible and appropriate. The task throughout is to conserve the patient's sense of safety in the relationship and to foster the patient's perception of the therapist as a receptive, warm, and trustworthy individual who will provide help through times of crisis, even if the patient's worst fears are realized.

Credibility and Trust

Therapist credibility and trustworthiness are also significantly and positively associated with patient outcomes (Beutler, Crago, & Arizmendi, 1986; Orlinsky & Howard, 1986). The therapist's ability to establish a role as a competent and knowledgeable authority, who is sensitive and responsive to the patient's needs, facilitates sharing and lends the patient courage to make changes. Perhaps as much as being empathic, establishing the authoritative but benign role of guide helps patients set directions to their lives and instills them with confidence that they will find support if their efforts fail.

These persuasive therapist qualities may also foster changes in perceptions and beliefs that result in new perspectives. Beutler (1983) has suggested that the persuasive potency of the therapist who is different from the patient enhances the tendency for the patient to respect his or her own views of life. Moreover, a strong, competent therapist serves as a model for the patient seeking to understand confusing circumstances. While the therapist should closely monitor the degree to which patients are permitted to accept, unquestioned, the therapist as a model, the availability of a credible and assured therapist who presents an alternative world view both offers permission to question established beliefs and represents a contrast to the belief that safety is to be found solely in old positions.

Specific Ingredients

Setting the Agenda in Group Environment

The peculiarities of the group psychotherapy setting infuse additional complexities into the therapy relationship. That is, the therapist is required to convey a sense of confidence and trustworthiness to a number of individuals at the same time, all of whom may have their own particular needs and methods of distorting the environment. Unlike the situation in individual therapy, the therapist is not given the flexibility to adjust a therapeutic persona to fit each individual. Indeed, the behavior exhibited must optimize the possibility that all group members will see the therapist in a manner that will facilitate their willingness to involve themselves in the treatment process. Hence, aside from the common courtesies of respecting individuals' names, attending to patients as they talk, and exuding an air of confidence and regard, the therapist is well advised to solicit from group members an agenda at the beginning of each session. This agenda will assist the therapist to define patients who are willing to work, and who thereby have circumvented that initial barrier of distrust. Such agenda setting also conveys the therapist's respect for each patient's right to choose. By allowing patients to engage in the process of arranging agenda items in order of importance, the therapist further conveys the collaborative nature of the relationship. Once individuals have identified themselves as willing to work and have indicated the nature of their work tasks, and after the group has agreed upon a priority for each of the issues described, the therapist is then prepared to begin individual work activities with patients who have listed themselves on this agenda.

FEP assures that no one is prompted into working without being ready. In part, this is accomplished by designating a specific empty chair in the group to be the working chair. After identification in an opening round of those wanting time during the current session, the group is told that the floor is open for work. There may be a short period of silence as patients check to see whether they are willing to act on their previous opening-round commitment; a member may be waiting for the opportunity and will bring the agenda to the group immediately; or the group may turn to someone who looks particularly stressed and ask whether he or she wants to take the working chair. In this third case, the therapist must be sure that the person is not coerced into taking the working chair.

There is no clear and representative rule for implementing therapeutic procedures. The therapist should use whatever procedure appears to hold promise for facilitating the treatment process. Hence, both the therapist's judgment and the stage of work dictate the selection. In the following pages, we explore some of the finer aspects of selecting and utilizing treatment procedures at the beginning, middle, and end of the session. The reader is referred to the FEP Compliance Scale (Appendix 1) for a reminder of how the various stages of the session evolve and how the procedures interrelate.

Focusing the Experiment

The initial task of selecting an appropriate experiment begins with establishing the nature of the work to be done. It is important that this process be collaborative and interactive, as in these two examples.

PATIENT: Well, I just have to say this. After he was able to breathe, I was screaming at him. I was, 'cause I'm so angry that, you know, I was angry that he almost died. I was angry. So I think that it was—I'm angry. The anger did that to him.

THERAPIST: OK. All right. What are we after here? If we do a good piece of work together, what's gonna happen?

P: Well, what I'd like, I'd like to let go of this fear, this terrible fear of— see, I have fear anyway, you know, it's in here, of something happening to him. I worry a lot about that, but then when something like this happens—

T: So the work is to help you find ways to be less fearful, is that right?

P: True, I'm scared so much of the time. I don't like it.

THERAPIST: OK. So, what I'm hearing is more than one part of you.

PATIENT: I'm all mixed up (*laughing*).

T: Yeah, and besides, I'm just gonna see if I can list the parts—

P: OK.

T: —and then we can proceed from there. One is this inside part that you like. I'm not quite sure that I know too much more about what that part's like, but there is an inside part to you that you like. There's an out-side part that you feel is real ugly to other people and to yourself too, it seems like. And then there's this judge out there, this kind of amorphous judge that is looking at you no matter what you're doing. Is that judge inside you, too?

P: Is that judge inside of me?

T: Is that a part of you too?

P: Oh, yeah. I'm very critical of myself.

T: So there's the beautiful part, and there's the ugly part, and there's the judge. Any more that you can think of?

P: Well, I want to be—I, no, not really. I just—I would like to be, like, the normal person. I also wrote about I'm resentful of people that are healthy. Not that they're healthy, I'm resentful of people that are healthy and that don't use their bodies to the full potential. And I wrote about this, that if I see a person that's so lazy they won't jog or exercise or ride a bike, because I would give anything to ride a bike, jog, walk, and so I'm resentful when I see or hear somebody who goes, "I won't exercise."

T: I'm gonna ask you to make a choice about where to focus 'cause you seem—

P: I know, I have a lot of stuff that—

T: —confused. One of the choices—and you've been thinking, ob-viously you've been working on that project, and that leads us to get a whole, you know, sometimes a whole bunch more things going in our heads than otherwise. One choice is that we can focus on these different parts of you and see what happens with that.

P: I think I'd like to do that.

T: OK. Another one is what you said earlier, which is to go back and focus on Peter again. One reason I think that's relevant is because that was at a time when you were healthy, and so there's—last week, when you were working on that, that was one of the things at the top. So I'm willing to work with you there—

P: Well, do you think it's better to—

T: I don't think there's any "better," I just think there are two ways to go. Why don't you just make a choice, and I will—

P: I'd like to work on the different—

T: —parts of you?

P: Yeah.

As these examples suggest, restatement, an ability to condense information to its essentials, and the willingness to set a direction from what is presented are useful in avoiding becoming foundered in verbiage devoid of a therapeutic task. FEP relies on the therapist's benign directiveness, interfaced with caring sensitivity to the patient's issues, when establishing a treatment focus.

Applying the Experiment

Initially, once a piece of work has been defined, the therapist's task is to maximize and magnify present feelings and sensations, and to break through the impasse or constraint against unfinished emotional reactions. Although this is a very general rule, it is difficult to make it more specific. Each therapeutic transaction dictates the next sequence, since all are viewed as experiments with an unknown outcome. Nonetheless, some guidelines are possible in implementing procedures. For example, it usually helps to begin slowly, with a gradual escalation of the process of magnifying affect (Zinker, 1977). The least resisted procedures are the most easily implemented at first, and the opportunity generally accrues for the gradual addition of more powerful and initially resisted procedures. Hence, dialogue between the patient and therapist centering on present experience is easily accepted, whereas physical enactment is often more difficult for the patient to accept initially. Dialogue between patient and therapist is more comfortably followed, for most individuals, with a dialogue between the patient and a significant other. Maintaining a dialogue between two or more internal aspects of one's self is somewhat more difficult for most patients, with physical enactment following in close proximity on the scale of difficulty.

Interventions

Consistent with the foregoing principles, it can generally be assumed that evocative procedures are eminently more compatible with the patient's initial tolerance level than are directed procedures. Evocative strategies consist of verbal behaviors on the part of the therapist that are designed to provoke and expand on the verbal behaviors of the patient. Questions, reflections, restatements, and verbal reframing of what the patient has said are useful evocative interventions. Among evocative procedures, interpretative statements are the most confrontive (e.g., "It looks like you are still letting Dad control you"). They are quite easily rejected by the patient, and hence require the strongest therapist–patient bond in order to implement.

A therapist must be creative in order to introduce a series of procedures that progress gradually from evocative to directive in the service of producing emotional escalation (Zinker, 1977). Evocative procedures ordinarily progress from reflections, to questions, to clarifications, and lastly to restatements and interpretations, as in the following examples:

- Reflection: "Seems to make you nervous to be interacting with Dad."
- Question: "Do you experience any nervousness as you begin to interact with Dad?"
- Clarification: "Are you saying that when you are near Dad you become anxious and scared?"
- Restatement: "It's almost as if you're expecting and afraid that your father will cut you off and ignore you."
- Interpretation: "You seem to be nervous around Dad because he never showed you any tenderness."

Directed interventions are more difficult to catalogue than are evocative ones. Partial listings have been provided by Beutler (1983), Stevens (1971), and Greenberg (1980). In addition, a summary of directed techniques that are commonly utilized in FEP has been given in Table 4.2. Although this list is neither comprehensive nor exhaustive, it does provide a general index to guide each set of procedures. The menu of techniques on the right-hand side of the table can be used interchangeably for the purpose of accomplishing the therapist's objective at each stage. As a therapist's objective changes from moment to moment, based upon the outcome of prior experiments, so will the techniques being used change. If, for example, the therapist becomes aware of an unconscious bodily movement on the part of the patient, the focus may shift to releasing suppressed emotion by exaggerating motoric responses. By the same token, verbal dialogue with the therapist may well serve, in the early part of the work experiment, to initiate the patient's involvement, but at the end of the experiment, the same process may be targeted at helping the patient reorganize his or her perceptual system or Gestalt.

To impose a procedure onto the therapeutic relationship without the patient's cooperation is extremely problematic. The rule of thumb is "Don't fight with your patient." The imposition of a procedure on the flow of emerging experience smacks of "gimmickry" rather than of "therapy." The ideal therapeutic session is one that proceeds in small steps, escalating the degree of difficulty at a rate that taxes the patient's emotions but that never provokes him or her to abandon the task. As a guide, the therapist is well advised to obtain the patient's permission before moving on to each new therapeutic experiment. Experiments sometimes are flat, and the therapist needs to make more than one attempt before the right experiment for the moment is found.

[Talking to herself as an imagined "old woman," the patient first directs a couple of remarks to the old woman. She then speaks of an uncle who complained constantly about his pain, and then moves to recalling her friend's reactions to her ability to cope with pain. All this happens in a brief span of time.]

THERAPIST: Do you feel that this is going anywhere for you right now? Is this getting in touch with anything for you?

PATIENT: No, I think I—sometimes I get angry—I'd like to maybe curse. No, I don't want to curse. I want to tell my arthritis something, that I hate it.

T: Yeah. That's—I was gonna suggest a change in the experiment that we're doing. OK?

P: OK.

T: The change would be to see your arthritis out here, or something that symbolizes it. All right? Perhaps see an aspirin bottle out here, or a crutch, or whatever.

P: Can I put this out there? (*Pointing to wrist brace*) This will help me, 'cause this thing I hate. This is something I really hate, so I'll just put this thing out there—if I can get the contraption off! (*Removes wrist brace*)

T: And let it be—let this thing be a symbol of your arthritis, so that it stands for all the arthritis in all of the different parts of your body. OK? And what I'm going to ask you to do is to see what it's like for you to look at this symbol of your arthritis and to say, "I'm angry at you."

Dialogue and Role-Playing Techniques

Resolution of existing anger entails integrating past experience with present existence. This process is impaired by strong sanctions against emotional experience. This overcontrol of feelings keeps patients stuck in the prior experiences that gave rise to the unwanted feelings. The dialogue techniques listed in Table 4.2 are used extensively to help patients revisit past experiences and free the bound emotions, reliving them in the present. These techniques have been described and illustrated by Perls (1969; Perls, Hefferline, & Goodman, 1951) and more recently by Greenberg (1979; Greenberg & Rice, 1981). These procedures must be conducted in the safety of an environment that is accepting of efforts to complete an emotional reaction, without the danger either of harming the target of one's anger or of risking the relationship. These objectives are possible, in part, because significant others are not present and can be reconstructed in fantasy or excluded at will. This characteristic is attractive for patients and reinforces the power they have over their disturbing fantasies. Indeed, Greenberg and colleagues (Greenberg & Clarke, 1979; Greenberg & Dompierre, 1981) have found that Gestalt two-chair experiments evoke more beneficial outcomes in therapy than do simply empathic reflections, perhaps reflecting this sense of control and ownership. The therapist can build on this attraction to encourage the patient to take the risk of acting out difficult emotions. One may redo or re-enact a past scene for the purpose of integrating these experiences within a new frame of reference, as suggested in the redecision therapy model of the Gouldings (1979).

Role-playing techniques have also been refined and demonstrated to be effective in working with groups of various types (Bohart, 1977; Satir, 1967, 1972). Role-playing strategies allow individuals to involve more of their sensory and behavioral systems in the interplay of activity, and also to engage other group members in significant ways. Of particular note, role-playing strategies may help patients to try on new behaviors and to experiment with their newfound feelings.

From a vantage point that is still distant from the patient's resistance, the therapist may encourage a patient to project hidden feelings through the use of puppetry or nondirected visual imagery. These procedures may produce much less threat than actual enactment or role playing. Puppetry, art, and use of a sand tray are especially useful with children, and Oaklander (1978) has described the use of these and other enactment techniques to maximize projective processes with this latter population.

Engaging Behavioral Systems

Since experiential therapeutic philosophy assumes that individuals behave as interactive, wholistic units, it is imperative to engage as many of the individuals' cognitive, sensory, and affective systems, as possible in therapeutic work (Kaplan & Kaplan, 1985). Various kinds of "acting-out" techniques can be productive in escalating emotional experience by releasing the inhibitions that individuals have against assertive or strong physical behaviors. What process is chosen often depends upon the unique needs of the individual patient. Some patients release the angry emotions through hands and fists, whereas others find release in the use of their feet. Often the therapist is alerted to the right mode by listening to patients' verbal cues: "I'd love to kick him in the ass"; "I feel like choking her"; "It's all stopped up in my throat, and I just want to scream and scream." Some such active techniques include kicking the floor, a pillow, or a cushion; hitting inanimate objects with a rolled-up magazine or a bataca; punching a pillow; and pushing against a wall or cushion. Throwing (cushions, pillows, bean bags) or tearing (newspapers or magazines) can be helpful in increasing the individual's awareness of sensory experiences that may signal the presence of angry emotions. Moreover, the process of tearing or throwing may leave the patient with a sense of satisfaction; it provides a reassurance of power, while at the same time engaging both tactile and auditory senses. We must reiterate that therapists must be careful to avoid reinforcing physical aggression and impulsive behavior in patients who already are poorly controlled and overresponsive. In the interest of caution, these strategies are best applied to overcontrolled patients who have no history of destructive behavior and who do have reasonable ego resources.

Batacas, or encounter bats, are very helpful instruments to have available for the therapy process. There is often a need to move from verbal expression to physical expression of anger in order to attain full release. Several authors (Enright, 1970; Perls, 1947, 1969; Smith, 1986) note that the interruption between the awareness portion and the expressive portion of the contact–withdrawal cycle involves constriction of the musculoskeletal system. Retroflective behaviors, in particular, diminish or totally prevent muscular movement. Reactivation of muscular movement may assist in the release and completion of retroflected movement. However, such physical activity on the part of the patient may need to go through a deliberate "acting as if" phase before the patient moves toward spontaneous release.

The following session excerpt provides an example of adding physical expression to verbal expression to obtain a fuller release:

THERAPIST: What's your body doing right now?
PATIENT: Relaxing. I feel a little better.
T: OK. A little better.
P: My stomach isn't shaking as much. I feel clear-headed. Before, I was—
T: How much of this do you want to be free of this morning?
P: I'd like to be free of the whole thing. But it's an ongoing thing because—

T: No, answer my question.

P: OK. I'd like to be free of it all. I'd *love* to get rid of it.

T: OK, then let's stay with this. Are you willing?

P: OK.

T: What I'm going to ask you to do is up the ante.

P: Sounds good.

T: All right. I'm gonna ask you to do something physical along with what you're saying. OK?

P: OK.

T: Because if you want to finish your anger and your resentment toward this man, you may have to be physical with it. OK?

P: Sound great. I'll do it. I don't need it cluttering my life!

T: OK. I'm gonna move this chair back out of your way. Come and stand right in front of him. We'll just get this out of your way here. Begin by saying what you need to say, and use the bataca.

P: I *hate* you! You are horrible! (*Using bataca—weak voice and tentative stroke*)

T: Now—bring your voice from your gut and say that again. Use the bataca stronger.

P: I *hate* you!

T: That's it.

P: Don't you understand?

T: "I resent you when you don't understand." Say it as an "I" statement, OK? And say the words and use the bataca at the same time.

P: I *resent* you! I *resent* you when you don't understand me! I *resent* you when you treat me like a child!

T: Keep going. "And I also resent you for . . ."

P: I resent you for being nasty to my mother.

Occasionally, the physical expression can be used to prompt the anger to the surface where the patient can deal with it. For example, the following patient was moving between anger and hurt.

THERAPIST: Oh, watch the hurt coming back!

PATIENT: I'm going back to hurt, yeah.

T: Yeah. Watch the hurt come back in, OK? And you can get into your hurt right now, or you can stay with your anger about that and finish the anger. Do you feel the hurt—yeah, you caught it there.

P: It went back—I—that same feeling as when I was sitting in the chair when we started.

T: Right. And that leaves you unfinished then, OK? If you want to get finished, stay with the anger, OK? Just let it be there (*Pause*) Trouble finding it again?

P: Yeah, I've got the hurt, and it won't go away.

T: OK, all right. What I'm gonna ask you to do is just take the bataca and hit the chair like you're just gonna split wood, just as hard as you can, about three or four times. Find the words now, and go on.

P: (*Swings the bataca a number of times and then bursts into anger mixed with hurt*) You're miserable! I *hate* you!

T: OK. Yeah, feel the hurt trying to creep back in there. Say it again— "I *hate* you!"

P: I *hate* you! You're not good, and you're not good for me or my mother! (*Sudden change in posture and facial expression*)

T: Tell him what happened just then.

P: I feel broken from him. I really feel—(*turning to the imagined significant other*) you may enter my life, but I don't think that I'm going to feel the same way about you. And I don't—it doesn't bother me.

The use of such physical display not only assists the patient in completion of residual anger, but illustrates and identifies retroflexive and deflective avoidance processes that are utilized to prevent the resolution of anger. Observations of how one approaches the task, for example, may reveal ambivalence, impulsiveness, denial, diversion, and other defensive patterns. A detailed description of working with the defensive patterns is found in Chapter 7.

A critical assist in the release of emotion is found in development of a specific focus. Much anger can be released, for example, through physical exercise. However, release is enhanced when there is a focal target (e.g., when the patient visualizes the target person's face on the golf ball, tennis ball, or cushion). It also enhances release to sharpen the verbal focus from statements of generalized anger to specific anger: "I resent you for . . ." or "I resent you when . . ."

When batacas or other instruments of anger expression are used in interpersonal encounters, certain rules should be established for the sake of safety and effectiveness. Some of the quidelines described by George Bach can be useful (Bach & Wyden, 1968). These include using the nonpreferred hand, maintaining physical contact, and avoiding particularly vulnerable bodily areas.

Engaging Language Systems

Many patients utilize language structures and words to avoid encountering their disowned feelings. This process is often noticed in verbal expressions of tentativeness. Disarming the patient of this defensive strategy requires that the therapist encourage the patient to change the structure of language by using less tentative and more definitive words. Even encouraging the use of extreme words is useful in bringing the patient into contact with the meaning that may lie behind tentative language. In a similar manner, it is often helpful to remove qualifying language that minimizes reactions (e.g., "a little angry," etc.) when these words are attached to emotional labels. The use of helpless language such as "can't" is often changed in order to acquire a more powerful and responsible posture of ownership (i.e., "won't"). In a similar way, removing or changing conjunctions, such as replacing "but" with "and," helps the patient reintegrate the alternative arguments on each side of the conjunctive word. Changing the word "but" to "and," in particular, has the characteristic of disarming the patient's effort to cancel either negative or positive comments with those that have an opposite valence.

Another method of achieving verbal distance from one's emotions is to attempt to incorporate others within one's field of responsibility. This pattern is frequently noticed in the use of the word "we" when a patient is really talking about "I." Asking the patient to experiment with the use of "I" in such circumstances aborts this effort to avoid responsibility.

Alternatively, sentences beginning with "you" are frequently seen both as projections and as efforts to prevent contact with important feelings. The comment "You make me angry," for example, denies personal responsibility and externally attributes the source of one's behavior. Asking the patient to restructure such sentences to begin with "I" forces the individual to express resentments more directly and to take responsibility for (i.e., to "own") feelings. Changing the question "Why do you resent me?" to "You resent me" and then to "I resent you" represents the type of progression that proceeds from language restructuring. One can see in this process how a patient's reaction may increase as the sentence becomes more personal and more directly owned. Here is another excerpt from the transcript of the patient with arthritis who was doing an experiment with her wrist brace:

PATIENT: It's so ugly.
THERAPIST: Try this: "You scare me."
P: You scare me.
T: Again.
P: You scare me.
T: Just stay with that one sentence and say it as it comes up for you.
P: You scare me.
T: Now I'm gonna ask you to stay with that sentence, but to turn it around slightly and say, "I'm scared of you."
P: I'm scared of you.
T: Again.
P: I'm scared of you (*Face begins to look young and fearful*).
T: Did you feel your face change as you said that?

P: Yeah, I'm *scared*.

T: Oooh, yeah. Feel that. Say it again.

P: It gives me the shivers.

T: Yeah, let your—

P: I'm *scared* of you. You're so creepy-looking. Ugly-looking. You look worse there than on my hand. I think I'm really scared of looking at you—it's scary. It's so—

T: OK, come back to the sentence "I'm scared of you."

P: I'm *scared* of you. I hate what you look like. You don't belong on me. But you do belong on me.

T: Try this on: "I don't want you there, and you're there."

In the process of personalizing language, as in any circumstance when the method of avoiding emotions is removed, affective experiences are typically escalated in accordance with the therapeutic objectives. Often a statement such as "I feel sorry for you" is a low-grade form of anger and resentment. It usually induces a sense of being superior to the target person, but does not allow for release and completion until the anger and resentment are fully owned and expressed.

A cardinal guiding principle in the integration of Gestalt therapy procedures with one another is the understanding that anxiety signals avoidance. If a therapist can move a patient toward anxiety (e.g., increase the anxiety arousal), the provoking content serves as a cue for discovering those things that the patient is avoiding. If patients dislike comments that they have been asked to make, for example, it may bespeak the presence of some sensed or anticipated danger in the remark. This can be noted in the following excerpt from the early part of an experiment, in which the patient's husband was in the empty chair and the patient, who had chronic back pain was addressing him.

THERAPIST: OK. Is it all right for you to stand up?

PATIENT: Yeah.

T: OK. Usually anger is done a lot better from a standing position than on our rumps. And I'm glad you put that Kleenex down just now, 'cause you only need that for the sad side, the hurting side. Just hang on to this bataca and I'll show you how to use it. "Jerry, I'm mad at you for . . ." (*Therapist hits empty chair with a loud bang, and patient has a strong startled reaction to force of the noise*) You OK? You still with us?

P: Yeah (*some hesitation and fear in voice*).

T: All right. Hit with the bat while you say things like, "Jerry, I'm angry at you for not listening to me. I'm angry at you for making me into a nonperson." Now just try it out, you know, just let yourself do something physical along with the stuff you're saying to him.

P: Oh, I don't feel very good about doing that.

T: OK. Just notice what your head's saying to you right now. What's the message? [The therapist elicits the parental injunction.]

P: I don't know. (*Pause*) "Nice ladies don't do that."

T: You bet. Nice ladies just get a lot of pain in their bodies and a whole lot of stuff inside. Eh?

P: Yeah, right. (*laughing in acknowledgment*).

T: OK. Now I don't think there are any judges in here, as far as I know, and Dave [the cotherapist] and I certainly don't qualify as judges, so, you know, there's no judge here to judge you as bad for doing that. So—

P: Just *me*.

T: Just you, and you've got a heavy one there, huh?

P: Mmm-hmm.

T: He's a tough judge, or is it a "he" judge?

P: No, it's me (*nervous laugh*).

T: OK. All right. Now, if you're willing to, you could send her outside the door till we get some work done.

P: OK.

T: Want to do that?

P: Yeah.

T: Try it out loud. "Hey, judge, get the hell out of here!" or whatever.

P: Hey, judge, get off my back! [After 16 years of chronic back pain!]

The therapist can assist patients through the process of expression by asking them to complete unfinished sentences with spontaneous comments, to change wishful language to acknowledging "what is," to reidentify or relabel feeling language, and to make statements of commitment rather than effortful statements (e.g., "I will" instead of "I will try"). These language-based procedures tend to move the patient toward this increasing anxiety, while cognitive content often becomes tuned to the source of anxiety. Patients frequently direct statements to their significant others about what they want. It is important that a therapist help a patient to see and experience the difference between what *is* and what *is not*. Each time the patient uses the words "I wish" or "I want," the therapist can approach that phase as an incomplete statement and ask the patient to supply the missing part. "I want" or "I wish" statements generally leave off the part of the thought that includes the reality. "I want you to listen to me" generally means "and you don't." "I wish I could allow myself to cry" includes "and I don't." By having the patient verbalize both halves, the therapist helps to make the split between the wish and the reality apparent. This can easily be done by feeding the missing part of the sentence to the patient, thus encouraging the patient to attend to the whole statement.

PATIENT: I want you to share responsibility for the kids.
THERAPIST: "And you don't."
P: And you don't.
T: "And when you don't, I feel . . ."
P: I feel upset—no—angry. I feel angry when you don't.

PATIENT: I wish you'd listen to me.
THERAPIST: "And you don't."
P: And you don't.
T: Attend to how you feel when he does not listen. Tell him what goes on. "I feel . . ."
P: I feel shut out.
T: And what else.
P: Resentful. I resent you when you don't listen.

The ownership of the real rather than the hoped-for situation often evokes the emotion lurking beneath the surface.

Engaging Systems of Nonverbal Communication

In addition to attending to the patient's verbal patterns, the therapist may attend to various nonverbal cues. Often a person can be energized to break through the barriers to feelings by raising or modifying voice quality or intensity, becoming physically active, or exaggerating the observed symptom of anger. Table 6.1 briefly describes some of the nonverbal behaviors that the therapist can routinely observe.

The therapist must be aware of variations in smoothness or flow in the patient's respiration, particularly in exhaling. Whereas inhaling occurs naturally, exhaling often signals the presence of affect through a sigh or a noise. When the patient prevents expiration, the affect associated with that process is also held. The therapist can release the process by drawing attention to the breath holding and asking the patient either to exaggerate the holding or to release and breathe out. Exaggerating observed nonverbal behaviors such as this may provoke magnified affect and enhance affective awareness. For example, observing breathing in the midst of crying may index the presence of lingering, aborted affect. Sucking after each sob suggests a competing emotion, which may be further pursued by drawing attention to sensory cues in the patient's mouth and throat. Frequently, when so directed, the patient can observe what appears to be a choking sensation in a struggle to suppress emotional response, and thus to keep rather than release the emotion. Either exaggerating this sensation or providing a counter against the defense itself will frequently facilitate the treatment process. For example, clearing the

TABLE 6.1. Possible Nonverbal Cues to Emotional Arousal or Control

Area	Cues
Appearance	1. Dress
	2. Grooming
	3. Personal care
Posture	1. Stance (slumped over, erect, off balance)
	2. Closed–open (legs, arms)
	3. Shoulders, chest areas
	4. Feet
Breathing	1. Shallowness
	2. Gulping
	3. Sucking in
Face	1. Forehead (frown, surprise, questions)
	2. Ears (movement, flushing, head cocked)
	3. Nose (nostrils flaring, wrinkling)
	4. Eyes
	a. Shifting—contact
	b. Squinting
	c. Moistening
	d. Reddening
	e. Pupils dilating
	5. Mouth (dry, lips pursed, controlled, etc.)
	6. Chin (quivers, jutting)
	7. Jaws (muscle flexing, teeth grinding)
	8. Throat and neck ("pain in the neck")
	a. "Catch"—clearing of throat
	b. Tightening of muscles—strain
	c. "Adam's apple"—swallowing
Voice	1. Pitch/sound (high, squeezed, choked)
	2. Wavering
	3. Whining
	4. Stuttering
Hands	1. Clutching, wringing
	2. Drumming
	3. Expressiveness
	4. Hand shakes
	5. Pushing–pulling

obstruction with a firm "no" can be suggested and repeated by the patient in order to reduce overcontrol of the feelings.

Similarly, a whining and complaining voice can be seen as a method for avoiding disowned emotion. Frequently, therapists observe patients to be drawn between a sense of hurt and the expression of anger. By exaggerating a patient's voice, directing the patient to reduce the whine or complaint, or directing a change in the accompanying helpless posture, a therapist can frequently speed the patient's contact with the feelings that these behavioral patterns serve to avoid. Raising the level of a week voice may help contact the other side of the emotional coin and may provoke an overt display of tears and hurt. By the same token, magnifying the verbal and postural behaviors that accompany hurt may reciprocally provoke the expression of anger. Once the patient is firmly in touch with the anger and has a commitment to move from "talking about" it to actual physical expression, it is beneficial to have the patient stand and address the empty chair verbally (and, if necessary, physically) from that position. A change in stance helps the patient shift from the usual hurt position to the unexpressed anger.

Magnifying or exaggerating verbal behaviors by directed screaming or yelling may further escalate a patient's disowned sensations and injunctions by bringing feelings into focus very rapidly and by breaking through inherent barriers that inhibit and control expression. A patient's unwillingness to utilize such suggestions may emphasize the amount and type of constraint and control that he or she employs to manage feelings. Resistances or struggles against such suggestions may thus serve as points of focus for defining another angry split.

The therapist should also attend to other physical manifestations of conflict besides posture and voice. Both seating distance and clenched hands, for example, are often indicators of efforts to restrain anger. Body signals of an emotion usually precede the patient's conscious awareness of that emotion (Zajonc, 1980). The use of dialogue with those bodily parts that seem to express a denied aspect of self has been described by Perls (1969). In such dialogues, the patient should be encouraged to give hands or other bodily parts permission to do the unexpressed. Often, simply asking the patient to attend to tight muscles may bring attention to those aspects of self that are represented therein. Significant signals of excessive anger control are teeth grinding, weak or restrained voice, shakiness, and stuttering. In all of these examples, the patient's attention should be brought to bear on the bodily area of manifest conflict, and responsibility for that impulse-inhibiting activity should be increased by invoking personally directed language (e.g., "I" statements).

Since the face is also a vehicle for nonverbal communication, it is frequently one of the first indices of a split or contradiction between feelings and constraints. Flushes, changes of skin tone, a frown, tics, and changes in the eyes and mouth that seem to contrast with what the patient verbally expresses can all be indexed as referencing potential splits and internal struggles. When the patient's attention is brought to the focal area, affect can often be heightened. Similarly, establishing dialogues around the split or exaggerating the observed behavior serves this same purpose. Throughout, the therapist's task is to think of the observed behaviors as efforts to inhibit or control emotional arousal. Following the mandate both to move the patient closer to the object being avoided and to remove the method of avoidance, focusing upon the avoidance pattern and either directly exaggerating or reducing that pattern have a high probability of increasing the patient's sensitivity to the avoided feelings.

Closing the Experiment

As the therapy session progresses toward closure, a series of closure strategies is useful. In FEP, the "goodbye" process is used in two contexts. The first of these is to indicate a conclusion to an individual piece of work that involves another person. The therapist solicits the specific use of the word "goodbye"; this allows the therapist to see how cleanly the patient concludes the work. If the "goodbye" is firm and clean, it most often signifies that the patient is achieving some closure. If, on the other hand, the patient avoids using the word or substitutes some other phrase, it can be an indication that there is still an unfinished matter that prevents the patient from letting go. This is a part of the patient's process, and some process comment such as "I'm aware that you did not actually say goodbye" can expose the avoidance. This line of work can lead to an exploration of how the patient keeps from saying goodbye. It can mean that there are difficult underlying emotions that need to be expressed, or it can mean that the patient may have some "secondary gain" in keeping the unfinished business with a significant person in an unresolved state (Tobin, 1975). Thus, by asking the patient to say goodbye and then by attending to how the patient handles that task, the therapist has an assessment tool for understanding the present state of the patient.

The second context in which the "goodbye" process activity is important is in releasing someone who is no longer physically available (e.g., because of divorce, death, or abortion). This goodbye must be preceded by work in which the patient has the opportunity to express all the unfinished emotions and thoughts. The work involves expression of grief, hurt, anger, or resentment that has been unexpressed. Many patients are actually unaware of how they felt when a relationship ended (Tobin, 1975) until they are asked through an experiment to say what they need to say. One woman found herself finally able to accept her hysterectomy when she was able to speak with the child that would never be and then to say goodbye.

In the next example, the patient had worked hard in dealing with his deceased father and was ready to end the session.

THERAPIST: If you have finished your old business with Dad, I would like for you to do a special kind of "goodbye" to him today—OK?

PATIENT: Sure—what do you mean?

T: You *physically* buried Dad 10 years ago; today I want you to *psychologically* bury him in a symbolic ceremony by using this blanket to cover him as you say your final goodbyes to him.

P: OK. (*Holds blanket*) Well, Dad, I am ready to cut the cord with you now that I've finally told you what I really feel. I am no longer scared of you and I won't be blaming you for my life any more! (*Looks surprised*)

T: Tell him how that felt.

P: Great! I just realized that I really have been blaming you instead of showing my anger toward you. So . . . I'll say goodbye, Dad, and let you rest in peace. (*Takes blanket and carefully, tenderly covers the empty cushion*) Goodbye, Dad . . . I love you. (*Embraces the covered cushion as he cries softly*)

T: Just allow yourself to stay with those feelings as long as you need to.

Experience has shown that this type of ceremony is profoundly effective in putting the "period" at the end of completed work. If patients have deluded themselves into believing they have finished when in reality the work is not complete, they will have difficulty in the exercise. This lack of completeness can be noticed by such acts as partially covering the focal chair/cushion or rejecting the process midway through it. The use of this burial process aptly symbolizes separation itself and may underline the importance of the grieving process. Time should be allowed within the therapeutic environment to attend to the grieving experience; the patient should be permitted to explore the anger, disappointment, and hurt that are embodied in this experience.

A final benefit of saying goodbye is that it allows the patient to be able to initiate a new "hello" experience with someone else. One man who had been divorced by his wife was not able to say hello to possible future relationships until he was able to talk about her as his "ex-wife," to express all his anger and grief, and finally to say goodbye.

At the conclusion of each piece of "work," a "goodbye" statement directed to the object of one's dialogue can facilitate returning to that interaction at a later point, if indicated. It is often helpful for the therapist to encourage the patient to express a goodbye in order to signal a partial resolution of the difficulty, even though the patient may resist doing so. If the interaction is still unfinished, such that the feelings embodied in the dialogue are not yet integrated into a revised view of self and others, the patient's "goodbye" dialogue should be accompanied by a verbalization of an additional contract that will be used to return to and complete this work, perhaps outside of the treatment session itself.

Evaluating the Work

Often the evaluation of the work experience can take place within the experiment itself. The value of this procedure is that it assists the patient in assessing how the end-of-session experience compares with the beginning-of-session experience.

THERAPIST: Before you say "goodbye" to John, would you tell him what you did for yourself today?

PATIENT: I finally got to my anger. I've been putting it on myself; I realized that today. It felt good to tell you what I'm angry about. I'm not all torn up inside. I'm breathing again. You don't frighten me—I'm not shaky inside now. I'm glad I brought you in here today (*laughing*).

T: Are you ready to say goodbye?

P: With pleasure (*large smile*). Goodbye, John!

The session itself should end with a termination process, which will be paralleled in the closing sessions of the therapeutic contract, in order to provide ongoing evaluation as well as to close out the treatment. These terminations symbolize separations, which, it is assumed, re-enact important separations in the patient's experience. Numerous methods have been devised for working with these separations, but dialogue, enactment, and fantasy are particularly valuable.

Summary

A therapy relationship that is seen as unsafe by the patient cannot have a consistent psychotherapeutic effect. Therefore, it is necessary for the FEP therapist to convey this sense of safety to the patient, both in the therapist's presence and in the introduction and implementation of methodology. We refer the reader again to Appendix 1, where the various tasks of the therapist are presented, along with descriptive criteria by which to address the adequacy of their completion. These tasks begin with the group's setting an agenda for the therapeutic activities and identifying unfinished business in the opening round of each group session.

In the experiment, the task is to maximize present feelings and sensations in order to break through the impasse and complete unfinished business. Generally, the therapist uses evocative strategies of verbal statements to stimulate the dormant response system, then gradually and sensitively escalates to more directive procedures, since imposing a procedure onto the therapeutic relationship is at best problematic.

Many experiential techniques, ranging from verbal (i.e., dialogue) to imagery (i.e., fantasy) to nonverbal (e.g., bataca work), are available to the FEP therapist. The therapist needs to be informed as to the appropriateness of each method and should have a rationale that fits the patient's immediate condition before engaging in any particular methodology. It behooves the therapist to be an astute and keen observer of the patient, since verbal and nonverbal behaviors are the most reliable cues to identify the areas of emotional blockage.

Closing techniques are useful and necessary for productive integration and utilization of the work within the session with the roles required in the outside world. Closing techniques, therefore, move the patient forward to the application of learning, and work to help differentiate experiences and interpersonal boundaries.

7

Fine-Tuning Therapist Interventions

A major problem of all psychotherapies is to motivate the patient to do what must be done, and to stay on task (Perls, *et al.* 1951). In Gestalt therapy generally, and FEP specifically, the defensive maneuvers of the patient away from task are not viewed and labeled as "resistance" but as "struggles" designed to avoid experiences that threaten perceptual constancy. The therapist is taught to notice *what* the patient is doing and *how* the patient is doing it. It is assumed that the patient can be motivated to stay on task, once the trained, alert therapist catches the particular mode of "contact interruption" and teaches the patient how to be aware of that process as well.

In FEP, the goal is to achieve a "primary" state of arousal of the motion associated with "unfinished business." When the patient is attending to the sensations, thoughts, and emotions of the moment and allowing them to be experienced and expressed as they move into conscious awareness, the patient is in a "primary" mode of expression. For example, the successful patient may allow the experience of unexpressed grief at the death of a parent, or the unexpressed fear associated with the increasing physical deterioration resulting from chronic disease, to enter and be retained in awareness. The less successful patient, on the other hand, remains in a state of unfinished emotional release and continues in that condition through the use of emotional configurations that prohibit or restrict the natural cycle of (1) arousal, (2) expression and release, (3) recovery, and (4) relief. These configurations that restrict emotions are analogous to the Gestalt "contact boundary interruptions" described by Perls *et al.* (1951) and by Polster and Polster (1973).

Contact Boundary Interruptions

The forms that contact boundary interruptions take have been briefly discussed in Chapters 1 and 4. The present chapter spells out these processes in more detail and outlines specific interventions that we have found to be generally helpful in keeping the patient on task. The delineation of the specific interruption, along with appropriate interventions, begins to examine the microprocesses that several authors believe must be monitored in the process of psychotherapy (Mahrer, Nifakis, Abhukara, & Sterner, 1984; Rice & Greenberg, 1984). Appendix 2 of this volume contains a rating scale for assisting the clinician in identifying various configural processes. An examination of this scale will help the reader to identify various disturbances in perceptual boundaries, and also to differentiate among the various types of anger that have been identified in previous chapters. Repeated assessments of therapy sessions over time may also help identify patterns of change as they occur.

The "contact boundary" is an important Gestalt concept, but somewhat difficult to define, because it is a process rather than a state concept (Frew, 1983). However, Frew, drawing upon the various Gestalt authors, has found four consistent characteristics of the contact boundary.

First, the person experiences perceived differences from others. The boundary is the point at which the individual experiences "me" in relationship to "not-me." Here are some examples of individuals with blurred boundaries:

- The man at work who disowns his anger and projects it onto his supervisor is not aware of the boundary between himself and the other.
- The woman who has accepted family proscriptions prohibiting the expression of emotions has blurred her boundaries and instead is confluent with family boundaries.
- An eighth-grade boy who constantly defers to his mother for answers to questions that the counselor is asking him has no solid sense of self.

Second, in a healthy or adjusting individual, the contact or "I" boundary possesses the characteristic of permeability or flexibility. This is the ability to relax the contact boundary momentarily and accept input from the environment. This is evident in the following examples.

- The child who accepts parental information not to play with the family dog in the street accepts valuable information from the outside.
- There is permeability when a group member receives and accepts feedback from another about unconscious ways in which his or her behavior has been antagonistic.

Third, interaction is initiated and experienced between people. People interact through their senses and through speech and movement, as in this poignant example:

In a therapy session a husband is touched by his wife's pain as she talks about the death of her mother. He reaches over and takes her hand. She briefly smiles at him through her tears and then leans into his body for comfort as he begins to tell her what he has missed because of her mother's death. She breathes a long, deep breath and seems to let go of something. (Here the actions and words continually evoke deepening responses in the interaction with each other.)

Finally, there is a "common figure," which is the emergence of common interest or experience point between one person and another. Healthy individuals are well aware of these contact factors and engage others at the contact boundary in a manner consistent with the continuing needs of both the self and others. For example:

- The grieving couple mentioned above create a common figure resulting from their grief.
- A housewife expresses to her husband her core need to go to work part-time. In the past he has resisted, but now he hears and becomes attuned to the importance of this and gives her unqualified support.

The neurotic organism has developed chronic interruptions of the contact process. If the therapist examines the contact boundary process carefully and discovers how the patient is interrupting the contact, then appropriate interventions, exercises, and experiments can be created, with increased potential of helpfulness. The development of an experiment is not a random, gut-feeling process, but a deliberate attempt to set up a facilitative intervention for a particular person who is engaged in a particular form of contact boundary interruption.

Undifferentiated or Confluent Emotions

The emotion most often constricted by contact boundary interruptions is anger. Moreover, Kaplan, Brooks, McComb, Shapiro, and Sodano (1983) point out that women may be especially susceptible to configural patterns that constrict anger expression. Women live in an "angerogenic" milieu, where the social reinforcement of suppression of rage is a given. Such patients, when encouraged in the psychotherapy situation to express their unfinished anger, find that initial efforts often produce a mixture of anger with sadness or hurt. Such mixtures are referred to as "confluent configurations of emotions." The patient with confluent emotions may express angry words, but the tone of voice is one of pain or hurt. Sometimes the patient says, "When I get really angry, I cry," and reports that tears were acceptable in the family, whereas open expression of anger was not. The result in the therapy situation is that the mix of hurt and anger remains undifferentiated. The therapist hears the incongruence of angry words and hurt affect, or hears the patient complaining or whining.

The task of the therapist is to help the patient to experience the differences between sadness and anger; to become aware of which one is stronger (more figural) at the moment; to shift with the patient as the patient's sensations shift (hurt to anger, and vice versa); and finally to move completely into each emotion as it emerges.

PATIENT: (*Sobbing and addressing her brother in the empty chair*) Why did you say that to me? Why don't you want to talk to me? I come home as often as I can, and just because you feel that you—you're stuck with our mother, it's not the truth. I've asked her to come and stay with me, I've asked her to live with me, and you insist that I don't love her. You don't know anything that goes on in my life at all.

THERAPIST: I'm gonna ask you to try out a sentence. "I *resent* you for implying that . . ."

P: (*Hurt voice*) I *hate* you! I don't resent you, I *hate* you. You just don't understand.

T: Ann, I hear your anger coming through your tears. Are you aware of that?

P: Yes.

T: OK. So I'm gonna ask you to separate out those two emotions, the hurt and the anger.

P: OK. You just want me to get angry instead of showing hurt?

T: Well, not necessarily get angry instead, but I'm going to ask you, if you're feeling more hurt, to allow yourself to move totally into the hurt. If you're feeling more angry, then be clearly angry. Otherwise, those two feelings get all kind of scrambled up in there, and then you're stuck with them in an unfinished kind of way. If you're feeling more hurt than anger, talk with your brother from that chair. If you're feeling more angry than hurt, I'm gonna ask you to stand up and talk to him. OK? So that you can separate the two feelings out for yourself.

P: I think I feel hurt.

T: OK. Stay with that.

P: OK. I love—Why don't you understand that? Why are you so nasty to me? [The patient continues in this vein for a while.] I don't even feel like 5 years old! All you do is make me feel—you belittle me all the time. All the time! I don't think you believe I have a brain in my head! Everything that I say, you know better. I resent that. (*The hurt is less, but the voice is flat*)

T: Stand up and say that.

P: (*Standing*) I *resent* that. I really resent it.

T: OK. Hear the hurt still in your voice. I'm gonna ask you to say it with resentment in your voice.

P: Jeff [the brother], I *resent* that! (*Angry voice emerges*)

T: Feel the difference?

P: Yes.

T: OK. Keep going.

P: Look, I'm an adult. I understand everything that I'm doing. I have perfect control of myself, and I don't need you around.

T: "I resent it when you're around."

P: I resent it when you're around, you know that? (*Voice drops off again and sounds hurt*)

T: Whoops! Your voice—do you hear it?

P: Yeah.

T: It's gotten real hurt again.

P: Yeah. I *resent* it when you're around (*Strong, angry voice*)

T: Does that feel different to you?

P: Yes. Yes. Honestly, I feel better.

T: Do you hear the two different voices?

P: Yeah.

Once patients are able to experience a difference between anger and hurt, they have the ability to explore each emotion separately, and to come to emotional completion.

Retroflection of Emotions

SQUEEZING OFF EMOTION

Two types of "retroflection" are defined in the Gestalt therapy literature. The first form can be described as squeezing off the expression of emotion. The organism is pushing toward completion, but the person interrupts and constricts emotional release processes. Smith (1986) believes that this type of retroflection is of special interest because it involves the musculoskeletal system. Retroflection diminishes or totally prevents muscular movement. The therapist facilitates by helping the patient attend to what sensations are being constricted in the moment and attend to the effects of that constriction.

PATIENT: (*The patient is picking at her arm. She is collapsed forward in the chair; her voice is almost inaudible; her look is stoic*)

THERAPIST: I see your body slumped forward. You look as if you feel very hurt. I see how you are outside and I'm wondering how you are inside.

P: I'm tough inside. I'm tough. I don't feel it any more, but as a kid there was a certain satisfaction that they [her parents] couldn't get me. They could give me blisters, but they couldn't get me down. (*Her feet begin to agitate and her shoulders tighten up*) I wasn't tough on the outside, I was tough on the inside, 'cause I didn't let them know. They'd give me blisters and I'd say, "You didn't hurt me!" (*Body continues to agitate. Her face tightens up after a brief look of fear. Her hands are tightly clenched*)

T: Just notice what happens when you recall very painful experiences and then tighten your body around those experiences.

P: I don't think I can do this.

T: What do you imagine would happen if you let your body release the feelings? If you let your hands wring the pillow instead of each other?

P: I just know that inside I'm strong and nobody can get to me.

T: And yet it must be awful to have to be strong all the time. I see what your body is doing. Would you be willing to experiment with not having to be strong today? Would you be willing to say something to your mother that you couldn't say as a kid?

TURNING EMOTION TOWARD THE SELF

In the second form of retroflection, the person turns the anger expression against the self rather than toward an appropriate target in the environment. In essence, the person becomes both the "doer" and the "done-to." Contextual cues give evidence of the appropriateness of the patient's anger at people in his or her life. Thus, often there is reason to be angry, but the anger is not expressed at that appropriate target. Instead, the patient develops a subject–object split.

The therapist will hear retroflexive behavior in the self-harassing language of the patient ("I don't like myself," "I kick myself around about that") or observe it in self-punishing physical cues (pounding fist on knee, picking at skin on the arm, etc.). The therapist must help the patient become aware of the self-harassment and help in the identification of an appropriate target in the environment (i.e., a specific person and situation about which the patient is angry).

PATIENT: (*To mother*) I hated you growing up. I felt so much anger at you. I hated the way you treated Daddy.

THERAPIST: Do you feel those feelings in your body now?

P: Yeah—right here. My stomach is all twisted.

T: Would you express your feelings to your mother and experience what happens.

T: Direct your feelings toward your mother.

P: (*Picks up the bataca and then suddenly changes*) It's not that I really hate my mother, I really hate myself. More than anything, I hate myself. (*To mother*) You did such good things for me. (*To therapist*) I feel so terrible to say I hate her. I'm really terrible for hating her.

T: I understand the love you had for your mother, and the appreciation. I'm encouraging you to explore the other side of that, the anger that you haven't expressed.

P: I'll try.

T: Let yourself start with your resentments and let them out of your body one at a time.

P: I resent your always being perfect. I resent you treating Daddy so unfairly. I resent that you killed yourself and would not take your medications. I resent your treatment of my sister. (*Stops abruptly*) Somehow it's *my* fault. If I could have been a better daughter, you would not have done those things.

T: Are you aware that each time some anger emerges you start blaming yourself? You make yourself the target.

Sometimes with this latter type of retroflection, a patient can be helped to turn the anger away from the self by using the bataca, which gives the organism concrete evidence of a willingness to direct the anger toward a significant other by hitting the cushion rather than the self. The therapist should watch for a special kind of retroflective hitting where the patient hits the cushion first and then hits, or discounts, himself or herself on the backswing. When this happens, the therapist should bring the retroflection to the patient's attention and give instructions on using the bataca without self-retaliation.

Instrumental Anger

Although instrumental anger is directed toward an identified subject, close listening reveals that the *goal* of the anger expression is not to reduce intensity and achieve peace. Instead, the intent is to blame, change, or punish the target person. The tone of voice and the words themselves are full of blame. Most statements are prefaced with the word "you" rather than "I."

The expression of instrumental anger often has the appearance of release, but it tends not to come to closure. The focus is on the "awful" behavior of the target person, rather than on the patient's moment-to-moment need for emotional release and relief.

THERAPIST: (*Feeding a line*) "Eddie, I'm angry every time you walk away."

PATIENT: Eddie, I'm angry every time you walk away! You ask me for communication, and then I try to act like an adult and I tell you we need to talk like adults, we can't just walk away. "Let's discuss it," and you walk away, you close the door, you start reading your book. You stick your nose back into your book, and you're always going into the bedroom, and you're always reading your books, and you always leave me out there with my feelings and I say, "Don't leave with my feelings!" I can't go to sleep at night, and you say, "I'm tired, I have to get up in the morning," and I say, "Well, I'm tired too, but dammit, I can't sleep while you're not listening to me, and I want you to listen to me so you can let me get rid of my feelings so I can relax too!" But it doesn't seem to make any difference to you. You're perfect, everything that you do is right and everything that I do is completely wrong. You're not fair.

Later in this same session, when the therapist checked on progress, notice that the patient reported relief, but immediately continued to move back into blaming and demanding that the target person change.

THERAPIST: Tell him how you're doing right now.
PATIENT: Eddie, it feels good to let this anger out, because it feels like you had to sit there and listen to me; you had to sit there and hear that you're just—you say you're listening to me. I remember the angriest, one of the angriest you ever got at me is when I didn't listen to you because I didn't know what feeling was. I didn't know what feeling and primal therapy was. But you know what you did after that? You got angry because I asked you a question and I didn't know I was supposed to keep my mouth totally shut, and then you drove off and you wouldn't talk to me and you never gave me a chance to make up, and I kept saying, "It's all right," I kept saying, "Eddie, you can talk." [The patient continues in this vein for a while.] Eddie, I told you, and I told you just in this past week, that we have to learn how to deal with our problems differently, because it's killing me. It makes me feel pain in my shoulders and in my neck. I feel the pain go down into my elbows. I can feel the pain in my knees and it wasn't there before I told you.
T: Tell him what you're going to do about it.
P: You've gotta be—I want to talk with you; I want to communicate with you, but I can't do it unless you are going to agree with me. [The patient goes on in this manner for a while.] I want you to really understand, Eddie, how much this affects me, how angry you make me; how important it is to be me and just discuss things, communicate more and maybe meet each other halfway. If that's a solution, you will change.

The anger expressed by the patient throughout this example tended to blame and demand change of the target person. The therapist who hears only anger and not its goal may believe that such a patient is releasing and progressing because his or her voice and manner are angry. Such a therapist will not often succeed in getting the patient to attend to the in-session experience. Suggesting statements such as "Tell him what you are going to do about it" promote a focus on out-of-session experience, which should be reserved for the homework phase. The following evaluation of the session's work by the patient above reveals her failure to work through instrumental anger. No new ground was broken; there was only a repetition of old complaints.

THERAPIST: Tell him what you accomplished today and then say good-bye.

PATIENT: I don't know, Eddie, that I've actually learned—I don't really know that I've learned any more than I knew before. I know all these things; I've said all these things; I sleep or I don't sleep with all these things, but I know I have to make some kind of decision 'cause I don't want to live with pain.

To be effective with such a patient, the therapist needs to help the patient move from "you" to "I" statements. This shift reorients the focus from the "there-and-then" of the target person's behavior to the immediacy of the felt experience for the patient. Consider the example given earlier of the patient talking to her brother about her mother:

PATIENT: (*Sobbing*) Why did you say that to me? Why don't you want to talk to me? I come home as often as I can, and just because you feel that you—you're stuck with our mother, it's not the truth. I've asked her to come and stay with me, I've asked her to live with me, and you insist that I don't love her. You don't know anything that goes on in my life at all.

THERAPIST: I'm gonna ask you to try out a sentence. "I *resent* you for implying that . . ."

P: I *hate* you! I don't resent you, I *hate* you. You just don't understand.

This alteration of language provided access to the patient's present affect, and also evoked the potent word "hate" for this particular patient. Often the therapist must continually nudge the patient out of blaming or instrumental language and into the language of present ownership. It is necessary for the therapist to repeat such interventions as often as it takes to help the patient shift away from instrumental anger.

THERAPIST: OK. Just tell your father where the hurt is right now. "I feel the hurt right in my throat."

PATIENT: Well, I feel a hurt in my throat when I talk to you, and I didn't used to hurt like that when I talked to you. I felt I could tell you anything. There was nothing we couldn't talk about. And it bothers me that now I have reservations about being open and honest with you, because I don't think you're being open and honest with me. I don't like that feeling. I don't like that that type of thing could separate us, 'cause I'm finding I don't want to be around you, and that hurts even worse.

T: Try out a line. Again, if it doesn't fit, throw it away. "Dad, I resent your hypocrisy."

P: Dad, I resent your hypocrisy.

T: Does that fit?

P: Yeah! I *don't* like hypocrites. (*Voice get stronger*) Yeah, it's very hard to cope with.

T: Did you feel your voice change?

P: Yeah.

T: OK. Say it again.

P: I resent your hypocrisy. I don't like hypocrites, and I don't like people that say one thing and do another. You remind me of the parent that says, "Do as I say, not as I do," and I don't want that kind of parent. I just want an honest parent.

T: "And you're not."

P: And you're not. You're definitely not. Like now I think you're fooling me, and you're lying to me, I think you're trying to spare me something that you think is gonna hurt me, but it can't hurt any worse than this did. So don't—

T: "I resent you for fooling me."

P: I resent you for fooling me.

T: Is that true?

P: Yes.

T: OK. Stay with that, with what you resent. Focus on how that affects you, what *your* response is, and tell him directly "I resent you for . . ." or "I feel . . ."—OK?

When patients are totally stuck in instrumental anger, it is sometimes necessary to challenge them to confront this dynamic directly. In the following example, the therapist had made many attempts to encourage "I" language, but the patient continued instrumental anger:

PATIENT: I hate you. I don't resent you, I hate you *and* you ought to listen to me so you could understand what is really going on in my life. Until you do that you shouldn't judge me. [Patient continues telling the significant other what he *should* do, etc.]

THERAPIST: (*Dropping further attempts to encourage "I" language*) Tell Tony you would rather give him your blaming and complaining than give him your stored anger.

P: (*Looking stunned*) No—why would I want to do that? (*Looking at therapist*) Am I doing that? (*Back to Tony*) *I am* doing that. (*Pause*) I've held on to my anger all these years, and I thought I could unload it if I just complained long enough and loud enough.

Deflection of Emotions

Those who deflect are able to take the "heat" off anticipated expression of emotions by expressing the emotion in an indiscriminate manner, either by changing the target or by changing the nature of the emotional arousal altogether. In the former type of deflection, the patient engages the environment on a hit-or-miss basis—for example, by being angry in many situations but never focusing the anger toward primary, unfinished situations. In the latter form of deflection, the patient changes the topic, intellectualizes and rationalizes feelings, or will only "talk about" feelings. Those who deflect in this way often present themselves as being troubled, but they seem to lack a clear focus, constantly shifting from one subject to another. Another way of deflecting the focus away from emotional arousal is the use of humor to lighten the impact of the issue on the person's life. At times this is noticed when the patient laughs while discussing serious, painful, or traumatic material. In each case, the process is one of quickly backing away from the experience or expression of emotions.

In FEP sessions, a common form of deflection is for the patient to move constantly out of the established experiment and to talk with the therapist or other group members, rather than the target person in the empty chair.

PATIENT: (*Turning from empty chair to therapist*) And that is exactly why I don't want to have anything to do with her.

THERAPIST: Would you tell her that?

P: She knows, I think, 'cause she's probably aware that I have avoided her lately.

T: I'm aware that you are avoiding her right now, by talking to me instead of her.

P: You want me to speak with her?

T: It sounds as if you have some unfinished business with her, and this may be a way for you to take care of things.

P: But she doesn't listen to me, it's sort of—I guess I feel that I've done what I can do.

T: Here in the experiment, you can create the experience of having her listen to you so that you can finish what you need to do for yourself.

P: I just feel so damn frustrated with the whole thing.

T: Would you be willing to tell her that? "Gina, I'm frustrated with you. I'm angry with you."

P: (*Returning to the experiment*) I am, Gina. I've been angry a long time.

At other times, the patient deflects by moving away from persistent, strong emotions and by talking about all the details of an event except the feeling, thereby keeping the emotion at arm's length.

THERAPIST: In the opening round a minute ago, you said you were upset with what was happening with your daughter. And you said you wanted some time.

PATIENT: Yeah. (*Pause*) I feel like I'm to going to cry.

T: If you're wiling, see your daughter there and tell her what you are feeling right now.

P: (*To daughter*) Well, we thought this was a good marriage, but we found out a lot of things after you got married, of course. But he's a—(*to therapist*) her husband is extremely moody, he gets very depressed, but he won't go for any help. She went on ahead with her degree in psychology, and she was going for her master's and her doctorate eventually; she's a very bright girl, but right now he's going to school and so she's working and taking care of their 7-month-old baby. He works too, but he's a person who has had a difficult time finding his niche. We thought he finally had found it in sports medicine. He was a football player, a star at the high school and a "preferred man" and all this, you know. And he's a good person, but he's just—he gets so moody and then he lashes out at her and he's never liked me, for some reason. I've made a real point to try to, you know, be accepting and so on, but when I went up there when their baby was born, every time I'd hold her he'd say, "Well, don't drop her," or "Watch her head," or something, and I finally said, "Now, Andrew, I've taken care of six of my own babies and a lot of other people's, I know how to take care of them." And—

T: I'm aware that as you talk you seem more distant from your feelings. A moment ago you felt like crying. What—

P: I have had it—well, I don't know. (*Resumes her story*) Well, I guess I feel badly for Kate, she's had a lot of things happen in her life, which she has taken in stride. She's a very strong person, but she called this morning, she called collect, very early, so I knew there was something wrong, and she couldn't even talk for a long time. Finally she said that he told her last night he didn't love her. They—right now, I suppose, they have a meeting with the church leader tonight and are hoping to resolve some of this, but my feeling is, I don't know if I want her to stay with him or not, because he's up and down and you never know what he's gonna—

T: I am wanting to know, as you talk about this, what is it that you feel in your body at the present moment. And would you be willing to talk to your daughter, rather than about her?

P: Well, sometimes I get a pain up here, but I feel it in my stomach right now.

T: You feel it in your stomach?

P: Yeah, my colitis. I hadn't felt it until now.

T: Would you move back to your daughter and tell her what you are feeling right this moment?

P: I guess I hurt a lot. (*Pause*) I am worried sick about you kids. (*The emotional pain returns to her face and eyes*)

Another form of deflection occurs when the patient weakens the affective response with humor or a smile. Here it is appropriate for the therapist to ask the patient to report what he or she is saying without the humor: "Be serious as you speak to your mother and see if that is different for you," or "Take the smile off your face and say the same thing to her."

Physical signs of deflection of anger are evident when the patient is using the bataca with a back-and-forth, glancing stroke. The appropriate intervention at this point is to instruct the patient to aim the bataca directly at the cushion, as one would aim a hammer at the head of a nail. This will often break up the deflection and bring more focus to the work.

With deflection, the therapist can facilitate the process by making process comments about what is happening: "I'm aware that you just changed the subject," or "I notice that you are moving into your head and analyzing what's going on, rather than expressing your feelings." When these comments are made in a nonjudgmental way, patients learn to be aware of what they do and how they do it, and the therapist runs less risk of seeing the patients as resistant (Lauver, Holiman, & Kazama, 1982). At this point, the therapist can then assist the patients in keeping the direction of the expression on target, rather than deflecting it to the side.

Defensive Anger

Defensive anger is a special form of deflection, in which the patient presents anger as a mask for another emotion, such as fear. The patient presents himself or herself as angry at the target person or at the therapist, but careful monitoring will reveal verbal or nonverbal signs that another emotion is being masked. Verbal signs often suggest that the patient has made a decision not to allow herself to be vulnerable—"I'm not going to allow you to hurt/scare me again!" The expression of defensive anger often does not fit the context of the life experience described by the patient. In that context, the expression of intensity is out of proportion to the context or does not make sense. The patient may sound angry while looking very fearful or sad.

PATIENT: (*To husband in empty chair*) It was like, um, I think I was screaming [she is describing an incident in which the husband choked on some food] and I threw this pot of soup in the sink. You got angry at me 'cause I made a mess, and you said I get so out of control. "You *never* do that in an emergency," you said. Well, how do you know what you do? You're 47 years old and you've never lost anyone close to you in your life, never, no family, everyone is alive (*angry voice*).

THERAPIST: "And I'm angry."

P: And I'm angry. I'm so angry that you don't listen to me when I tell you about cutting something up or whatever. And I'm so angry that I could be so scared by it. And I'm angry that you don't understand my fear. That really makes me angry, 'cause you think I made so much of it.

T: Are you aware of your anger in your body right now?

P: Mmm-hmm.

T: Where?

P: Well, all over, in here, nausea, and like, jumpy.

T: OK. The question is, are you going to keep it inside your body or are you going to let it out right now?

P: (*Sighing*) That sigh felt better.

T: You still look troubled.

P: But I don't know how to get rid of the anger. I mean, physically I feel really sick. I don't even have—I mean I don't even have the strength to use one of those things (*pointing at the bataca*). My hand is hurting so bad from yesterday. That's the other thing. Today, you know, my hand is really swollen today and, you know, it's like, I'm not mad that my hand's swollen from what I did, but it's like, that aggravates me.

T: Uh-huh.

P: Because, at the moment, I would never think of my pain, if somebody was hurt. I mean, I could get up and help them, but today I'm suffering. It hurts.

T: Tell him about that.

P: My hand hurts so bad. My hand hurts from whacking you yesterday, but at the time I never thought of anything. I mean, I just thought, you have to breathe. I—I just can't believe this has happened twice; two times! Two times! (*Voice angry again*) Most people don't choke one time in their life, and twice! Two times! It's so—you don't know how scared I am to be left alone. I have been left by so many people that I have loved, and then I was so scared that you were going to leave me alone.

T: Keep talking to him.

P: (*Angry voice*) You don't know what it's like to be alone. You don't know what it's like to lose someone you love. And I depend on you for so many things. And it just—it just scares me so much. I have always had this fear that you would die and leave me. (*Voice changing*) I think—you're older than me. I'm—there's a chance I'll be a young widow, but I'm so scared. I'm so scared of being by myself.

T: How old do you feel right now as you are feeling scared?

P: I feel young.

T: How young?

P: I think I feel like when my mother died, when I was 10.

T: How did you know that she died? Did you see her?

P: I think so, I think she was dead. I mean, she was sitting in the chair and I was slapping her face, but I think she was dead.

T: Right now, make a choice of going back to your mother and saying what you need to say, or stay with your husband and tell him how scared you are of losing him too.

In this example, the therapist had the option of moving the patient from present defensive anger to the unfinished fear experienced when her mother died. She could now re-enact either old scenes involving her mother or recent scenes where she was fearful. By owning her fear, she could give up her inappropriate mask of anger.

Defensive anger is often a cover for sadness or hurt. In either case, it is the job of the therapist to encourage the expression of the covered-up emotion. This task can be accomplished by softly but persistently supporting the patient's exploration of the possibility of tears hiding behind the anger. The therapist may suggest, "I am hurt by (about, etc.) . . ." sentences, at the same time drawing the patient's attention to body responses, especially in the throat, chest, and face areas.

Projected Emotions

From the emotional configuration of projection, the patient perceives that an "unwanted feeling" is embodied by others in the environment. Perls (1973) has described the process as like living in a house lined with mirrors and yet believing that one is looking outside. The stance of such a person is often one of self-righteousness and of hypersensitivity to anger from others. The behavior of the patient, because of the projection, is reactive rather than active. The projection interrupts excitement and subjects the patient to stress of a kind and degree that activates the patient's belief that he or she cannot cope. The behavior is perceived as being embodied and owned by others rather than the self, because the "I," without realizing it, is forcibly interrupting outwardly directed impulses.

In Gestalt therapy generally, and FEP even more so, the projecting patient is asked to "play out the projection." One basic experiment is to reverse the roles of the projector and the object of the projection. In this process, sometimes the patient is asked to be as he or she thinks the other person is, and at other times the patient is asked to experiment with a reversal of that stance. That is, the patient is asked to assume the posture of either the target person or the self—to be a "doer" rather than a victim, or a victim rather than a victimizer.

PATIENT: (*To mother, with angry look*) You had that hatred in your eyes. Every time I tried to do something and it wasn't right, I'd see that hateful look in your eyes. You just couldn't accept anything I did! I did everything perfectly and you wouldn't accept it. You were just cold and unfeeling toward me. I felt your hatred.

THERAPIST: Experiment with something. Say, "You hate me."

P: You hated me—you did.

T: Now, would you look at her, as angry as you can, and say the opposite: "I hate you."

P: I hate you.

T: Is that true for you?

P: Well, I hate never knowing where I stood.

T: Tell your mother that.

P: I hated never knowing where I stood.

T: Try out, "Mother, I hate you when . . ."

P: Mother, I hate you when you are silent.

T: Keep going.

P: I hate you for never praising me—never acknowledging my efforts.

Use of the two-chair dialogue technique can be helpful in breaking the projection. To implement this procedure, the patient is asked to become the projection of a significant other in the other chair, so that the patient experiences the dialogue as the significant other would directly from that chair. The goal here is the same as in the foregoing examples—that is, to move the patient's verbal stance from "you" to "I" for ownership. In the following example, the patient was stuck in denial and unawareness of feelings.

PATIENT: I don't know why—I just can't find my feelings toward my father right now.

THERAPIST: Sit in the other chair for a moment and be your father.

P: (*Moves to empty chair*) I don't know what he'd say.

T: Don't hurry. Just sit there for a moment and allow yourself to create what you believe he might say and do.

P: Do you want me, as my father, to talk to me?

T: Yes.

P: (*As father—stern, distant tone of voice*) I don't know why you never lived up to your potential. You wasted so much time. By now you should be well on your way to security. You disappoint your mother and me in so many ways. (*Face begins to change and emotions begin to surface.*)

T: Change chairs. Say something back.

P: Boy, do I feel something now.

T: Say it to him.

P: I'm angry. I could live up to my potential only if I did what *you* wanted. You *never* consulted me about what I wanted.

T: "And I resent you for that."

P: Do I ever. I resent you for never once asking me—asking what I wanted to do with my life. You had me programmed before I could walk.

T: "And I resent you for that."

P: Yes. I resent you for that. And I resent you for putting down anything *I* ever chose to do. (*To therapist*) Boy, I feel my anger now.

T: Fine. Keep talking to him.

By becoming the projected part, the patient is able to stimulate the suppressed emotion hiding under the projection.

Introjecting Beliefs about Emotions

Introjections about the expression of emotion also interfere with the successful completion of emotional experience. Although these introjected beliefs in themselves do not constitute a contact boundary interruption, an introjection may lead to a configural stance that does interrupt contact (e.g., deflection, retroflection, etc.). Hence, in order to prevent continuing interpersonal difficulty, it is assumed that once a contact boundary interruption has been undermined, the therapist must help the patient understand and reorganize the beliefs that are embodied in the patient's introjections.

Fagan and Shepherd (1970) define "introjections" as complex ways of behaving and believing that are adopted wholesale from significant others by the developing organism. They believe that introjections constitute one of the main transmitters of pathology across generations. Yet unrealistic introjections are manifest as a discrepancy between what the person has been told to experience and what that person actually experiences. For example, the parental introjection that "Good girls don't get angry" leaves the daughter either denying any anger so she can be a "good girl" or accepting that she is a "bad girl" because she experiences anger as a normal person does. Unfortunately, the nature of introjection assures that the personal experience will be disowned in favor of the introjection itself. It is difficult to throw off the introjection because of the often-perceived threat of disapproval. The therapist, therefore, when working with a patient's introjection, must help the patient attend to the behaviors that are self-interrupting. Generally, that means first helping the patient hear the "should" or "should not" message. Only after this message is explicit can the therapist engage the task of assessing how much of that message is true for the patient at this point in time. In addition, the therapist helps the patient explore the "catastrophic expectations" that usually are attached to the introjected message. Once patients are aware of both what they are doing and how they are doing it, it is easier to create experiments where patients are willing to "try on" the inhibited behaviors (e.g., to be angry at mother, to express sadness publicly, to say "no" to people).

THERAPIST: Your face reddens as you talk to your father (*in empty chair*). Tell him what you experience.

PATIENT: I feel all tight inside and my face feels hot.

T: Tell him what emotion goes with that.

P: I'm angry at you (*restricted voice*).

T: I see you hold it in and not express it.

P: (*To therapist*) I could never be angry with him.

T: Tell him, please.

P: I could never be angry with you.

T: What stops you?

P: Because it just isn't OK. You never allowed us to be angry. You would tell us we were awful to feel that way.

T: Feel the struggle in you between the part of you that flushes and is angry and the part of you that follows your father's rules.

P: That's exactly it—I feel pulled in both directions.

T: OK. Excuse your father from the chair for a moment. I'm going to ask you to change the experiment. Would you speak from each of those parts of yourself to the other part? (*Sets up two facing chairs*) Start either place.

P: (*From the introjected chair*) You know it's not right to feel angry. Nice people just don't do that.

T: Change places and speak from the other part of you.

P: (*From other chair*) It may not be nice, but sometimes I really feel angry.

T: Tell what it's like to hold it in.

P: When I hold it in I feel tight and confused.

T: Change again.

A dialogue between feeling experience and introjection can be encouraged to continue until the patient achieves integration and willingness to experiment with changing the introjected beliefs. When the patient arrives at a sense of what is true and not true, in his or her own experience with the expression of anger or other emotions, then the patient can return to present interpersonal dialogues in order to experiment with and reinforce the reformulated beliefs.

Setting Up Experiments

Much has been written in the Gestalt literature about the subtleties of setting up experiments (Levitsky & Perls, 1970; Zinker, 1977). However, the transition from talking about an experience to the actual, felt experience is a crucial one (Roden, 1985; Van de Riet et al., 1980). Therefore, we restate some of the key elements in establishing experiments in FEP.

First, experiments need a rationale. Otherwise the patient does not understand what is being asked or suggested (Polster, 1985). If the patient is told, "Talk to the chair," there is no rationale for understanding the directive. But if the therapist says, "I hear you talking about your ex-husband and believe we both could learn more about your experience if you were to talk *to* him, rather than *about* him," then there is a rationale for the patient to change what she is doing.

In FEP, much attention is given to "unfinished business," but the therapist must listen to the patient's story long enough to be able to tell whether the unfinished business is indeed problematic. When unfinished business has been identified, the therapist can easily move from the patient's story to an experiment with configural emotions by explaining the purpose of the experiment: "At times all of us have experiences that we have not been able to finish. I hear you talking about a multitude of unfinished feelings you have toward your ex-wife. I believe that moving into a dialogue with her can give you a way of finishing some of the issues that constantly haunt you."

Another rationale for the experiment might center on the patient's sense of safety, as exemplified in the following:

PATIENT: I know that I have harbored many hard feelings toward my dad, but I can't afford to let him know that.

THERAPIST: What stops you?

P: Well, our relationship is shaky at best, and if I told him all my bad feelings I'd lose him for sure.

T: Would you like to get those feelings out of you and *not* run the risk of losing him?

P: Of course! (*Pause*) But that's not possible.

T: Yes, it is. We could set up an experiment in this room right now where you could verbalize what you have choked off all these years and not

drive Dad away. Here's how you can do that. [Therapist gives an explana-
tion and moves ahead to set up the empty chair dialogue.]

Using safety as a rationale becomes especially significant in marriage
counseling when one spouse is not present. The spouse who is present may
be worried that any actual confrontation will hasten the breakup of the
marriage. The therapist can present the experiment as a way to explore and
resolve some reactions without putting the partnership at risk.

Second, the therapist should be cautioned to construct experiments out
of what is going on (what is figural) in the session. That is, there must be a
context for the experiment. If the patient is speaking about the difficulty of
raising children as a single parent, the therapist's goal is to construct an
experiment that fits that context—for example, to have the patient engage in a
dialogue with her children or with the husband who left her in that position.

Third, the therapist must get an agreement from the patient to move into
an experiment, and must provide safety for the experiment. An explicit
agreement from the patient to experiment often serves as a check about the
clarity of the rationale (see above) and the amount of safety felt. If the
rationale is muddy, then patients may be reluctant to agree to work. No
experiment will be therapeutically productive if there is lack of safety. Safety is
provided by reassurance, but also by addressing all of the general group needs
for confidentiality, trust building, and so on. Safety for a particular exercise is
created by explaining that the patient controls the experiment and can stop it
at any point. Safety is also provided by carefully matching the risk of the
experiment to the current self-support of the patient. If the patient is reluctant
to move toward an experiment, it may indicate a safety issue rather than a
"resistant" patient. The difficulty experienced by some therapists when they
invite patients into experiential and expressive behavior can often be tempered
by working from a clear, shared rationale and context for each experiment
and by obtaining a clear agreement to engage in the experiment.

The other side of the safety issue is that the therapist must also be
comfortable with a particular experiment. An important caveat is this:
Never set up an experiment in which the therapist feels at risk! The odds are
heavily against the chances of such an experiment's succeeding, since the
therapist cannot provide unqualified support.

Heightening and Releasing Emotional Expression

Once a patient has agreed to and has entered into an experiment, the
therapist's concern is that the experiment will be a productive experience for
the patient. The functional objective is to heighten present experience, in the
belief that the ultimate objective (change) will be realized when the patient

fully experiences the present (Daldrup & Gust, 1988; Polster & Polster, 1976). Therefore, a repertoire of interventions that can help the patient to enter into a complete experience of the moment is helpful. Here we would like to suggest some therapist behaviors that keep the patient in the experiment and enhance moment-to-moment experience.

1. It is generally helpful, once a person is in a dialogue with a significant other, to make "process suggestions" rather than "process inquiries." If the therapist makes an inquiry, the patient searches for an answer to the inquiry, turns to the therapist, and makes a reply. The therapist must then encourage the patient to re-enter and resume the dialogue.

    a. Process inquiry: "What are you feeling as you say that?"
    b. Process suggestion: "Tell your father what you feel as you say that."

Another example:

    a. Process inquiry: "What did you hear in your voice just now?"
    b. Process suggestion: "Tell your mother what you heard in your voice," or "Take the tears out of your voice and say that."

The process suggestion keeps the patient highly focused on the significant other and allows the therapist to move into the background and to assume the role of coach. Highly focused attention to a significant other enables the intensity of the experience to emerge.

2. Feelings can be intensified by asking the patient to exaggerate body sensations or behaviors:

    a. "Tighten your stomach even more as you speak."
    b. "You are pointing your finger at your son. Continue to talk to him and exaggerate what your hand is doing."
    c. "Stand up, move around as you talk. See if that feels different for you."
    d. "Say that again!" (a particularly germane statement)
    e. "Say it louder."
    f. "Say it from deeper inside."
    g. "Use the bataca to strengthen your words."
    h. "Do something physical to emphasize what you are saying."

Feelings can also be intensified by giving the patient permission and support:

    a. "Stay with that feeling."
    b. "Give yourself permission to go as far as you will with that."
    c. "It's OK to cry (shout, etc.) in here."

3. When a patient is having difficulty capturing the essence of his or her reaction to the significant other, role reversal (becoming the significant other) can often re-evoke the depth of unfinished feelings in the patient.

   a. "Sit over here a moment and be your father. Say and do what you imagine he would say and do. . . . Now change back and react to that."
   b. "Stand up like your mother and say that as she would."

4. Language is particularly potent in enriching present experience. The therapist should always ask for "I" language from the patient:

   a. "Say 'I' instead of 'it.'"
   b. "Begin sentences with 'I' rather than 'you.'"

5. The specificity of language also enhances and intensifies experience. The therapist should ask the patient to change global complaints to specific resentments.

   a. Global "you" statement: "You always say things to hurt me."
   b. Specific "I" statements: "I am hurt when you tell me my feelings are silly," or "I resent you when you walk away when I'm upset."

Changing general statements to specific statements creates a sharper focus for the work experiment and provides an environment in which figure (specificity) can emerge from background (generalization), thereby forming the Gestalt around which work takes place.

6. The therapist should assist patients in cleaning up "fence-sitting," tentative, or qualified language, as in the following:

   a. Tentative statement: "It almost makes me angry when you . . ."
   b. Definite statement: "I am angry at you when . . ."

   a. Qualified statement: "I feel a little resentful when you put me down."
   b. Unqualified statement: "I resent you for putting me down."

Feelings cannot be heightened or intensified as long as they are being restricted by qualifications or diluted by tentative verbalizations.

7. Helping the patient develop focusing and attending skills also will enable the patient to know the richness of his or her experience.

   a. "Be aware of your voice—hear how it trails off as you speak."
   b. "Go back to the knot in your stomach and see how it is doing as you express your anger."

c. "Notice how your head is lying on your left shoulder. Tell your husband what that is about."

d. "Tell Mom to stay out of this while you are dealing with Dad."

8. The therapist can also help to enrich the patient's experience by sharing behavioral observations. This process brings attention to "obvious" behaviors that may not be apparent to the patient.

a. "I'm aware that you take in lots of air and then hold your breath."

b. "I hear the words you are saying, and I'm most drawn to the tears in your eyes."

c. "I'm aware that as you talk about him you are hitting your leg with your fist."

d. "What is your head shaking 'No' to as you express yourself verbally?"

9. Heightening and intensifying feelings can sometimes be aided by feeding a specific sentence to the patient as a "try-on." This process generally aims to make explicit what seems to be only implied in the patient's manner and dialogue.

a. "Try out this sentence: 'I resent you when you treat me that way.'"

b. "See if this fits: 'I feel abandoned when you walk away from me.'"

c. "Try on: 'I'm afraid to tell you what I feel.'"

10. Finally, the process of clarifying feeling states can be aided when the therapist makes personal observations or guesses about the patient's internal struggle. Again, the results of these statements can be to make the implicit explicit, thereby bringing the material into sharper focus.

a. "My sense is that there are two parts of you caught in a struggle with each other. Does that fit?"

b. "I have a hunch that you constrict your anger because you are afraid of it. Is that true?"

Or the therapist can self-disclose reactions to patient behavior.

a. "I feel more in touch with you when you look at me as you talk than when you don't."

b. "I feel bored with your victim role."

If the therapist has a full range of responses to enhance the here-and-now experience of the patient, then the therapist enables the patient to experience the richness and intensity of the moment. The unrealized needs of the organism can be played out, and the patient can come to a sense of completion. Table 7.1 provides further suggestions to assist in this process.

There are times when the therapist needs to be sensitive to the development of emotional reactions that are experienced by the patient as surges, flushes, or rushes of emotion. Sometimes these reactions are made evident to the therapist by a reddening in neck and face areas, or by moisture developing in the eyes, or by a change in voice quality. When the therapist observes any of these physiological signs, it is helpful to draw the patient's attention to the physical response and to connect this response to the emotion attached to it. Then the patient is encouraged to allow the full development of the emotional reaction to a completion point.

In the same vein, the therapist should be alert to the "ebb-and-flow" phenomenon of crying. Often the patient experiences crying in cycles. A buildup of grief or hurt starts gradually, increases to a peak point, and recedes as the organism goes into quiet relaxation; within moments, the cycle begins to repeat itself. The therapist can be encouraging by helping the patient see this cycle as analogous to a wave approaching the beach, building into a swell that breaks over the shoreline, and then receding back to the ocean. In this way the patient is able to move with the organism's natural and spontaneous rhythm.

PATIENT: (*sobbing*) I love you so much. (*Stronger rush of tears*)

THERAPIST: Feel the buildup of tears inside of you.

P: I feel like I could cry forever and never get over the loss of you (*much crying as she talks*).

T: Just allow your tears to go as far as they want to go.

P: (*Deep sobbing as tears flow*)

T: That's it—just ride that wave of emotion as long as it lasts—all the way into the shore.

P: (*Tears go on for extended time, and then body starts to relax*)

T: That's right—just notice how your body tells you when the wave of emotion reaches shore. Now just stay aware of yourself in the quiet waters for a while.

P: (*Remains still and quietly resting; then face begins to contort with more sadness*)

T: OK, now—this is just another wave coming in so you can ride it into shore like the last one—trust your body—it is doing its natural thing.

P: (*Tears build to a peak and recede as before*)

This process continues until the patient's body indicates satisfaction by staying quiet rather than bringing forth more waves of emotion.

TABLE 7.1. Interventions to Increase Emotional Arousal

Types	Examples
1. Catching affective changes (that the patient seems not to catch)	"Did you hear your voice change just then?" "You look different. What just happened?"
2. Modeling for the patient	(Therapist stands) "Would you stand and speak with your friend?" (Therapist raises voice) "Say that again, say it louder."
3. Keeping a continuous check on physical benchmarks	"How is the pain in your gut? Just stay with it. Feel it." "You are still biting off your words and tightening your jaw. Experiment with opening your mouth as you speak."
4. Asking patient to move to a different physical position	"Notice how you are doubled in on yourself. Would you sit tall and speak and see how you feel?" "Stand up and continue to say what you resent."
5. Repeating statements and gestures	"Stay with that sentence. Say it again and notice what happens." "Continue to point your finger as you are doing now . . . again . . . again."
6. Exaggerating contact	"Make your voice larger; fill the room with it." "I see your foot move as you say what you're angry about. Keep doing that with your foot . . . now make the movement larger."
7. Exaggerating withdrawal	"You are shrinking into the chair. Just continue to do that. Pull up into a ball." "You are holding your breath. Continue that and notice what goes on."
8. Eliciting movement into specific scene	"You are talking about what happened at home last week. Be there in the scene and tell it as it unfolds." "You look/sound very young. Do you feel it? Be that age and tell me what's going on."
9. Encouraging role reversal	"Change places and be your mother. Say what she would say. Use her voice. . . . Now change back and respond."
10. Focusing on incongruence	"I'm aware of your angry words and polite smile. Say the words again without smiling them away." *or* "Say the angry words again and smile more as you do it." "I hear you say you are not resentful and I see you hitting your knee with your fist."
11. Moving into the constriction	"Just feel where you hold all your sadness. Move right there in your throat/eyes." "Don't let any of the anger/sadness slip out right now. Contain it all."

Alternative Strategies for Release of Heightened Anger

THE PROBLEM

It is clear from our work with FEP that the release of anger involves heightened verbal expression and physical release. When teaching these procedures to therapists who work in a variety of settings, trainers are faced with practical issues that may be problematic for the use of FEP strategies. Some therapists work in crowded office spaces, where privacy is created more by partitions than by soundproofed walls; some work with hospitalized patients who are confined to bed with limiting physical problems; and some work with patients who clearly are willing to do something about their anger and who clearly say "no" to the use of a bataca. We have been challenged to devise ways in which therapists can use FEP in spite of these and similar constraints. Here are some alternatives we have found to be useful.

ALTERNATIVES

First, drawing is a very effective alternative. This has worked well with some patients who feel anger and yet will not allow themselves to release the anger with pillows or batacas. Large sheets of heavy newsprint and the oversized crayons developed for small children are helpful. An angry person can hold the large crayons in a fist, which can represent an angy gesture. Once the arousal level is increased using the techniques described elsewhere, then the therapist can introduce this strategy.

> "I'm aware of your present anger, and I'm going to suggest a way for you to release it. I know you have said 'no' to the bataca. Here are some crayons and newsprint. Pick colors that to you are angry colors. Then take one of the colors and hold it in your fist. Now stay in touch with the anger, let it mobilize in your body, and let it move to your arm and hand. Make angry strokes on the paper. Don't draw your anger, let your act of drawing be angry. . . . Good, make the strokes more angry. Make them larger. Continue to let the anger in your body come out through your hand. Continue to do that . . . check in with your body and see how much of the anger is out . . . continue until you feel that anger flow out of you."

This form of anger release can be done in a hospital bed, in an office with sound constraints, or with patients who choose not to use other methods.

Another effective medium for intensifying arousal is clay (Oaklander,

1978; Rhyne, 1984). Inexpensive potter's clay or the plastic nonhardening types both work well. Clay offers a great tactile and kinesthetic experience; a person can really get his or her hands into it, thus creating a great bridge between senses and feelings. Clay works equally well for adults and children. It can be punched, molded, squeezed, pounded, cut, stabbed, pinched, or squashed. A child can be invited to create a figure of an abusive older sibling and can then be invited to release onto that figure whatever the child wants. A woman or girl who has been sexually abused can be invited to create a figure of the perpetrator and then vent the anger. Sometimes patients give these figures large genitals and then destroy the clay figure and genitalia. Rape victims may find this kind of work productive.

A woman who lived in a halfway house for chronically mentally ill adults discovered that clay was very useful. She found that if she expressed her anger in her room by pounding pillows or being loud, she was misunderstood by fellow patients and was thought to be "acting out." She learned to take the anger and focus it in her hands, and then privately and quietly work the clay until she transferred all the anger to the clay. While she worked the clay, she would focus on the target person of her anger, and work each resentment out one at a time.

Sometimes, items as simple as an ordinary towel can be useful in working with anger. A towel is easily portable, and a therapist can keep one in a desk drawer or attache case. The therapist can ask the patient to take the emotion and wring it into the towel, as if wringing water out of it. Towels can be used by people with limited mobility, such as people with back pain, who may not be able to use their arms and bodies to release the emotion through batacas. Towels can also be used to hit or tear. The therapist who is working with an emotionally aroused patient in a confined work setting can give a towel to the patient with a simple instruction to the patient to make the best use of it. "You are feeling a lot of anger right now. Take this towel and do with it whatever you need to do to release that anger. Twist it, squeeze it, or whatever; just continue to focus on your anger toward your father as you do that."

Sometimes there is a destructive drive associated with the expression of angry feelings. Therefore, it can be helpful to have and to use things that can be destroyed. Cardboard boxes, newspapers, phone books, or old magazines are useful. Again, these items can be used to exaggerate and release anger in those situations where noise may be an inhibiting factor. Once the person is focused on the unfinished business and has enhanced the feeling of anger, then a phone book, a newspaper, or a magazine can be given to that person with the same instructions as above: to stay focused, to take one issue at a time, and to express the feeling physically using the item at hand. The therapist continues to monitor physical and emotional changes and to follow the other steps of the model. Boxes are especially valuable with people who feel their anger release in their feet and legs rather than in their voice or hands. As noted elsewhere, the patients often reveal their individual modalities in their language ("I'd love to give him a kick in the ass," "I could just strangle him"). Patients occasionally report the helpfulness of being able to destroy something with the aggressive angry feelings. To be surrounded by crumpled, shredded pages of an old phone book can give visual evidence to a patient that he or she has been doing something real and physical with previously constricted feelings. Therapists should be alert to patients who are into instrumental anger and want to destroy something as a manipulation rather than as a means of letting go of the anger. In this case, patients can be asked to bring their own material to destroy as a way of breaking up the instrumental anger. If patients are instructed to bring something of their own of considerable value, they soon realize that physical destruction is not a prerequisite for release of old anger.

Patients who are seen in situations where noise or privacy is an issue can also use writing to express their anger. A patient can write the anger in the form of a letter, which helps him or her to stay focused on the significant other. The therapist as coach can help this method to be successful by telling the patient (1) to continue to focus on the significant other ("See that person in your mind"); (2) to be specific about the angers and resentment; (3) to use "I resent you for . . ." statements; and (4) not to move to lengthy discourses to explain things; but to work from an emotional point of view. It also helps to tell patients that since they will not send their letters, they can write "unedited versions" where they do not have to watch what they say and how they say it. This process can be used in the therapy session or suggested to patients as homework; in the latter case, patients are instructed to bring their letters with them to the next session, where they can decide whether they have finished or need to do something more with the letters. People sometimes choose to drop their letters in the wastebasket or to take them to the fireplace or outside and burn them. If a patient is reluctant to make a final disposal of a letter, it is worth exploring how the patient may yet be hanging on to the anger with the significant other.

Patients in hospital beds must cope with a wide range of emotions, and clay or art may help them with the expression of feelings. If they are struggling with anger, sometimes something as simple as a Styrofoam cup may help them to enhance and release it. A patient does not have to be physically strong to tear it, poke it full of holes with a pencil, or crush it with a hand. But this can assist in the release of some of the emotion resulting from confinement, pain, or loss of function.

Screams, yells, and loud verbal noises are important to many in releasing their anger, especially when they experience the anger constricted in their throats or jaws. Again, noise can inhibit the therapist, the patient, or both; however, the use of a large pillow is an effective way around this. The therapist can instruct the patient to take a large breath, to bring the pillow to his or her face, and to let the scream, yell, or noise come. If the patient is not sure that this will work, the therapist can demonstrate and let the patient hear. The noise inside the pillow is louder than that heard outside. It is important to listen for a full release from the patient.

THERAPIST: (*To patient screaming into a pillow*) I'm aware that you began to scream and then suddenly stopped. Did you notice?
PATIENT: Yeah, I started to scare myself.
T: OK. Are you willing to do it again and not cut it off?
P: Yes—I need to do this.
T: Take a breath and scream into the pillow again.
P: (*An extended scream, which is still cut off*)
T: You got further.
P: I was more aware of not finishing that time.
T: Go ahead and do it as many times as you need to to get the feelings out.

All of these methods can broaden the possibilities for patients who feel constrained by the limitations of the setting or by their own physical limitations. As therapists work with these and other options, they often develop a feel for what works best for them. All of these methods ask the patient to do something physical to express the feelings: write, scream, draw, tear, twist, punch, poke, cut, and so on. This is critical in getting the patient to move from "talking about" the emotion to actual present-moment experience of and actual release of the emotion. Involvement of the body in the act fits the wholistic approach of FEP. Again, the therapist monitors the patient's process to assess whether the patient moves into a flow of release or whether the process is interrupted or aborted. When there are interruptions, the therapist makes appropriate process comments:

- "I am aware that you began to twist the towel and then you suddenly stopped—are you aware that your hand is smoothing it out? Do you try to smooth things over with your wife?"
- "Do you feel yourself come alive as you are punching the clay?"
- "Tell your father what you are experiencing as you tear that piece of paper."
- "Now that you have released your anger in the drawing, come back to your body, and then when you are ready draw a new picture that expresses your new feeling."

Any restrictions placed upon the experiment by the setting or by the condition of a patient can be counterbalanced by the creativity of the therapist and patient in collaborating with each other.

Summary

An essential goal in FEP is to achieve a "primary" state of arousal of emotion associated with unfinished business. A knowledge of contact boundary disturbances is critical for the FEP therapist, so that appropriate interventions can be designed to assist the patient with the impasse.

Confluent emotions occur when emotions such as anger and hurt are mixed to the point that the patient is unable to discriminate one from the other. The therapeutic task here is to help the patient experience the difference between being angry and being hurt.

Retroflection of emotions takes one of two forms: Either the experience of an emotion is squeezed off, or the emotion is turned against the self. In this case, the therapist must aid the patient in identification of an appropriate target person to whom the emotion can be directed, so that the expression moves away from the patient rather than against the patient.

In instrumental anger, the intent of the expression is to blame, manipulate or punish others rather than to complete the emotion. In this situation, the therapist must move the patient from making others responsible for the patient's own feelings to taking ownership for the choice of response, thereby regaining potency to deal with the issue in any way chosen.

Deflection of emotions is a form of denial of feelings in which the patient makes light of the emotional response, distracts by changing the subject, or stays at a cognitive level when dealing with emotions. The therapeutic goal here is to keep the patient in the here-and-now experience while keeping the direction of the work on target.

Projected emotions are those that the patient sees in others but is actually experiencing himself or herself. The goal of therapeutic intervention in projection is to establish ownership for the patient through experiments such as role reversal or playing out the projection.

Introjected beliefs about emotions are often manifested as a discrepancy between what the person has been told to experience and what is actually experienced. Here the therapist must help the patient to recognize the "should" messages and to explore any catastrophic expectations attached to introjected beliefs.

To be successful in setting up experiments, the therapist must attend to the key elements of productive experiments:

1. Appropriate and understandable rationale.
2. Construction of experiments within the proper context.
3. Provision of enough safety to enable the patient to agree firmly to collaborate.

The fundamental objective of the experiment is to heighten present experience so that change can be possible; in this respect, process suggestions have been found to be more helpful than process inquiries.

Since at times there are restrictions placed on the experiment, such as privacy, noise factors, and/or physical limitations of the patient, the FEP therapist must be flexible and creative in establishing the experiment. Helpful alternatives to bataca work include drawing, working with clay, tearing paper, wringing towels, kicking boxes, and writing out feelings and thoughts. In all of these methods, patients are asked to do something physical as well as mental, in keeping with the wholistic posture of the model.

8

Evaluation

In Gestalt therapy, an emphasis is placed upon process diagnosis as opposed to nosological diagnosis. Process diagnosis implies a constant cycle of clinical evaluation and experiment. It also suggests that temporal phases of therapy cannot be governed by a precise and preplanned agenda. Nonetheless, systematic evaluation of progress and change may occur at particular points throughout the process.

When to Evaluate

For example, at the beginning of each continuing session, the therapist may check the progress and status of patients, particularly with respect to the homework assigned at the previous session. Each patient in the group may also be queried relative to his or her current feelings or any remaining feelings from the prior week's work, as well as any integration of the work from the last session.

Moreover, at the closing phase of each piece of work, again at the termination of each session, and still again in the closing session of each course of therapy, there is a need for specific evaluation and feedback. At these points, the patient may be encouraged to report current experiences, to describe anticipations of the future that are built upon those experiences, and to observe and monitor any changes that have occurred as a function of therapeutic activity. Observing changes in tension levels, pain, or internal sensations with reference to earlier temporal points allows the therapist to check his or her impact and allows the patient to assess progress on a moment-to-moment basis. Such observation of in-process experience is also designed to heighten patients' awareness of sensory cues, in order that these cues may become more pronounced and more easily integrated with prior experiences into revised formulations of the world.

The evaluation of experience is particularly significant at the actual conclusion of a piece of work, during which time that experience is processed with other group members. Particular attention is given at this point to the changes that the patient believes have occurred because of the work. In this phase, an emphasis is placed upon reconceptualizing work experiences in view of the heightened and then reduced affect that has occurred over the course of the work. The patient is asked to report here-and-now awarenesses of physical, emotional, and cognitive activity. Any "benchmarks" that were identified in the initiation phase may now be checked to see whether there have been changes since the beginning either of the session or of the work experience. Two examples follow.

PATIENT: (*To an imagined colleague*) I know when I stand here and talk and feel completely, completely relaxed and in control, and I know when I feel that you have control of me. You aren't gonna have control of me any more. *Nothing* at all.

THERAPIST: How's your throat doing right now?

P: Fine.

T: OK. Anything else you need to say to him right now?

P: I'm glad you're gone.

T: Tell him what you did for you this morning and then say goodbye.

P: Jeff, I made myself more of a whole person. I don't have to walk around worrying about you, about how I'm going to react to you, or what you are going to do to me. You are physically in my life, but emotionally and mentally, goodbye. I don't need you any more. (*Silence*)

T: What's going on now?

P: It's really strange. You know . . .

T: Notice the difference between what you felt when you sat down in the chair and what you feel now.

P: It's different—really different, you know?

T: Just stay with it and notice what it is. Be aware of what those differences are, and as you're in touch with them say what they are.

P: Control. I mean it's like I'm—he's not controlling me any more. You know, I feel free. I feel—I feel like I can talk about him and not cry. And, you know, you could ask questions about him and I wouldn't fall apart.

THERAPIST: I want you to do one more thing, Jon. Would you see yourself at his graveside, as if that's his gravestone? I want you to stand there for a moment and see if there is anything else you need to say or do before you say goodbye to him and let him be buried.

PATIENT: It's like there's—you say by his graveside; I see graves everywhere else and his is, like, nondescript, like nothing.

T: All right. Tell him that.

P: Here I see all these other graves and I see tombstones, and I see signs where people have left their mark. Some say "He was a good man," and others say "May he be with God," and yours has nothing on it. I guess that describes the type of person you were. You were just nothing, and that's all I have to say to you.

    T: Would you say goodbye?

    P: Goodbye.

    T: Now just take a moment to see how you are doing.

    P: I feel good. I just feel relieved.

    T: Remember the pain in your throat?

    P: Feels pretty good.

    T: Any pain left?

    P: No. I feel fine.

Indications of Finished Business

An important indicator of finished business is a shift in the stance of the patient's relationship to the target person. One type of shift is identified as acceptance of the events and of the significant others as they are, accompanied with an enhanced affirmation of self. A person may never come to love an abuser or rapist, but can get to the point where he or she can accept what occurred without feeling overwhelmed and without losing the sense of self. A second type of shift is the spontaneous ability to express love or appreciation toward a person about whom only anger or resentment could previously be felt.

    PATIENT: [After an extended period of anger expression and release about many specific issues involving her grandmother] I don't feel any more resentment toward you.

    THERAPIST: Is there anything else you want or need to say before you say goodbye?

    P: (*Spontaneously*) I love you. I really do. You did many nice things for me when I was small. I hated to live with you because of your craziness, but I know also that you loved me . . . at least as you knew how. I feel some love toward you right now. (*Pause*)

    T: Anything else?

    P: No.

    T: Would you say goodbye, then?

    P: I'm glad I brought you in here today. Goodbye, Grandma.

If there is no softening of the initial or presession stance, it is a clear signal that the work is not yet complete, and the therapist should note this fact and share his or her observation.

THERAPIST: I am aware that you are having a difficult time finishing. Each time you have begun to stop, you cycle through the resentments once again. Are you aware of doing that?

PATIENT: Yeah. . . . There is just an awful lot that I'm angry about.

T: Well, we're approaching the end of time today. Would you be willing to tell him that you are still holding on to some anger?

P: I guess I'm still mad.

T: Tell him that and then tell him how much you did release—that is, what you accomplished. And then tell him whether you are willing to bring him in again.

P: I'm still angry at you. I can still feel the pain in my jaw. But I started . . . at least I did that. I have a *lot* more to tell you, so I'll bring you back again.

T: Say goodbye and then let me know what you experience in your body right now.

The work phase can be terminated for at least three different reasons: (1) The patient has concluded all he or she needs to say to the significant other; (2) the patient has not concluded but does not wish to go farther at this time; or (3) there is no more time left in the session. Therapists should lead the patient through the same type of wrap-up (including assessment of what was accomplished, any needed contracts for future work, and a good-bye) in any of the three terminal situations described above.

Homework

In initiating the homework phase of the therapy session, the patient may be asked again to determine the value of the session just completed and to answer questions relative to how the learning can be applied to his or her life. This discourse can lead naturally into a construction of homework activities that may take the experiences into the patient's living environment. As much as possible, a close relationship between the work experiment and the homework experience should be preserved, and the patient should be engaged in designing and developing a relevant homework assignment. If this is done, there is an excellent chance that the homework will assist in the completion of the work highlighted in the working phase. The homework assignment, however, rather than emphasizing emotional escalation as the work itself has done, usually emphasizes letting go of the emotional experience, giving up defenses, or encountering other people who may provide support and feedback. This, it should be underlined, is the essence of a reintegration phase.

In the following example, the patient had just finished an emotionally charged piece of work with her uncle. She reported feeing the ability to now talk about her uncle without being upset.

THERAPIST: OK. Why don't you have a seat over here? Right now I'm thinking in terms of some homework. What you just said about talking to your uncle without tears may be a bridge into that homework. I think it's important to take what we do here and find a way to do something with it outside the group. Otherwise, sometimes what we do here is a "So what." Would you be willing between now and the next time we meet to find someone that you would talk to about your uncle?

PATIENT: That I would talk to?

T: Yeah.

P: Sure. Mmm-hmm.

T: And just experience yourself talking to that person about him without the tears.

P: OK.

T: And then come back and report how well you did on that. If the tears come back, then we may need to do some more. OK?

Reintegration and Reformulation

Hoehn-Saric et al. (1972) have aptly observed that attitudes and perceptions are more easily and readily changed following intense emotional experiences. The consolidation aspect of therapy appears to be important to the reformulation of a patient's Gestalt following the work experiment. The stage of evaluation needs to be firmly interfaced, therefore, with the stage of homework. This process is designed to keep both the therapist and the patient from being misled to believe that the value of therapy is in emotional arousal alone. It is anticipated, in fact, that emotional arousal simply provides a vehicle for the patient to reintegrate and reformulate experience and to derive a new representational model through which the world can be observed.

As this reintegration and reformulation of experience occur, it is expected that the results can be evaluated by attending to changes that patients experience as various types of movements (see Chapter 5, "Dynamics of Change" section). The therapist should look for changes from a narrow range of affective response with little awareness to a broad range of emotional response with fuller awareness. Another change to be assessed is in the area of spontaneity, as patients experience a heightened sense of energy once the unfinished business of the past has been completed, allowing them to live more fully in the present. Patients who have restructured their schematic emotional memories cease to deny or distort their experience, thereby providing a new view of themselves and others. Patients may also change from a passive posture to a more active and responsible position in their experiences. Sometimes there may be a positive change from a life of illness to a movement toward health. A sign of movement may be a more realistic view of the world as it "is" rather than as it "should be." A helpful sign is moving from victimization to potency in coping with life. A move from blaming and complaining to acting or doing is often another part of a patient's changes. Patients often change from feelings of deadness or depression to feelings of vitality and aliveness, and from a guilty posture to a stance of responsibility. As positive feelings increase, patients are much less self-abusive and abusive of others, and become more caring and sharing with themselves and with others.

Summary

In FEP, there is constant clinical evaluation of the patient's work. At the beginning of each weekly group, progress with homework is checked, along with any remaining issues from the preceding week.

Evaluation is especially important at the conclusion of each individual piece of therapeutic work. Here physiological changes are particularly useful indicators of change. Assessment of these physiological benchmarks also teaches patients how to monitor themselves outside the therapy session.

Particular attention is paid to the completeness or incompleteness of each patient's work; a shift in stance toward the significant other provides an indicator of finished therapeutic work.

The session's work is terminated when the patient has finished unfinished issues and has shifted emotionally; when the patient has decided not to go farther; or when time runs out.

Homework bridges the therapy session and the patient's life. Homework is constructed to assist the completion of unfinished tasks. It usually emphasizes giving up defenses or using environmental reinforcements rather than emotional escalations. The function of homework is to help in the cognitive restructuring necessary to successful therapeutic change. This change can take many forms, such as movement toward a fuller emotional experience; more spontaneity and energy; more time spent in the present; less denial and distortion of experience; more active participation in life; better health; less blaming and complaining; more vitality; less abuse of self and of others; and more caring for self and for others.

9

Summary and Example Transcripts

Summation

The foregoing chapters have presented a psychotherapy model that is designed specifically to deal with suppressed, stored, or denied feelings. This approach to psychotherapy is based upon the general principles of Gestalt therapy, and the procedures described have mainly emanated from that position. Of particular concern to the current approach, however, is the focus upon individuals who possess or display a limited range of anger-related affects. The resulting procedures emphasize the importance of clarifying, magnifying, and highlighting these affects through a series of psychotherapeutic procedures that also extend the range of available and accessible feeling states. In order to help retain this emphasis, we have adopted the label "focused expressive psychotherapy" (FEP). We have described the role of the patient and of the therapist, and have addressed the process of sequencing psychotherapeutic procedures and of anchoring these procedures to a series of expected outcomes or objectives. The model presented here defines a process for the therapist to follow while applying the strategies, as well as a series of guidelines for evaluating that process as it evolves.

FEP is primarily designed for use in short-term (20-session) group therapy, although it is equally applicable to individual therapy. Indeed, work within a group setting is primarily in a therapist-to-patient format; hence, relative consistency of application can be maintained across a variety of treatment modes. The strategies described have been applied in a wide array of settings, including schools, prisons, detoxification centers, geriatric centers, chronic pain clinics, and private clinical practice, with a wide age range of patients. The procedures defined here, however, are particularly suitable for those patients who experience difficulty in the expression or inhibition of angry impulses. The procedures have been applied to patients who experience chronic pain, partially or totally as a result of the psychological influences of anger on the pain experience. It is our anticipation that alleviation of emotional constraint, the development of a modulated method of integrating current and past experience, and a more refined view of expressing current emotional awarenesses in the context of interpersonal relationships will produce substantial benefit to patients.

Throughout previous chapters, small portions of therapist–patient dialogues have been included to illustrate various FEP concepts. It is fitting that this summary should end with examples of FEP sessions presented in their entirety, with annotations in brackets. The presentation of a single session is just that—a single session. All pieces of FEP work are unique expressions of the interaction of a specific therapist and patient, but we hope to illustrate that the basic steps of the process we have discussed in the foregoing pages can be achieved in a single session.

Example of a Brief FEP Session

The patient in this example, Beth, was a 40-year-old married female. This was her first experience with FEP group therapy. This was one of the early meetings of a series of group sessions. She attended this group as a trainee in the FEP model. On this particular day she chose to be the patient and to address an unfinished personal issue. (An excerpt from this transcript has been presented in Chapter 7.)

PATIENT: When we first made rounds I thought of my mother-in-law, but I'm gonna do some work with my father. When I was watching Ellen work I was trying to decide. I don't think I'm angry at him as much as I am disappointed, or it could be a combination of the two. Probably the reason I'm having trouble with it is that I might not have made up my mind which one I am—angry at or disappointed with. I think that he brought me up in a religious environment, he gave me a lot of good advice, and I respected him for it, and it was really traumatic for me to find out at 17 that all of that damn advice was hypocritical. And I guess all of us, when we're children, respect our parents, and I respected him and I listened to him and, maybe I had an unrealistic image of him as a person, or maybe as a parent. I put him on a pedestal and followed all that advice to the letter and then it was—is very tragic for me to find out that he didn't live the kind of life that he had told me was the kind of life people should live.

THERAPIST: And before we finish today, what do you want to do for *you*?

P: Well, I guess I want to get rid of some of this anger and disappointment. I'm just real tired of carrying all this stuff around. [Note the patient's tentative commitment.]

T: Would you bring him in here? [This is premature—neither commitment nor rationale has been established as yet.]

P: First I want to tell you a little of what happened. [The patient is not ready to move to the experiment.] My parents got divorced. I lived with both parents, back and forth. But when I was in seventh grade I lived with my mom and then a friend of mine's father died, and I realized that from his father's death—and I was very close to his father—that I didn't know a lot about my dad, so I decided to go live with him. That was OK with my mom. They didn't seem to have a big emotional thing or a lot of anger between each other about it, and she said "OK." And I liked my dad. He was a professor at college, and he also was a minister and he got his master's from a school of theology and gave me a good foundation for a lot of things. Instead of screaming and yelling, he was a talker, you know. He felt that I was a certain age and we could talk and we developed a good relationship, and I was glad that I came to live with him. He and my stepmother started having problems where they would yell a lot. Then when I was about 16, one evening I came home and—we had one car and he usually had the car—and when I got home, she said we had to go for a walk. And I didn't know what the hell was going on, but I went for the walk and we seemed to be searching the neighborhood. It was for my dad. After I put it all together, looking at where we were stopping, we were stopping at the homes of certain single women in town or down the block, looking over at their homes. And that upset me.

T: Would you be willing to stop and go back, Beth? Be in that scene again, you know, walking those streets with your stepmother?

P: OK. All right. [The patient makes the commitment to move to an experiment.]

T: Be there, you're 16. Talk to her.

P: What are we doing? Where are we going? What's going on? And she'd say, "Well, just come with me. I just need you. There could be dogs or men around, it's dark. Just come with me." And I remember getting real angry, not knowing what the hell was going on. I said, "Well, who are we looking for? What are you doing?" So she said, "Just come with me." And so that's when I started watching her and then that's when it—so I said, "We're looking for Dad!" And there was a lady named Anne Green and we were standing down by her house. And this was in a little country town in the South, and then I remember it hit me, and I said, "That's Miss Green's house!" And I said, "What do you think he's over there for?" And she said, "Never mind." And I remember being real angry, not knowing what the hell was going on. [She still is reporting her story rather than experiencing it.]

T: Be there.

P: OK.

T: See Miss Green's house. Stand in front of it.

P: Well, I remember getting real angry and saying, "Why the hell do you think he'd be there?" And she started yelling and screaming for me not to curse her, and she went off and I said "Well, I don't know what the hell you want from me! I don't even want to be here." I said, "If he's doing that, that's your problem. I want to go home." And she just—

T: How are you feeling?

P: Well, I'm feeling frustrated, you know? So I said—[The patient is deflecting and returning to reporting family rules about emotion.] At that age you're supposed to do what people tell you, and you're not supposed to be rude, and you're not supposed to disobey, and, you know, all that other crap that you're taught that you're not supposed to do to adults or say to adults, and—

T: Now, Beth, if you're willing, bring your father in here, and I'll give you a line to say. If it doesn't fit, throw it away. OK? [Therapist attempts to get a focus on the significant other.]

P: OK.

T: "Dad, tonight we were looking for you in Miss Green's house."

P: OK (*shows signs of emotion coming over her face and eyes*).

T: Yeah, feel yourself experience that statement.

P: [The patient is continuing to deflect feelings and report the story to the therapist.] Well, you know, I got a thing. It's like, when it first dawned on me that that's what we were doing, well—no, it's—OK, it's like after I discovered that was true, my first feeling was, "I'm a kid and that's not something I should be telling my dad about."

T: Yeah. And so you stuck there.

P: Right, 'cause, you know, it was—uh, when we were talking about how kids are brought up—

T: Yeah, but that's still—that memory and that experience are still there for you.

P: Oh, yeah.

T: OK, and that's what I'm asking you to do, to move back into that memory. Here's a chance for you to say what you, as a kid, had to stop.

P: OK. Dad, tonight we went walking the street, and do you know what we were doing? We were looking for you. [First direct contact with the father.]

T: "And when I realized how I felt . . ."

P: And when I realized that, I was hurt and I was disappointed and I didn't like you very much any more. And I didn't like—

T: Do you feel it as you're saying it right now, Beth?

P: Yeah.

T: OK. Just be aware of where you feel it in your body. Do you know where? [This question establishes the first set of benchmarks.]

P: It's like it's in here, coming up (*pointing from stomach up to throat*).

T: It's right in there? OK. Just stay in touch with that. So it's right in your gut—

P: Well, it's like it sort of comes up and I ease it back down.

T: OK. All right. And we'll just follow that, and just see if you can get to the point where you don't ease it back down. You just let the feeling come all the way up and all the way out. OK? [Therapist provides support so that the patient can allow the emotional surges.]

P: All right. (*To father*) You know, I didn't come here to see you do all of this kind of stuff, you know, I'm just a kid. You know, I don't want to be talking to you about who you're sleeping with, and I don't want to be getting in the middle of this. I thought we had a good life, and you and your wife had a good life, and then I come here and find that you're doing this, you know. And don't talk to me like you talk to me, where you give me all that nice bullshit. I want to talk to you and I want you to be honest with me and not give me a lot of intellectualization, 'cause now I'm starting to feel that that's what you do (*voice is rising*). You're a good talker, but you don't say anything.

T: Come and sit over here for a moment. [Role reversal can sometimes evoke a strong emotional arousal.]

P: OK (*changes chairs*).

T: Be your father. What would you be saying back to Beth right now? Be your dad.

P: Your stepmother's been upset lately. You know, when you're young and you're a member of the community and you're involved, people think these things. Now see, you didn't see me. You didn't see the car at any of those places, did you? You know, I don't know why your stepmother would do this to you and get you involved in this, but just don't you worry about it, we'll take care of it, you know?

T: Change back.

P: OK (*moves back to original chair*). I don't want you to "take care of it" and I don't want you to talk to my stepmother, I want you to talk to *me* (*stronger voice*).

T: "And you don't." [This adds the reality to the wish.]

P: And you don't. You don't at all. It's like you're trying to shield me from something, or you're trying to not let me know that you're human and that people make mistakes and people do things, you know? That's all I'm asking you to do, is to be honest. I don't want to know the gory details of what in the hell you're doing. I just want you to be honest and not fool me. And now I'm starting to rethink a whole lot of things and that hurts. Maybe you haven't been telling the truth all along. Hell, you're a minister! And I don't think ministers are saints, but I don't think you should sit here and lie to your kid. You tell me not to lie and to be honest and I try to do that, and now I found out that you might have been lying all along. And that hurts. That really hurts. [The patient's emotional arousal is intensifying.]

T: Yeah. Feel where the hurt is, Beth, right now.

P: Well, it moved up here.

T: OK.

P: It moved from my gut to my throat.

T: Right to the base of your throat? [The therapist continues to clarify psychophysical benchmarks.]

P: Right.

T: OK. Just tell your father where the hurt is right now. "I feel the hurt right in my throat."

P: Well, I feel a hurt in my throat when I talk to you, and I didn't used to hurt like that when I talked to you. I felt I could tell you anything. There was nothing we couldn't talk about. And it bothers me that now I have reservations about being open and honest with you, because I don't think you're being open and honest with me. I don't like that feeling. I don't like to think that that type of thing could separate us, 'cause I'm finding I don't want to be around you, and that hurts even worse.

T: Try out a line. Again, if it doesn't fit, throw it away. "Dad, I resent your hypocrisy." [The "try-out" process moves the patient toward "I" statements and increased arousal.]

P: Dad, I resent your hypocrisy.

T: Does that fit?

P: Yeah! I *don't* like hypocrites. (*Voice gets stronger*) Yeah, it's very hard to cope with.

T: Did you feel your voice change?

P: Yeah.

T: OK. Say it again.

P: I resent your hypocrisy. I don't like hypocrites, and I don't like people that say one thing and do another. [The patient slides from the specific to the general.] You remind me of the parent that says, "Do as I say, not as I do," and I don't want that kind of parent. I just want an honest parent.

T: "And you're not." [Again, this adds reality to the wish.]

P: And you're not. You're definitely not. Like now I think you're fooling me, and you're lying to me. I think you're trying to spare me something that you think is gonna hurt me, but it can't hurt any worse than this did. So don't—

T: "I resent you for fooling me." [This suggestion, using the patient's phrase, moves her back to "I" statements.]

P: I resent you for fooling me.

T: Is that true?

P: Yes.

T: OK. Stay with that, with what you resent. Focus on how that affects you, what *your* response is, and tell him directly, "I resent you for . . ." or "I feel . . ."—OK?

P: I resent you for violating our trust that we had. I resent you for lying. I resent you for disappointing me (*voice weakens*).

T: Now—right now, I hear the resentful words, but I don't hear it in the tone of your voice anymore. Do you feel the difference when it's there and when it's not there?

P: Yeah. It's like I started out strong and then I—

T: Yeah, uh-huh. Tell your dad what happened.

P: When I did that?

T: Yeah. "I started out strong with you and then I . . ."

P: I started out strong and then I felt like I was a kid lecturing my parent, and that makes me feel like I should go back and be a kid again. And I'm mixed up about which role I'm supposed to have here. I want to be your kid, but I don't want to get involved in a mess like this. [The patient gets to the introject "Kids shouldn't . . ." and to the split that results.] And I don't like you for making me feel the feelings I feel about it (*face changes*).

T: What happened just then?

P: Oh, I just had a feeling of, you know, "I don't know what else to say to you."

T: Mmm-hmm. Tell him that.

P: I don't know what else to say to you, 'cause I've been honest. I've said what I felt and I really don't feel you've said anything that meant anything.

T: And where is it in your body right now? Still in your throat, or is it— [The therapist is checking back on benchmarks.]

P: Oh, yeah, I think it's up here.

T: Still up in the throat? OK. Want to get it past your throat this morning, Beth? [The therapist seeks the patient's renewed commitment.]

P: Yeah.

T: OK. Then I'm gonna ask what I asked of Ellen, and that is to move toward doing something physical with it. I think that's the way we get past the point where you are. OK? I'm gonna ask you to stand up and use the bataca.

P: All right.

T: Move that chair back out of the way.

P: Sure.

T: Now as you pick the bataca up, just pay attention to what you feel, what you're telling yourself, and what you're feeling right now. And what I heard you say a while ago is that sometimes you scare yourself about releasing your anger because you feel—

P: Oh, I don't scare myself about releasing it. I just know the potential of it.

T: OK, all right.

P: I mean, I still—I mean I get angry now, and I yell and—but I yell with a certain amount of control 'cause I've been in some violent situations.

T: All right.

P: It's sort of like the Incredible Hulk—you wouldn't like me if I was mad (*large smile*).

(*General laughter.*)

T: And this morning I'm trusting that you can let it out in the amount that you can handle it. [The therapist provides safety.]

P: It's like, I'm not feeling angry, I'm just feeling disappointed. [The patient's moving away from her anger.]

T: Yeah. And—I'll share my sense of that. My sense of it is that disappointment is a polite way of experiencing your anger.

P: OK.

T: Then you don't have to deal with him directly and say "I'm angry with you." You can say "I'm disappointed—"

P: Oh, but I told him that. We discussed as an adult.

T: And you still get an emotion all choked up in your throat, and then it stays there. [The therapist keeps the benchmark in view.]

P: Yeah.

T: OK. And that may be a sign that there's something stuck in there, and it's more than disappointment. [The therapist gives a rationale.]

P: Well, I know I'm angry in the sense that as we discussed it as an adult. He admitted it, but it was like, "Don't judge me for it." You know? It's like he finally told me, but it was like I was trying to tell him how I felt and he was telling me, "I never judge you."

T: And Beth, if you want to get to that point, where you no longer judge him, sometimes what we have to do is go back to those unfinished situations. Go back and be 16 and take care of what you felt then and let it go here, so that then you can catch yourself up to date and be with him in a nonjudgmental kind of way. [The therapist provides a rationale for expressing the unfinished material.]

P: All right. Well, at 16—

T: Just move back to that age.

P: See, at 16 I find it very hard to, it's like striking my dad. [The patient moves back to introjection and split.]

T: Yeah, yeah, at that point in time, there are parent roles and child roles.

P: See, when I get angry, I don't get loud. I get very quiet when I get angry.

T: OK. The important thing is whether you find a way to release it or whether you keep a part of it. I don't care how loud you get. What I'm concerned about is, does it get stuck in your throat and then you end up with a piece of it still in there, or do you get it all the way out so that you're clear?

P: All right.

T: Anger does not necessarily have to raise the roof.

P: Right. Yeah, I mean I know we all got our own ways of dealing with it. I'm not sure what I'm really hitting, 'cause as long as I see him it makes it very difficult at 16 to hit that.

T: Right. Yeah. "I can't do that, you're my father."

P: (*Uses the bataca and makes several heavy blows—no words*)

T: Try it again.

P: (*Several more blows and then stops*) I just don't understand why you'd do that.

T: "I resent you for doing that." [The therapist evokes the "I" language.]

P: I resent you for doing that. I really do.

T: OK. Say that and use the bataca at the same time.

P: I *resent* it. [The patient slides to "it" language.] It really makes me angry when you do that. (*Hits with bataca*) It makes me angry when you lie to me and when you treat me like I don't have good sense. (*Hits again*)

T: "I resent you for . . ." Use words and the bataca at the same time. [The suggestion moves her back to "I" language.]

P: (*Using bataca repeatedly and speaking*) I *resent* you. I really resent you. You really make me *angry* when you do that. God—(*Face changes dramatically*)

T: Tell him what happened just then.

P: I just feel like I knocked the hell out of him.

T: Tell him that.

P: I feel like I just knocked you on your ass for hurting me like that, and I felt *good* about it (*standing tall and looking proud*).

T: Say that again!

(*General laughter.*)

P: (*Laughing heartily*) And I felt—

T: Tell Dad: "Well, I felt good!"

P: I felt *good* about it. It felt *real good*. (*She breaks into laughter, and the group joins in strongly*)

T: How are you doing now?

P: I'm doing great! (*More laughter from both her and the group*)

T: Anything in your throat? [The therapist checks the benchmarks established at the beginning of the experiment.]

P: No, my throat is absolutely clear—and my gut is calm.

T: Yeah, before you sit down, pull your other chair back over here, and leave your father there for a moment and tell him what you just did for you. [The therapist encourages assessment.]

P: You know, I think I just released years of feelings about you that I've been carrying around that weren't as important as I thought they were. And it feels nice to let that go and get rid of it, because it's not only about what you did but also how I conduct myself as a mother and a wife. And you have to be you and I have to be me, and I don't need to carry that around any more.

T: "So the next time I see you . . ."

P: So the next time I see you, I can be your daughter and you can be you and I can love you for the way you are and the way you respond to me, not how you conduct your life with other people. And I like that.

T: Anything else you want to say to him before you say goodbye, Beth? [The therapist elicits a goodbye.]

P: I look forward to calling you and seeing you again. Hope you get your jaw fixed. (*Laughs a strong, hearty laugh*). Goodbye.

(*General laughter from the group.*)

T: All right. [The therapist establishes homework.] Let's talk about homework for a moment, OK? Do you have any ideas about what you could do to build on what you did for yourself today? Like, do you want to go home and give him a phone call and just see what it's like to talk to him without all this anger, or do you want to write him a letter, or do you have something else in mind that could help you?

P: I think I'll call him.

T: OK.

P: I think I'd like to call him and talk to him.

T: OK. And just see what it's like—

P: And see what it's like and to see how I handle it and maybe tell him about it.

T: OK. And then come back and report in and see how it goes.

Beth came to the following meeting and reported two things. First, she spoke about the preceding Father's Day, when she had bought the most "neutral" card possible. Second, she related that she talked with her father that week and that it went well. Her father thanked her profusely. Beth reported that she remained "unhooked" when her father started making numerous promises, which Beth knew might never be fulfilled. Her husband was amazed that she was able to reach out to her father in such a direct manner, after the previous years of alienation.

At the end of the work reported above, Beth broke into spontaneous laughter. This is a common psychotherapeutic occurrence, and the few studies that are available support its therapeutic benefit; they have found that there is a positive relationship between outcome and strong in-therapy expression of feelings, including laughter (Mahrer & Gervaize, 1984; Nichols, 1974; Nichols & Bierenbaum, 1978; Scheff, 1979).

Example of Working with a Patient with Chronic Disease

The FEP therapist will generally find that the unfinished business of patients is with significant others in the patient's life. However, when the patient has a chronic disability or disease, the resulting pain, loss of role, limitations on daily living, and devastation of self-image may cause the disease to demand more attention than other episodes of unfinished business. Achterberg-Lawlis (1982) and Rogers (1983) believe that in chronic disease situations, the focus must first be on the pain or disease experience and then shift to other unfinished issues. Often pain patients are caught in a bind: On the one hand they feel angry, scared, hurt, or crazy, with lots of feelings to be expressed, and on the other hand they believe that no one wants to be burdened with the saga of their suffering. Sometimes they predict the loss of friends if they openly discuss how they really feel. Then, too, they may receive support from others for not expressing their feelings: "I admire how you never complain about your arthritis."

Included here is a transcript of an FEP session with a woman with rheumatoid arthritis. (Excerpts from this transcript have been presented in Chapter 6.) In this patient's case, the FEP work did not result in a disappearance of the pain. She did, however, report achieving a reduction in the pain, as well as a sense of relaxation in which she could cope more effectively with her pain. The relaxation followed the heightened experience of and expression of her fear and her anger. What is not reported in the transcript is the feedback from other group members (pain patients also), who disclosed to her that they too experienced fear and anger and appreciated that there were places where they could be honest about feeling, sharing, and expressing their emotions. Through FEP, pain patients gain the knowledge that all their feelings are valid, learn to monitor the negative effects of nonexpression of their feelings, and realize that they have choices. They learn that they have a choice of expressing or not expressing their feelings, and a choice to express the feelings directly (to a friend or spouse) or symbolically (as in an FEP session). The skills involved in symbolic expression and release are readily transferable to home life, where the patients can learn to release the hurt and anger about the disease in symbolic, safe, and productive ways.

PATIENT: Right now I feel that my body's really hurting, and my eyes are burning, and I just feel lousy. [The patient starts the session with here-and-now awareness.]

THERAPIST: Mmm-hmm.

P: I don't know why I'm telling you that, but—

T: All right. Where does your body hurt?

P: All over.

T: All over?

P: All over.

T: Any exceptions? [The therapist asks for specificity.]

P: No. No, it doesn't hurt right there (*pointing to her scalp*), but all the way down.

T: OK. So except for your scalp—

P: Yeah, my neck, all the way down, yes. Everything hurts.

T: In a kind of a dull pain, or a sharp pain?

P: No, kind of just an—I always describe my arthritis when people say "What does arthritis feel like?"—I always say "Have you ever had the worst flu? Well, I would say take the worst flu and make it a trillion billion zillion times worse than that." Like the flu, but—right? So that's what my body's feeling like.

T: All right. And you experience that generally throughout your body. Any parts of it more painful than other parts? [The therapist establishes benchmarks.]

P: My legs, and right now my wrist is really hurting.

T: OK. So your right leg and your left wrist.

P: No, both legs.

T: Both legs.

P: Yeah.

T: In your knees?

P: Uh-huh, knees, yeah.

T: OK.

P: And my eyes are very tired. I don't know if you can see; they look kind of heavy. They feel heavy; I don't know if they look heavy.

T: Some, yeah.

P: Yeah. But, like I said, I'm tired of being tired, if that makes any sense. Like, I tire very quickly today. It was like, when I'm coming here, I try to stay home all day and do my things around the house and not actually leave the house until I'm coming here. But today I had a couple of errands to do and I noticed as soon as I was out, in 30 minutes I was exhausted, and I had a real hard time coming here tonight. I kept contemplating, "I don't think I'm going." I'd say, "You're going." Here I am.

T: And here you are.

P: Yeah, I do tend to push myself.

T: What I heard you say before you came up and sat here is that what's in focus for you is a lot of resentment about having this arthritis, having the disease.

P: Mmm-hmm.

T: [The therapist develops a rationale for an experiment.] You know, if you're resentful at a person, like there are times when you've worked on anger toward other people—the guy in the grocery store who stole your purse—you put him out here and you direct your resentment at that person in order to help you get rid of it. If you're angry at your disease, and if we were to put something out here that would represent your disease, what kind of image, what symbol, what thing could you put over here that would represent your arthritis?

P: Well, there are a few things. You want only one?

T: Well, if there's a list—

P: Well, to me, something very ugly (*indicating wrist brace*), and then maybe a wheelchair and some crutches, one of these. Something very deformed, a pile of garbage.

T: So a pile of all of these. Medical aids, wheelchairs, and crutches, and such as that. [The therapist suggests aids to focusing the patient's attention.]

P: Yeah, medical aids. Somebody old, too, sitting there. [She adds another possible focus.]

T: Oh, you see somebody old there.

P: Even though it's really somebody young, it's a—you know, it's like the young, I feel old.

T: Uh-huh. Is that the arthritic part of you that you see over here?

P: Mmm-hmm, yeah. Yeah. The arthritic part. Otherwise, I feel young.

T: Uh-huh.

P: It's like I look young, but I really feel old.

T: All right. Just take a moment to look over here in your imagination and to see those things that you've described.

P: Mmm-hmm.

T: What do you feel going on inside you?

P: A sick feeling, scary. It's like I almost don't want to even look at those things.

T: Mmm-hmm.

P: And I also feel like they really don't belong to me. [The patient indicates denial of reality.]

T: Would you say that to them? "I don't want to look at you and I don't want to believe that you belong to me."

P: I don't want to look at you and I don't want to feel like you belong to me. But I know you do, or you will and you don't fit me. You don't belong to me, you don't—this is getting mixed up—you do belong to me, probably, but I don't want you there.

T: Mmm-hmm. Come over here for a moment. Sit over here (*pointing to the empty chair*).

P: OK.

T: Be that old person that you—[The therapist encourages the patient to work the split.]

P: (*From the empty chair*) Hope I can get out of this thing!

T: Well, we'll give you a hand up if you get stuck, OK?

P: OK. Be the old person?

T: That you saw over here.

P: Be that person? I don't know if I can do that. It's kind of hard to do that.

T: Mmm-hmm. Would you rather be the wheelchair? Imagine yourself being that wheelchair?

P: NO.

T: OK. Stay with the person that's over here.

P: OK. It's really strange. It's like, it's hard to explain, but I feel young, but I feel like an old person. It's like, you know, getting up (*groaning*), like that.

T: Do it. Exaggerate that.

P: Getting up like an old person would?

T: Yeah.

P: Before, I wasn't gonna be exaggerating getting out of this thing. (*Exaggerated groaning*) You know, something like that. (*Stands and goes back to original chair*)

T: Uh-huh, OK. Now, say something back to her.

P: You're sure crabby. That's a terrible thing to say. [The patient demonstrates retroflection.]

T: You're judging yourself right now, or you're judging what you're saying.

P: Yeah, that's true. That's true. Yeah. I don't like what that person did. It reminds me of what my uncle used to do with his arthritis. I don't like that. That's why you never hear a sound out of my body. [The split evokes a memory of another relationship.]

T: Mmm-hmm. Tell her that.

P: I don't like it that you were calling attention to yourself. You could have done the same movements in silence, just like I do. You don't have to exaggerate it. I can't stand that. And when my Uncle Phillip did that, with his arthritis, the whole neighborhood knew he was getting out of a chair. And I was a child, watching him, and I just—oh, I hated that. I hated looking at him. That's why no one will know I'm in pain, because of that. [The patient states an early decision regarding expression of feeling.] I always keep it to myself. This friend that was with me over the weekend— may I say this one thing?

T: Yeah, go ahead.

P: This friend that was with me, she told me that—she said I'm amazing, and I said "Amazing?" and she said, "Knowing you're in chronic pain and all the time, I can't believe how you handle things, how fast you do things." [The patient is presenting her vulnerability to an old introjection.] And she wasn't talking about walking, she was talking about cooking or whatever, and I said "And that's why, when my wrist started, it just scared the hell out of me because this is something I really need to do my things," you know, and that's why I got so frightened with the wrist starting. That's like, will I be able to continue doing all my things?

T: OK. [The therapist feels a need to check on focus and commitment.] Do you feel that this is going anywhere for you right now? Is this getting in touch with anything for you?

P: No, I think I—sometimes I get angry—I'd like to maybe curse. No, I don't want to curse. [The patient identifies a more basic split.] I want to tell my arthritis something, that I hate it.

T: Yeah. That's—I was gonna suggest a change in the experiment that we're doing, OK?

P: OK

T: The change would be to see your arthritis out here, or something that symbolizes it. All right? Perhaps see an aspirin bottle out here, or a crutch, or whatever. [The therapist makes suggestions for fine-tuning the experiment.]

P: Can I put this out there? (*Pointing to wrist brace*) This will help me, 'cause this thing I hate. This is something I really hate, so I'll just put that thing out there —if I can get the contraption off! (*Removes wrist brace*)

T: And let it be—let this thing be a symbol of your arthritis, so that it stands for all the arthritis in all of the different parts of your body. OK? And what I'm going to ask you to do is to see what it's like for you to look at this symbol of your arthritis and to say, "I'm angry at you."

P: OK. Could you turn it over? There's something about the other side that really bothers me.

T: This side?

P: No, these straps. Just the way—I think even if I just do this it looks more like, scary, to me or something. I don't know. It doesn't fit me. [Denial again.]

T: All right.

P: Oooh, I hate looking at that thing. It looks so strange to me. It doesn't belong on me. [More denial.]

T: Un-huh. Feel what's going on in your body right now.

P: I'm feeling scared.

T: Oooh, all right.

P: It's so ugly.

T: Try this: "You scare me." [The therapist suggests that the patient try on a sentence.]

P: You scare me.

T: Again. [The therapist encourages repetition.]

P: You scare me.

T: Just stay with that one sentence and say it as it comes up for you.

P: You scare me.

T: Now I'm gonna ask you to stay with that sentence, but to turn it around slightly and say "I'm scared of you." [The therapist encourages the patient to try on a sentence in reverse.]

P: I'm scared of you.

T: Again.

P: I'm scared of you (*face begins to look young and fearful*).

T: Did you feel your face change as you said that?

P: Yeah, I'm *scared*.

T: Oooh, yeah. Feel that. Say it again. [The therapist encourages escalation of the feeling.]

P: It gives me shivers.

T: Yeah, let your—

P: I'm *scared* of you. You're so creepy-looking. Ugly-looking. You look worse there than on my hand. I think I'm really scared of looking at you—it's scary. [The patient is beginning to lessen the denial.] It's so—

T: OK, now come back to the sentence "I'm scared of you." [The therapist suggests personalizing the language.]

P: I'm *scared* of you. I hate what you look like. You don't belong on me. But you do belong on me. [The patient reidentifies the split.]

T: Try this on: "I don't want you there, and you're there." [The therapist feeds a sentence that highlights the split.]

P: I don't want you there, and you're there. My arthritis is there, and I don't want it.

T: Uh-huh. Say it to your arthritis: "You're there, and I don't want you there." [The therapist directs the patient's focus.]

P: You're there, and I don't want you there. And I feel that I can't control you. [New material emerges.]

T: Yeah, OK. Stay with the feelings there, feel what's the pressure behind your eyes right now. Just stay with that. OK? [The therapist draws attention to physical reactions.]

P: You're a scary disease that's running my life, ruining my life and running it. I don't have control of you. I like to have control of things.

T: Uh-huh. Well, one thing you do have control over right now are your feelings towards your arthritis. You can take some time right now to be as angry as hell at it if you need to be. [This statement moves the patient from a victim position to a response-able position.]

P: It's funny, I don't know how much anger—it's like, it's just that I'm scared of the unknown or something. [The patient is not yet feeling the anger.]

T: Uh-huh, so you feel more scared than angry?

P: It's like I hate my arthritis, and I'm scared of it.

T: Direct it out here, "I hate you and I'm scared of you." [The therapist encourages a move from "about"-ism to "is"-ism.]

P: I hate you and I'm scared of you. Sometimes I just, oooh, I wish I could just—

T: Just what? [The therapist urges the patient to finish the sentence/thought.]

P: Just take you out of my body and just—

T: Now, tonight, for once, you can do that, OK? (*Moves bataca in reach of the patient*) [The therapist indicates one of the power-full attributes of an experiment.]

P: I don't know how much it will; I can only use one hand, I can't use my left hand.

T: OK. Well, if you wanted to squeeze this bataca, or just as if you could take your arthritis and let it be here right now and if you feel that sometimes you'd like to attack it or tear it up or tear into it— [The therapist suggests adding physical contact to words.]

P: Mmm-hmm. Yes. I wish I could grab hold of it and just squeeze the hell out of it.

T: Mmm-hmm. Let that symbolize your arthritis right now. Talk right to it.

P: I *hate* you.

T: Again.

P: I *hate* you. You are such a terrible pain. (*Tears come*)

T: Just feel the feelings there, just let yourself feel the tears, feel the hurt. [The therapist encourages escalation of the hurt feeling.]

P: You are such an *angry* feeling, it's such a—

T: Oooh, OK. So you're feeling the anger now. [The therapist catches the shift from hurt to resentment.]

P: Just so—it's such a mean feeling.

T: Talk to it. "I'm angry at you."

P: You are—I'm angry at you for invading my body (*hurt voice*).

T: Now say it again without the hurt. [The therapist urges a move from confluence to individuation.]

P: I'm angry at you for invading my body that used to be healthy. I *hate* you! You make me clench my teeth, it hurts my head.

T: Yeah. Now right now, you don't have to clench your teeth. If you want to yell at it, open your mouth and scream at it, you can do that. [The therapist encourages reversal.]

P: I hate you. I hate you. You're such a terrible thing.

T: Keep going, you're doing fine.

P: You're mean (*hurt voice*). [Hurt voice returns when this judgmental word is used.]

T: Now, are you feeling more hurt than angry right now?

P: I'm hurt, and I'm just—I am angry, I *am* angry. I wish I could take you out of my body and just rip you apart.

T: Right now you can do that, OK? For once, you can just feel yourself take it out of your body and rip into it.

P: Oh, it just—(*squeezing the bataca with her hands*)

T: Oooh, feel that. That's it. [The therapist encourages arousal of feeling.]

P: I *hate* you.

T: Say that again. [The therapist urges heightening of feeling.]

P: I *hate* you! Please leave me alone!

T: "And you don't." [This adds the reality.]

P: You don't. Every damn day I go to sleep with you, and every damn morning I wake up with you.

T: "And I'm angry about that."

P: I'm angry (*sobbing*).

T: Is that true for you? [The therapist is checking to see that she is not simply introjecting his words.]

P: Yes. I'm *angry*. I am sick of the pain. I am tired of the pain!

T: "I am *angry* about the pain."

P: I am angry about the pain and I'm angry at what you're doing to me (*hurt voice*). [Voice still indicates a state of confluence.]

T: Now you're feeling more hurt than angry right now? Is that true?

P: No, I'm really angry.

T: OK. And what I'm aware of is that I hear the anger and I also see the tears, and if you're feeling more angry, then let yourself be angry without the tears. OK? If you're feeling more hurt, then let the tears come. [The therapist encourages differentiation.]

P: OK. I *hate* you (*clearly angry voice*). [This breaks up the confluence.]

T: That's it.

P: I hate that you make me feel old. I'm young! Let me live my life without pain!

T: [The therapist feeds a line that adds the reality of the pain.] "And you don't, and I'm angry about that."

P: You don't, and I'm angry. I hate you! I hate you so much! You are ruining my life. You have—

T: Yeah, just let it come.

P: You have stopped me from doing so many things I want to do. I hate you more than anything. *Anything!* I swear I could *strangle* you if I could get my hands on you.

T: You've got your hands on it right now.

P: Oh, I just— (*returns to squeezing the bataca*)

T: That's it, just squeeze—

P: (*Sobbing*) I'm scared, and I'm hurt, and I want to stop!

T: Yeah, all these feelings are coming at the same time, right? Feeling scared, and feeling hurt, and feeling angry all at the same time.

P: I don't know what I'm feeling. I'm mad, I'm hurt, I'm— [More confluence.]

T: Yeah. What I see is that very quickly you move from feeling to feeling, because lots of feelings are coming up in there.

P: Oh, everything is in—

T: So, yeah, just take it one moment at a time, OK? [The therapist slows the experience down so that all parts can be felt and owned.] And whatever feeling comes up at that moment, just let it be there. So if you're feeling more scared one moment, that's OK. If you're feeling more mad the next moment, that's OK. [The therapist encourages her to track her own awareness as it shifts.]

P: (*To the arthritis*) I'm scared of you.

T: All right, just stay with the scared part.

P: I'm scared of what you're doing to me. Where am I gonna be in a few years? (*Silence*)

T: "And now I'm feeling . . ."

P: And I'm feeling mad.

T: OK.

P: I wish you'd leave me alone.

T: "And you don't." [This changes wish to reality.]

P: You *don't*! (*Punches the bataca*)

T: Do that again. Don't hurt your wrist, but—

P: You *don't* leave me alone.

T: —but let your anger out, OK?

P: You *don't* leave me alone! (*Begins to punch the bataca again*) You just keep on gnawing at my body, and sometimes I feel like I'm going out of my mind. Sometimes the pain is so excruciating I feel like I'm losing my mind. I feel like I'm gonna just die sometimes from you, but yet you don't kill me. You torture. You *torture*!

T: "And I *resent* you for that." [The therapist elicits "I" language.]

P: And I *resent* you for torturing me! You're so *mean*! I *hate* you! I hate you more than anything in this whole world. (*Becomes quiet*)

T: OK, now, just stay with what's coming up from moment to moment. You said a moment ago that all kinds of confusing things were coming up, so we're just gonna take it a moment at a time and see what's coming up for you right now, OK?

P: I think about what you've done to my life.

T: Uh-huh. "And as I think about that . . ."

P: And as I think about it I fit—I—I—feel *mad*.

T: That's it, let the anger be there.

P: I feel angry and I feel so resentful of you. You're a mean thing, mean and *nasty* and *cruel*. You're not letting me live my life. Let *go* of *me* already!

T: "And it doesn't." [The therapist encourages a move from what *is not* to what *is*.]

P: You just keep on gnawing at me. (*Voice changes—hurt emerges*) You never give me one moment, pain-free! (*Sobbing*)

T: Do you feel more hurt now than mad?

P: Yes, I was hurt.

T: Just let yourself feel the hurt, too. OK?

P: You never let me have one, single, solitary moment in a day. You never leave me alone. (*Voice begins to sound resentful again*)

T: Are you feeling more hurt or more mad?

P: Angry now.

T: OK. So let yourself move into the anger, OK? Just gonna take one feeling at a time, but if you keep moving from feeling to feeling, that's okay. We'll just keep identifying what it is and deal with it as it comes. [The therapist encourages her to monitor herself in the present.]

P: I'm sick of you. I'm sick of you.

T: Yeah. Change "sick" to "mad at you." [The therapist suggests a change from debilitating to potent language.]

P: I'm mad. I am mad at you, oh, and I hate you. I hate you more than anything in this life. You are ruining my life. But I won't let you. You try but I won't let you. Because I fight you. I fight you. [Beginning of emergence of a more potent position.]

T: OK, you look like you're trying to tear the bataca up. Is that—

P: I do. I feel—

T: OK. You know, one of the things that's around today are new phone books, and out in the hall are sitting all these old ones. I'll get one of those books and maybe we could use it right now, OK? [The therapist proposes another fine-tuning of the experiment.]

P: Mmm-hmm.

T: So we'll let John [another patient in the group] go look, but until he comes in with an old phone book, let's just keep doing what you're doing, OK?

P: I know one thing. You are trying desperately to stop me, but I won't let you. I will fight you every inch of the way. I'm a fighter, but so are you.

T: Uh-huh, and just feel the fight in you right now.

P: But I'm stronger than you are. I feel stronger. (*John returns with phone book*)

T: OK. (*Puts phone book in patient's lap*)

P: Want me to rip the pages if that's what I feel like doing? I couldn't rip the whole book.

T: Yeah. Not in one fell swoop, but it just seemed like you wanted to tear into it.

P: I want to tear—when I tear it's like I'm tearing it, like— (*tears pages in book*) like I'm tearing it out of me. It's like I'm just getting rid of it. It's like letting it—pulling it out, pulling it out of me.

T: That's it, and as you do that, just pay attention to what it's like, OK?

P: When I pull—when I'm tearing it, it feels good, and then, when I go like this (*crumpling paper*), it's that I'm throwing it off my body.

T: Yeah, that's it. Just stay with what's going on.

P: I feel angry (*tearing and crumpling paper*).

T: Yeah. OK, let it come.

P: I *hate* you!

T: That's it, just let it come. Keep feeling that anger. Stay right there with it and let your body do what it wants to do. Let your hands do what they want to do. [The therapist shares belief in the body's ability to know what needs to happen.]

P: I want to take you and I did—(*more tearing and crumpling of paper*) wring the life out of you and just throw you away off me.

T: Uh-huh.

P: You make me *shake* (*Body shakes all over*)

T: Oooh, just feel that.

P: (*Continues tearing and crumpling of paper*) It just feels so good to just—I'm taking you and I'm crumpling and just—this is what I feel you do to me, but now I'm doing it to you. (*Body begins to shake again*)

T: OK, and we're working from moment to moment, so just see where you are at this moment, what's coming up for you right now.

P: I'm scared of you. I am scared. I'm scared because I feel like even though I'm—even though I'm being mean to you, you're gonna get me in the end.

T: So when you feel scared, does your body feel like shaking?

P: I feel nauseous and then it just gets—

T: Nauseous? OK, just let that feeling be there, and if you want to shake, let yourself shake.

P: I feel like even though you're gonna get me, you are—that you're gonna win at the end. I don't like to think that. I'm getting angry because I'm thinking of that. [Each time she allows herself to experience the fear, anger emerges.]

T: All right.

P: And I don't really like to think it. I don't like to think it because I feel that I'm gonna get you at the end (*digs fingers into the phone book*)

T: Stay in the present moment, all right? And try this out. "A moment ago you scared me, but then I decided . . ." [The therapist feeds a potent sentence.]

P: A moment ago you scared me, but I decided to take control, I get that anger. Anger comes back and I am gonna fight it (*rips phone book more*).

T: OK. [The therapist feeds another line.] "I'm gonna fight you."

P: I'm gonna fight you. The anger—I'm gonna fight you. I'm gonna-I'm gonna fight you, I'm gonna do the best I can.

T: Now stay in the present moment. "I'm fighting you right now." [The therapist urges the patient to move into the potency of the present.]

P: I am fighting you. I am fighting you. You're not gonna get the best of me. You're not.

T: All right, now stay in the moment. What comes up next for you? Still mad, or is there something new there?

P: No, it's a lot of—I'm mad. I'm just—(*tearing pages of phone book*)

T: OK, then stay with it, keep going.

P: I'm mad, I hate you. Again, I hate you. I *hate* you more than anything I've ever hated in my life (*shivers*).

T: Oooh, just let that shiver come out. OK, do you feel that? OK.

P: I just, I want to, I want it—I don't know, I just—I want to strangle everything that you represent to me.

T: OK, just—that's it. Stay from moment to moment, what's happening right now.

P: Right now I just feel peaceful. [After emotion clears the system, organism goes to state of equilibrium and relaxation.]

T: OK.

P: Like, I just feel like some stuff I just—like, just relaxed, I don't feel angry.

T: All right. Stay with the moment. Just enjoy that feeling.

P: I feel relaxed. I feel like I almost took part of you out of me. It's like I—it's like right now I feel relaxed, really relaxed, not like when I sat down here—like I did get rid of some of that excruciating pain. I'm still in pain, but I feel relaxed. [The patient describes benchmarks of progress.]

T: OK. So tell that thing in your lap that represents your arthritis what you accomplished for you tonight, OK?

P: Well, I feel like I worked on you tonight. I feel like I got you because you're busy always getting me, but today I feel like I—I worked on getting you and hurting you, letting you feel what you feel like to my body. I think I let you feel what it feels like to inflict pain. I feel good about that. [The patient engages in assessment and acknowledgment of self.]

T: OK. Let me ask you to do one additional thing, if you would. [The therapist is remembering the strength of the image of the uncle at the beginning of the session.]

P: Mmm-hmm.

T: Would you imagine your uncle sitting over here for a moment, the one who let the whole neighborhood know that he was groaning up out of his chair, OK? And say two things to him. One is how the two of you are alike, and the second is how the two of you are different in the way you deal with your arthritis, or in having arthritis.

P: Tell him one thing how we are alike and one thing how we're different?

T: Yeah, how you're alike and how you're different.

P: Uncle Phillip, we both have arthritis in our 30s, and you had it in your 20s, 20s and 30s, young people with a really scary disease. We were alike that way. But where you and I differ is, you gave in and I fight. [The patient acknowledges her potency.] And I won't, I won't let it get the best of me. I will fight this, but as I'm fighting it, I'm gonna do it by myself, though. I'm not gonna look for the sympathy from people, and I'm not gonna tell everyone when they say, "How are you doing?" I'm not gonna tell them really how I'm doing. That's where you and I differ. You felt the need to tell everyone your excruciating pain, and why bother? They didn't understand anyway. Not me. I will never do that. [The patient achieves integration.]

T: OK. Say goodbye to him.

P: Goodbye. I love you.

T: OK. Yeah. I appreciate how you see a difference in how you want to express the fact that you have arthritis rather than to complain to the world about it, and I believe it's important to still find a way to sometimes get into the anger and the fear and the hurt that you feel about it, and to acknowledge that those things are there for you and allow yourself to express those things. I think that's critical, and I think it's a bind that people with a chronic disease are in.

The point to be emphasized in this example is that people have "givens" in their lives (i.e., arthritis was a given for the patient above) over which they have little or no control; however, everyone has absolute power over his or her choice of how to respond to the given. The patient with arthritis in this transcript found that out when she quit trying to control the arthritis (e.g., "I don't want to feel like you belong to me") and allowed herself to have her own response to the fact that the arthritis does belong to her (". . . but I decided to take control and when I take control, I get that anger. Anger comes back and I am gonna fight it"), she was able to accomplish some relaxation (". . . I did get rid of some of that excruciating pain. I'm still in pain, but I feel relaxed").

FEP Session Illustrating the Physiological Effects of Emotional Constriction

This patient, Fern, was a 40-year-old registered nurse with 16 years of chronic back pain; she had intermittently obtained relief through medications over that period. This was the first hour of the first session following the pretraining initial session. (Excerpts from this transcript have been presented in Chapter 5 and in Chapter 6.)

THERAPIST: What I'd like to start with, Fern, is what you're feeling right now—the kinds of emotions you're feeling and the kinds of physical feelings you have. [Therapist starts by eliciting psychological and physical benchmarks in the present.]

PATIENT: Oh, I can check. Physically, I feel terrible. My stomach is shaking, I feel nauseated, I have something that's not quite a headache but it's, no, more right in here above my eyes. It's not really a pain, but it's there and I know it, and it almost feels like it's being squeezed. I feel like *I'm* being squeezed. [Benchmarks: Shaky stomach, nausea, headache, squeezed feeling.]

T: There you go. Yes, you bet. Yeah. OK. All right. Those are very definite signs, then, that I'm gonna ask you to just remember, and we're gonna check those out at the end of your work to see if anything changed in that and in the stomach and anywhere. Are there any other areas of your body that are really giving you a hard time right now? [In terms of the tasks of a session outlined in Chapter 4, these symptoms are used as part of the asessment at the end of the third step (the work itself) and in the fourth step (assessment of the work done at the conclusion of the session), to determine any changes occurring in symptomatology.]

P: Yeah, my leg, my left leg, and that hasn't bothered me for a long time either. It's not really "pain" pain, but it hurts and I know it's there. [One more benchmark: pain in left leg.]

T: Do you sit over more on this side to kind of relieve your pain? Is that it?

P: Yeah.

T: OK. All right. That would be a good area, then, to pay attention to, and we'll see if anything changes there. Any other areas that you want to note right now before we go farther?

P: I feel like I'm vibrating from my hair down to my feet. [One more benchmark: body vibrations.]

T: OK.

P: I really feel like I'm coming apart.

T: All right. If you're willing to, if you feel safe enough to do that, I'd like for you just to stay with the vibrations and just let youself vibrate as much as possible. [The therapist gives the patient permission to be whatever she is.]

P: That scares me.

T: All right. What do you say to yourself that gets scary? What do you see as going to happen? "If I let myself vibrate, I'll what?" [The therapist elicits the predictive fantasies of the patient.]

P: I'll lose control of myself (*quietly*). [The patient indicates a critical introject—the control issue.]

T: I didn't hear the tail end of that.

P: I'll lose control of myself.

T: "Of myself." Yeah. OK—

P: —And everything around me (*gulping breath*).

T: That meant something there. Could you feel the sucking in on that one? Yeah. OK. All right. (*Patient is nodding agreement*) What does that mean in terms of what will happen, losing control? What will you do? Will you cry or will you yell or what would you do if you lost control here? [The therapist assesses the patient's predictions about "losing control."]

P: I don't know. Maybe yell and scream and carry on—

T: OK. All right.

P: —Be irrational. [The patient indicates another heavy introject—"be rational."]

T: Right. Are you ever irrational?

P: No, not totally. I'm always—you know, I do get some irrational, but not completely. I always have some kind of control on it. A leash, like.

T: Right, like a string that you can always pull yourself back, right.

P: Mmm-hmm.

T: To center or something like that. OK. One of the things that I hope to be able to do is to provide some kind of safe place here for you to go even past that string if you want to. You're not gonna have to, but it's all right. Nothing bad will happen is what I'm saying. OK? And that you can go past that string and then you can still come back and get in touch with your rational self. You won't be letting go of it that way. [The therapist provides safety in therapy for the patient, so that she can feel, think or do whatever is, rather than changing feelings, thoughts, or actions to fit her introjects.]

P: OK (*tentativeness in voice*).

T: What happened to you as I said that just now about going past the string?

P: It's hard to explain. I got frightened, very frightened, but then when you said it would be safe, then that felt like a warm wave. [The patient gives feedback on "safety" minilecture.]

T: All right, good. OK.

P: But then it went right back to being scary again. [The patient shows excellent awareness and self-honesty.]

T: Did you feel your mouth go—

P: Yeah. Dry?

T: Yeah, dry, and does it want to kind of squiggly or something? [The therapist explores the patient's sensory reactions.]

P: Mmm-hmm. Popcorn. Mmm-hmm.

T: Yeah. When I'm really feeling things, I can feel this part of my mouth just start to fall apart.

P: Prickly.

T: Oh, yours is getting prickly?

P: It's prickly.

T: [The therapist begins the first of the process—establishing a focus.] OK. All right. OK. I would like for you to pick one person who's important to you in your life to deal with today and just let your system tell you right now who that person is. There's no right one or wrong one; it'll just come to you, something that will pop up here in your head. [The therapist directs the patient's attention to unfinished business with significant others.]

P: I got a problem, 'cause two of them pop up, my husband and my daughter. [Both possible foci fall within the range of significant others in the FEP model—spouse and children.]

T: All right. OK. All right.

P: And it's kind of—

T: They go together, like bookends or something?

P: Right now, yeah, right.

T: OK. Are they on one side of the fence and you're on the other side, or are they just both—[The therapist begins the process of patient discrimination between the two foci.]

P: No. They're over there.

T: They're combined, huh?

P: Well, yeah. They're combined.

T: OK. All right. And like, is Dad giving daughter support against you or something like that, or how did they get combined like that in your head?

P: They're hooked up because they're both doing it to me, if you know what I mean? They're socking it to me, each in their own way.

T: All right. OK.

P: But the result is the same and that's why they're, like, bookends.

T: I see. OK. How does your husband do it to you? [The therapist begins separation of one focus from the other—work can only effectively deal with one focus at a time.]

P: Let me count the ways (*laughing*).

T: A lot of them, huh?

P: Yeah.

T: What's a good example?

P: He just, um, he ridicules my feelings. They're not even valid. If I say I feel thus and so— [The patient describes a powerful manipulation of her affective system.]

T: Yeah, then what do you get back?

P: If I said black, he'd say white.

T: Yeah, OK.

P: "And you're crazy, it's not." You know. [The patient mentions a label—"crazy"— she has "bought into" over years of conditioning.]

T: OK. That would be the statement, "You're crazy," when you get—

P: Yeah, "Don't be ridiculous."

T: Yeah. Be rational? Make sense? [The therapist refers to the injunction identified above.]

P: Yeah, make sense, be logical, don't be an "emotional female." Boy, it's really—[The patient describes the application of a societal label—"emotional female."]

T: I saw this finger come out. Is that the way you feel, that the finger's coming down on you? [The finger symbolized the "critical parent" coming down on the child.]

P: Right, that's, yes, and I feel like (*laughs and clamps her teeth as if biting off the pointed finger*).

T: I'll remember not to do that to you. How does your daughter get to you? [The therapist now attends to the second significant other.]

P: She does it differently. She—she commiserates with me, she gets me to open up and then—boom!

T: That's a tender trap, huh?

P: Right.

T: Just sucks you in and then all of a sudden you'll get it.

P: Right, and then she stonewalls me, you know, she'll do something really terrible or—and really hurts me. She'll get me feeling, you know, like, oh, it's OK and we really understand each other, and then she'll do or say something that makes me think she doesn't even care if I'm alive. (*Face contorts and tears well up*)

T: Yeah. Just notice what you feel right now. [Rush of emotion is caught by the therapist and is fed back to the patient.]

P: It hurts.

T: Just feel how much hurt is in there right now, Fern, so we won't rush past that and into just—[The therapist attempts to slow the patient so that the affect can be fully experienced.]

P: It hurts. They're both hurting. (*Fighting tears*)

T: I'll bet. Just feel how much, and just feel it as it begins to come up that center tube there. Can you just feel it rising right up through here? [The therapist attempts to keep the patient focused on the here-and-now experience.]

P: Yeah. It makes me feel sick. [Getting "sick" sabotages completion of the rising emotion.]

T: OK. You feel kind of queasy right now?

P: Yeah.

T: OK.

P: Nauseous.

T: Now as we work you may feel even more nauseous, because, you know, that stuff's trying to come up, and I know we got a bucket here that you can just puke into if you need to. All right? So don't hold it back. This is the time you don't have to hold the string on. OK? Today you can just let it come up. [The therapist gives the patient permission to "go all the way" with whatever comes, even if it means vomiting to complete the nauseous reaction.]

P: Oh, I don't think I can do that.

T: It's OK, just go with it as far as you can go today. And just feel any ways right now in which you might be controlling that feeling that's coming up. Can you feel the brake you have on it? [The therapist asks the patient to take ownership of her power to complete *or* to stop any reaction.]

P: Yes.

T: Where do you control it right now? Can you tell?

P: I don't know, I just keep trying to get hold of myself—you know, get myself back together.

T: All right, yeah. Uh-huh. Yeah. OK. Are you holding on to it? Just— that's OK (*patient exhibits rush of tears*), take your time; it's all right to make the sounds of crying. In other words, in here you don't have to keep your crying quiet, or secret, or anything like that. [As control is acknowledged, tears are able to move, in spite of the patient's continuing attempts to fight for control.]

P: Oh, it hurts so much!

T: You bet, and just feel what you're hurting about right now. Can you feel it? Remembering something? [The patient is asked to identify/specify focus of the tears.]

P: I care so much for them!

T: Mmm-hmm.

P: I feel like I'm on a treadmill. I keep trying, trying to be good (*crying is sucked in on the inhalation*), and turning it to do with me, they don't— (*overwhelmed with emotion*)

T: OK, now just feel that one, 'cause there's a lot of energy, now that one's gotta hurt all the way down. [The therapist encourages the patient to stay focused on what is happening to her.]

P: It's terrible, I've never felt so bad (*still sucking in air*).

T: Just feel what it's like to contain that much hurt in your body right now. Can you feel that, what you have to do to hold on to all that? [The therapist requests the patient to acknowledge the "cost" of such containment.]

P: I feel like I'm gonna fly apart now—

T: [The therapist solicits commitment to work with a specific significant other.] All right—OK. Let's see if we can get you a little relief on that, all right? You're just to pick one of these people to work with today, either your husband or your daughter. [The patient can only complete the Gestalt with one focus at a time.] And we'll just take some time to see if we can get some things finished off.

P: Oh, I don't know which one.

T: There's no right one or wrong one, so you can't go wrong either way, but you just need to pick one of them.

P: My husband. [Commitment is made.]

T: [The therapist initiates work on unfinished business identified by the patient.] All right. OK. I need his name.

P: Jerry.

T: I'm gonna ask you to think about bringing Jerry here into the room. I assume Jerry would probably never come to something like this. Is that right or not?

P: I don't think so.

T: [The therapist sets up the experimental part of the work phase.] Right. So it might take a pretty strong imagination, but I want you to just imagine that we've been able to get Jerry to come in here so that he can hear about the pain you're in and any of the reactions you have to being in all of that pain. OK? And so I want you just to imagine that he's seated out here in front of you right now. And I'm gonna move my chair a little bit here so that I can be behind you like a coach, all right? Let's just keep this right over there. (*Rearranges chairs*) OK, and, I want you just in your mind's eye to think about the fact that Jerry is sitting here waiting to hear from you, and this time you can talk to him without him shutting you off in any way. [The therapist establishes a rationale for what the patient is going to do.]

P: He laughs at me. (*Sucks in tears*).

T: Ah. Well, that's a pretty powerful one, isn't it? Can you feel it go down in there as soon as you think of that? Would he be laughing at you now? How would he handle this right now? What would he say—"Oh, for Pete's sake!"? [This refers back to the ridicule mentioned earlier—the husband controls her here in the session as well as at home.]

P: Yeah.

T: Yeah?

P: Yeah, he would, and then if I—

T: "Come on, Fern, it's not that bad," or what?

P: "Oh, you're exaggerating." [One can imagine how often the patient has heard this at home, after 16 years of psychogenic back pain for which no physiological basis has been found.]

T: "You're exaggerating." Right, OK. Now will you tell him how that makes you feel *toward* him—not *inside yourself*, but *toward* him when he laughs at you, when you're into your feelings. [The therapist distinquishes between "intra" and "inter" feeling.]

P: Oh, it makes me so mad.

T: Just try that, right at him, just tell him. I've forgotten his name! Jerry? That's what I was gonna call him, but it didn't sound right. "OK, Jerry . . ."

P: You don't have any right to laugh at me like that. It hurts when you do that. [The patient relates to her hurt rather than to her anger.]

T: Just try, "I resent you for laughing at me."

P: Ohhh—

T: Is that a little too strong?

P: Yeah. [The therapist's stimulus sentence was premature, so he has to back up to the level where the patient is stuck.]

T: Yeah, you're not supposed to do that, are you?

P: No.

T: No. Can you feel your hands rubbing and your body cringing away from me? Yeah, OK. Now notice just what happened when I suggested you say "I resent you, Jerry." [The therapist calls the patient's attention to her physical reactions to the strong emotion just expressed in the stimulus sentence.]

P: Yeah. (*Cringes as she hears therapist's loud voice*)

T: Yeah, what happens down in—

P: Well, it's spooky. It makes me nervous.

T: Yeah. This is something you're not used to saying, right?

P: Scary. Yeah. Yeah.

T: OK. Tell Jerry what happens as soon as I raise my voice and, you know, do that thing about "I resent you for . . ." [The therapist is testing for signs of physical abuse from the past, which may be indicated by cringing response to a loud voice.]

P: That scares me.

T: OK. Try it this way. "Jerry, you scare me."

P: Jerry, you scare me.

T: OK, just feel your body. Is it kind of—can you feel yourself pushing back away from him there?

P: Yeah, I'm shaking, and afraid. [The patient is entering the impasse between being a victim for all these years on one side and becoming an assertive, potent person on the other side.]

T: Yeah, OK. All right. Now, I want you—I'm going to just move back a little so I don't distract you, and I want you as much as possible just to talk to him about it. You know? "Jerry, I get scared when I start talking to you, and right now I'm feeling da-da-da-da-da," whatever it is. [The therapist is asking the patient to move from "talking about" with the therapist to *doing* by "talking" to the significant other.]

P: I'm afraid. I get scared.

T: Just tell him what you're scared of.

P: Oh, I don't even know. I don't even know why I'm scared.

T: Just tell him a few things you guess you'd be scared of. [If the patient doesn't *know*, she is asked to *guess*.] "I'm scared you'll hit me"? [Second inquiry regarding physical abuse.]

P: No.

T: "OK, I'm not scared of that one."

P: No.

T: Tell him what you're afraid will happen.

P: (*To therapist*) He makes me feel like I don't exist.

T: OK. Say that to him. [The therapist directs focus back to the significant other.]

P: Jerry, you make me feel sometimes like I don't—I'm not even here, like I don't even exist.

T: Tell him how he does that to you, what he does that makes you feel that way. [The therapist requests specificity from the patient.]

P: When I try to tell you how I feel, you act like I'm crazy, like I'm not entitled to have any feelings, like it's not important, and then you turn away and you make believe I'm not even there.

T: Try this on to him: "Today I won't let you turn away, Jerry." [An attempt to move patient from victim role to one of potency.]

P: Today I won't let you turn away (*slightly stronger voice*).

T: Notice how that felt to say that, and just tell him how that felt now.

P: I'm not sure.

T: OK. Try it again to him. Try it a little louder, just to see how that goes. [Repetition can help make a clearer contact with patient awareness.]

P: Today I won't let you turn away. I don't—he doesn't believe me.

T: Oh! Do you believe you?

P: No.

T: Oh, all right. OK. Would you be willing to make sure that he stays here until you get finished with the feeling today, till you get finished expressing yourself? Would you be willing to keep him right here? [The therapist seeks a deeper, more definite commitment to the work at hand.]

P: Yes.

T: All right? OK. Fine, because, remember, today you're in charge. This time Jerry stays here and listens to you. [The therapist reinforces her capacity to cope—not to be a victim.]

P: OK.

T: All right? He doesn't interfere with you in any way unless you let him do it.

P: OK.

T: Now tell him how that feels and tell him what you're gonna do today. "Today—"

P: That feels good. That feels good to know that you're gonna sit there and listen and that you're not gonna turn away (*much stronger voice*). [The patient takes a more potent verbal stance.]

T: Tell him how mad you are at him.

P: Oh, I am—it makes me furious!

T: OK. Now try that again, this time take the tears out of the voice. Just try it, like "That makes me furious!" [The therapist encourages separation of two competing emotions—hurt and anger.]

P: That makes me furious! (*Surprised look on face*) [The patient makes a real internal change toward the competent self.]

T: OK. Wow! Feel the difference in it? Did you feel the difference? [The therapist asks the patient to acknowledge the change.]

P: Yeah.

T: What did you do, just go over the cliff on that one, right?

P: Yeah.

T: OK, but you're still alive.

P: Yeah (*tentatively*).

T: OK. All right, try it again; this time, try it as "*You* make me furious, Jerry." [The therapist seeks repetition for reinforcement plus gradual escalation of ownership by changing "it" language (objective language) to "you" (more pointed and subjective language)—the final step is to move "you" language to "I" language.]

P: Oh, God!

T: It's all right, just take a deep breath and hold your nose and just jump.

P: You make me furious, Jerry!

T: That sounds really—

P: Oh, yeah! [The patient is beginning to realize that what she is doing is working for her.]

T: —strong. OK, now I want you just to stay on that place, and just stay in there, keep your voice up, and just tell him about everything that he makes you furious with—everything you can think of, and don't pass anything up. "I'm angry at you for da-da-da-da-da." [The therapist seeks specification on the patient's part.]

P: Oh, I don't even know where to start. I don't even know where to begin.

T: A list as long as my arm?

P: It's true, as long as my arm and as old as I am.

T: You just start anywhere your mind can catch something, you know? Whatever it brings up, just let him hear it.

P: You ignore me. You never talk to me. You talk at me, not to me. You don't listen.

T: Feel that anger as it begins to rise. [The therapist asks the patient to acknowledge developing affect as she cognitively verbalizes content.] Now I'm just going to ask you to change your sentence just a little bit. [This is the final stage of language development from "it" to "you" to "I," which is a full ownership verbalization.] Instead of "You don't listen to me," try "I resent you not listening to me" or "I'm angry at you for not listening to me" or anything like that. Just start it with "I am."

P: I'm angry at you for not listening. [A clear, clean statement of feeling.]

T: Just notice how that felt, and then try another one. Yeah, feel your body as it changes position just then.

P: I'm angry at you for treating me like a nonperson. [Another clear statement of feeling.]

T: Oh, boy. Try that one again. That one is a good one. [The therapist encourages imprinting by repetition.]

P: Angry at you for treating me like a nonperson.

T: Ah. Can you feel your body shaking with that one? [The therapist asks the patient to contact body sensation to what is being expressed.]

P: Yes.

T: OK. You kinda hit bull's-eye there. I want you just to stay with that, and I wonder if you—like, I don't know where your pain is. Is it on the left side, over here? [The therapist is checking out the patient's physical limitations.]

P: Yeah, somewhat—

T: OK. Is it all right for you to stand up?

P: Yeah.

T: OK. Usually anger is done a lot better from a standing position than on our rumps. [Since it is the position of FEP that the whole person—cognitive, sensory, and affective—is needed to complete a Gestalt, the request to stand is appropriate. Standing enhances the involvement of the body in the subsequent work, as well as providing a psychological antidote to the weak and victimized posture of the patient earlier in this session.] And I'm glad you put that Kleenex down just now, 'cause you only need that for the sad side, the hurting side. Just hang on to this bataca and I'll show you how to use it. "Jerry, I'm mad at you for . . ." (*Therapist hits empty chair with a loud bang, and patient has a strong startled reaction to force of the noise*). You OK? you still with us?

P: Yeah (*some hesitation and fear in voice*).

T: All right. [The therapist continues the modeling.] Hit with the bat while you say things like, "Jerry, I'm angry at you for not listening to me. I'm angry at you for making me into a nonperson." Now just try it out, you know, just let yourself do something physical along with the stuff you're saying to him. [The therapist suggests bringing the cognitive and sensory domains together.]

P: Oh, I don't feel very good about doing that.

T: OK. Just notice what your head's saying to your right now. What's the message? [The therapist encourages the patient to acknolwedge the cognitive part of the organism.]

P: I don't know. (*Pause*) "Nice ladies don't do that." [Another common societal injunction.]

T: You bet. Nice ladies just get a lot of pain in their bodies and a whole lot of stuff inside. Eh?

P: Yeah, right (*laughing in acknowledgment*).

T: OK. Now I don't think there are any judges in here, as far as I know, and Dave [the cotherapist] and I certainly don't qualify as judges, so, you know, there's no judge here to judge you as bad for doing that. So—[The therapist confronts the judgmental "critical parent" of the patient.]

P: Just *me*.

T: Just you, and you've got a heavy one there, huh?

P: Mmm-hmm.

T: He's a tough judge, or is it a "he" judge? [The therapist checks to see whether the judge may represent father and/or husband introjection.]

P: No, it's me (*nervous laugh*).

T: OK. All right. Now, if you're willing to, you could send her outside the door till we get some work done.

P: OK.

T: Want to do that?

P: Yeah.

T: Try it out loud. "Hey, judge, get the hell out of here!" or whatever.

P: Hey, judge, get off my back! [After 16 years of chronic back pain!]

T: That's so, right? OK. Now just see what it's like for you. Did you ever get hit as a child? [The therapist makes a final and direct exploration of physical abuse history.]

P: Mmm-hmm.

T: Yeah. OK. That jump sure looked like it.

P: Not real hard, though.

T: Not real hard, but enough to scare you, huh?

P: My first husband hit me a lot.

T: All right. OK. All right. Well, listen, that makes it a lot harder to do.

P: It's scary.

T: You bet, and it's even more important, then, that you're able to get over that hump of "this is not bad to do this." Now, if I was hitting you over the head, then that becomes bad. All right? [The therapist clarifies the difference between symbolic completion and completion face to face.]

P: Yeah, OK.

T: But here I'm just getting it out, so I don't have to hit anybody over the head.

P: OK.

T: All right? "So here we are, Jerry. . . . I am furious at you, man."

P: I am really angry at you. You don't know how angry I am at you. [The patient shows a new resolution to attend to the unfinished angers from the past.]

T: "But I'm gonna show you."

P: Yeah. I'm gonna show you, I think (*laughing*). [Great self-honesty from the patient!]

T: Oh, what did you think of to make you backtrack there? OK. Try it again. OK, try out, "I am going to show you my anger for a change." [The therapist calls for one more try.]

P: I *am* going to show you my anger for a change. I really am. [The patient makes an authentic and meaning-full commitment.] Ooohh. [She is surprised at taking such a risk of confrontation.]

T: So you just feel it when it's in there, see, 'cause that's your signal, that's your sign of what you're holding on to.

P: Boy, I'm really angry at you. Oh—(*strikes cushion, laughs*)

T: How'd that feel? [The patient is encouraged to process the physical response.]

P: That felt good (*laughing*).

T: To hit it? OK. You might get addicted to this, but—you can walk around with a bataca hanging off your hand all the time. Try it again.

P: I ought to take these shoes off.

T: Oh, good. Thank you. You're way ahead of me. That's good.

P: (*Mumbles*)

T: Yeah, you're down on the floor—

P: From the shoes (*laughing—removes her shoes spontaenously*).

T: Right. OK.

P: I'm really (*striking cushion*) angry (*laughing*). [Laughter tends to dilute the effect of the anger.]

T: All right, yeah, right. OK. So you don't get that left side to hurting or anything, see what happens if you come down this way more than you come across this way [Swinging the bataca in a brushing-away manner indicates the possibility of a deflective internal position.] All right? [The patient is asked to use the bataca so that she doesn't deflect her anger, but rather expresses it directly in a focused fashion.] Is that any different or is that—OK. All right, OK. Now I'm gonna get back so you can just concentrate on Jerry and I want you to tell him in a sentence as you hit, "I am angry at you for da-da-da-da-da. Another thing I'm angry at you for is da-da-da-da-da."

P: Oh, man, I can't even think of all the reasons.

T: OK. You just pick one at a time, just one at a time.

P: I'm angry because you make me (*strikes cushion*) feel like a nonperson.

T: All right. Yeah, let the air come out. [She has not been exhaling to this point.]

P: You make me feel like I (*strikes cushion*) don't matter. Boy! (*Strikes cushion*)

T: What was that one? 'Cause you started, you said "Boy!" and then you didn't tell him the rest of it.

P: Yeah, I'm trying to think of the words! [She is choking off her expression.]

T: The words? all right, all right, that's all right.

P: I can't even think of the words.

ANOTHER PATIENT: (*To focal patient*) Are you left-handed?

T: You're left-handed?

P: No, I'm right-handed.

T: OK.

P: No, I'm just trying—

T: Yeah, it's kind of hard to get both—these are bad bats in that regard, you can't get both hands up. But that's about as good a way to grab it as any way. [A side discussion on the use of the bat arises from comments of her fellow group members, who are trying to be helpful.]

P: Yeah (*laughing*). Two-handed.

T: Yeah, right. Two-handed. "Two-fisted anger, Jerry—that's what I've been holding a long time."

P: That makes me mad, too.

T: Oh, yeah. Tell him. "Jerry, I'm mad about . . ." [The therapist directs the patient back to the significant other.]

P: I can't even talk! (*Strikes cushion and suddenly lets out a shout*) [The patient achieves a breakthrough by opening up the vocal passageway.]

T: All right! Keep saying that to him. Get that passagway opened up there.

P: Mad! (*Strikes*) Can't even talk! (*Strikes*)

T: All right, go ahead. Keep working. That's it! Go! Go ahead! Go ahead! [The therapist reinforces the patient for use of verbal plus physical expression.]

P: Feel it! (*Repeated strikes with bataca*)

T: Go ahead, Fern! Go on! That's—yeah. Now tell him real quickly now how that felt before you lose it. "Jerry, that felt . . ." [The purpose here is to assist the patient in making the connection between emotional release and physiological response immediately following the release.]

P: That felt good. Boy, that felt like I was giving you back some.

T: Now you're on track, now you can get rid of as much as you want to today, and you don't have to take it with you as leave here. You can just leave it right here. [More encouragement by therapist.]

P: Oh, boy! (*Strikes*) there!

T: Tell him, "There, Jerry, that's for . . ." What? [The therapist asks the patient to specify the anger.]

P: (*Strikes*) That's for making me miserable!

T: All right, OK.

P: (*Strikes*) That's for making me feel sick!

T: OK. Just keep with the feelings, but I want to show you something you're doing. Watch me. (*Thereapist re-enacts patient's hitting herself with bat on each backswing*)

P: Oh, I hit myself! (*Laughs*)

T: Yeah, you give him one, then give yourself one, see, to keep it even! Now, if you really want to unload it, just keep it out here in front, see, and don't let yourself hit yourself. All right? Because it belongs to Jerry. [The therapist instructs the patient on how to break up retroflective hitting of herself with the bat.]

P: (*Turns to therapist*) Another thing I'm mad about—

T: Right. Tell him. [The therapist directs her to keep the focus on the significant other.]

P: I (*striking*) take it out on myself!

T: All right! "But right now I'm not!" (Retroflective self-abuse has been broken.]

P: I'm sick of being sick! (*Kicks the cushion*) [The patient adds more of her physical self to the work.]

T: That's it! Tell him how that kick felt.

P: That felt good, too!

T: I'll bet. Tell him if you've ever wanted to really kick him.

P: Boy, I coudn't tell you how many times I wanted to kick you.

T: Can you tell him where you wanted to kick him?

P: In the shin—

T: All right.

P: —Where it hurts. Boy! I just wish that you could (*strikes*) feel what it (*strikes*) feels like when somebody (*strikes*) laughs at you!

T: All right! "When you laugh at me, I get angry at you, man!" [The therapist brings the patient's verbalization back to herself.]

P: Oh, yeah, I get angry at you. You make me (*strikes*) feel (*strikes*) crazy.

T: "But today I'm not gonna feel crazy. I just feel angry." [The patient is encouraged to separate the feeling of "crazy" from the expression of anger.]

P: You make me angry, and (*strikes*) then, when I get (*strikes*) angry, you laugh! And then I think I am crazy. But I'm not crazy. Boy! [She has rejected that old message.]

T: How did that feel?

P: That feels good.

T: All right, now, are you keeping track of your stomach and your chest and your head? [The therapist asks the patient to check out the benchmarks established at the beginning of the session.]

P: Yes.

T: Can you feel anything changing?

P: My head doesn't hurt any more. [One benchmark is gone.]

T: All right, OK. We're on track—

P: And my stomach is not queasy any more. [Another benchmark is gone.]

T: All right, great.

P: I still feel a little shaky. [Another benchmark is still present.]

T: OK. You've got some more time, if you'd like to take it with him, and just give yourself another 5 minutes with him and see how much you can unload right here that you don't want to take home with you. [The therapist gives the patient a clue—"another 5 minutes"—that the session will be coming to a close.]

P: I don't want to take any of it home.

T: All right.

P: I'm (*strikes*) tired of it.

T: Give it to him, that a way.

P: Boy—(*strikes*) tired (*strikes*), sick and tired, tired!

T: All right. Now, let me suggest something, that, instead of getting tired about it, you get angry about it. ["Sick and tired" merely leaves a patient *sick* and *tired*—we recommend that patients try being angry instead.]

P: I am angry. Oooh!

T: All right, use angry words now. All right? "I resent you for . . .", "I'm angry at you for . . .", "I'm pissed at you for . . ." [The therapist instructs the patient in use of "I" language.]

P: I resent you for putting me in the middle between you and Kathy. [A "go-between" position usually produces resentment.]

T. All right. Get yourself out of there, don't let him do that. Hand that back to him.

P: Boy! You want to punish her, you want to do mean things to her, and you make me tell her! (*Air is coming out of her lungs now*)

T: "So what I'm furious with you about . . ."

P: Do your own damn dirty work!

T: Oh, boy, feel how that one felt! [The therapist asks the patient to acknowledge sensory feedback as soon as she takes a self respectful position on the issue.]

P: Boy!

T: Feel your body, 'cause it will tell you how you're doing. [The patient is encouraged to use the body for assessment of progress.]

P: Feels good. [The patient acknowledges change.]

T: Huh? Feels good?

P: Yeah, that feels good.

T: All right, good.

P: I don't believe it. (*Looks and sounds surprised*)

T: Tell Jerry—I want to call him Sam. Tell him—you got a Sam in your life by any chance?

P: Nope (*laughing*), not yet! [Certainly no traces of a victim in that response!]

T: OK. Watch those predictions.

P: Oh, boy, I'm angry at you!

T: For? [The therapist elicits focus through verbal specification.]

P: Angry because you try to make me feel old and ugly and unfeminine, like a piece of goddamn furniture!

T: All right!

P: Ohh!

T: Tell him how it's feeling. "Hey, Jerry . . . !" [The therapist asks the patient to acknowledge to the significant other that progress has been made.]

P: Boy, does that feel good! Let me tell you something, Jerry, how does it feel?

T: Tell him how it feels from your side.

P: Boy, it feels good. Let me tell you. I don't feel crazy, I don't feel out of control, I just feel mad! [The patient has destroyed some of the old "tapes" about being crazy and out of control.]

T: Beautiful! Right on!

COTHERAPIST (C): Would you try saying, instead of "It feels good," "*I feel good*"? Let's see if that's different for you. [Cotherapist asks patient to use "I" language.]

P: "I feel good"? I don't think I quite believe that. [Consistent self-honesty from patient.]

T: OK. Tell him what keeps you from believing you feel good right now. [The therapist urges the patient to identify the block.]

P: I know what it is. You got that damn hook in me, that's what it is.

T: There you go. Come on, feel that one.

P: You and that shittin' hook. Oh!

T: All right. Tell him.

P: Be a good little girl, Fern! Be a good little wife! [Society's injunctions are still in operation.]

T: "Don't you raise your voice to me, Fern!"

P: Don't raise your voice to me! Cook! Clean! Do all the bookkeeping [private business of the family] work!

T: Feel that hook. ["Hooks" are usually loaded with introjections plus predictions of what will happen if the introjections are disregarded.]

P: Don't live!

T: Yeah.

P: Just do what you want, and forget what I want! The hell with that! [The patient "unhooks" from the crippling injunctions.]

T: Yeah, that's it. Feel it as it boils to the surface.

P: Boy!

C: Just keep focusing on that—

P: Yeah, I know what that hook is. If you get mad at me, right? Big hook, and I'm gonna stop breathing, or something. Well, it ain't true! [Another unhooking.]

C: What are you gonna do instead? [The cotherapist leads the patient to own her power by committing herself to some type of behavior.]

P: I don't know (*laughing*). I'm angry at you because you make me feel like my whole life depends on whether you're happy or not! If you like me or not! (*To therapist*) That thing's going down my pants (*laughing—referring to videotape microphone*). I was wondering what (*laughing*)—

T: You thought you were really getting some changes in there, huh? (*General laughing in the group*)

T: Tell him about the hook and where it is right now, how deeply it's in there or whether you're getting it out, where you stand with it.

P: You and that hook. (*Strikes the cushion*) Boy! I'm not gonna let you have that hook in me any more! [The patients shows a firm commitment to change.]

T: Tell him how that felt before you lose it right now? [The therapist requests the patient to acknowledge any progress in the moment it is experienced.]

P: Boy! NO MORE HOOK! Boy! (*Hits cushion with force as she verbalizes*)

T: All right.

P: No more! I'm not gonna let you do that to me.

T: Yeah. "I am not letting you do that to me right now." [The therapist brings the patient to the here-and-now.]

P: No. And I'm not letting you do that to me now. And I'm not afraid that I'm angry at you. [The patient experiences release from her fear.]

T: Oh, boy. Feel that.

P: Boy, that—that's the truth. I'm not afraid. Oh, boy, that feels good. I feel good. I feel good.

T: OK. Yeah.

P: I didn't crack up. [The patient has tested her prediction of the first part of the session, and realizes it has no validity.]

T: You can lose control and not crack up, huh?

P: That's right. I'm still in one piece. [Verification of self.]

T: Now I know that you got things really going for you, and I'm gonna have to ask you to just begin to wrap up with Jerry, and the way I'd like for you to do is just tell him what you got done today with him. [The therapist initiates closure of the session—part of assessment is done by telling the significant other what was accomplished in the work.]

P: Well, if nothing else, you know how I feel now. *I* know how *I* feel. And I'm not gonna let you make me eat myself alive any more. *No more.* And you're gonna know how I feel, too. I'm not gonna let you laugh at me any more.

T: OK. "If you do laugh at me, I'll . . ." [Patient cannot stop significant other from laughing.]

P: If you do laugh at me, I'm just gonna tell you anyway. [Patient can express her feelings anyway.]

T: All right. Beautiful.

P: And I'm sure he will.

T: That may be, but you can still do your thing. Tell him how you feel about what you did with him today.

P: I feel good about what I did today. I feel really good about it. I feel like I've got my life back, it's back in my hands. And you're not pulling my strings. Oh! Boy! [The patient feels self-approval and competence; she no longer feels like a victim.]

T: Tell him about your body and what it's feeling right now. [Final check on benchmarks.]

P: Just telling you this stuff and bashing you like that, my body doesn't hurt, that headache is gone. [Two more benchmarks are gone.]

C: What about your left leg? Is that any different?

P: That is kind of—it doesn't hurt, it's kind of stiff or, no like when you use a muscle a lot and it's sore the next day, that's what it feels like.

C: OK. Tell him [her husband] what it feels like.

P: Pains in my leg, pains in my back, pains in my head, sick to my stomach, and all because I was afraid to be angry at you. (*Pause*) No more. No more. [The patient acknowledges the connection between her chronic pain and her suppression of her emotional system] I'm just gonna tell you, and I'm gonna keep telling you until you hear me!

T: Sounds fabulous!

P: Wow! You should know how good I feel. Oh boy, Jerry, you should just know.

C: You look like you're finished.

P: Yes. I think I'm finished.

T: Why don't you just thank him for coming in here and letting you beat on him for a while? [The therapist elicits the goodbye—closure of the work.]

P: (*Lauging*) Thanks for letting me beat on you. Thanks for coming.

T: Just say goodbye to him any way you wish to say goodbye.

P: OK. (*Makes a kissing sound, laughs puts arms out in a big hug, and closes eyes*) [Once anger is released, the loving part can be truly and authentically felt and expressed.]

T: All right! You can feel that even after you get all this anger out, right?

P: Yeah, I really love him. I really do.

T: I'd just suggest you just have a seat for a moment here and just feel what you've gotten out of the work that you've done, because you worked hard for it, you earned every bit you got. [The assessment phase was conducted after the session was over, since time limitations on use of the counseling room did not allow for that discussion in its usual spot following the closure of work.]

T: (*Turning to group*) If the rest of you just notice what you're feeling, I know we're running short on time, but I'd still like to just get some feedback from each of you. [The therapist sets up a "tailgate" possibility.] Ordinarily we'd have a little more time, and then if you had some work to do as a result of what Fern has been doing, then we'd go right directly to that; but today we won't be able to do that, because we don't have that kind of time. [A "round" of the group is conducted before ending the session, so that other group members can share their reactions to what happened to them as the work was being done; can briefly give feedback in terms of appreciation to the person who worked (analysis, interpretation, or evaluation of the piece of work is considered inappropriate); and can verbalize their commitment to a work contract, possibly in the next session.]

The fifth step of the procedure (carrying the work outside of the session) followed the fourth step (assessment) out in the hall after the counseling room was emptied. The patient asked whether her husband and daughter could review the videotape, since they were not present for the actual session. Arrangements were made for the three of them to view the tape 1 week after the session above. After the tape was over, the husband summed up his reaction in one comment: "I've been waiting 16 years for that to happen." This indicated that both she and he knew what was really going on in their relationship, but were afraid to confront it openly because of predictions based upon unrealistic introjections.

10

Training in Focused Expressive Psychotherapy

The body of Gestalt literature has expanded over the past several years (Heimelstein, 1982), but the portion of that literature given to training and supervision has remained relatively small. Greenberg (1980) and Harman (1977) have emphasized the importance of therapeutic methods that deepen experience and promote awareness; they believe that training must teach the specific skills necessary to implement those methods. Greenberg and Sarkissian (1984) believe that two types of skills must be taught. The first are perceptual skills (e.g., the ability to recognize common recurring events in the therapy process, such as a split or specific unfinished business). The second is a set of procedural skills needed to intervene effectively in the identified recurring events.

Those authors who address issues of training in the therapeutic methods of Gestalt theory are uniform in their belief that such a therapy cannot be reduced to a "bag of tricks" (Harman & Tarleton, 1983) or "a few gimmicks" (Mintz, 1983). The continual emphasis is on solid theoretical grounding in Gestalt theory and in experiential learning principles (Feder, 1980; Greenberg & Sarkissian, 1984). Mintz (1983) believes that the moment-to-moment focus of Gestalt therapy makes it important to introduce students not only to traditional lecture material, but also to experiential phases of training and supervision as well.

In previous chapters, we have discussed the importance of therapist warmth, caring, collaboration, and credibility. These characteristics are not easily trained; they are developed through years of social process. Yet we believe that they are essential and that technical proficiency in FEP or any other procedure will not make up for their absence. In our own programs, therefore, we attempt to recruit only those who are able to demonstrate these nonspecific skills in their lives and in screening interviews. We also believe that training in specific procedures should be founded on general knowledge and training in human behavior and should be preceded by specific training in those skills that will facilitate decisions about whom to treat. A familiarity with normal development, diagnostic systems, and assessment procedures should be combined with prior successful experiences as a helping professional to prepare for training in FEP. A terminal degree in a mental health discipline is not a prerequisite to beginning specific training, but does help insure that the foundations of knowledge are present. We find that for more advanced training, prior or contiguous graduate work is a virtual necessity.

Training in FEP consists of three phases:

1. Theory development.
2. Specific skill training.
3. Experiential learning.

Table 10.1 contains a protocol for these three levels of training.

Phase 1: Theory Development

Phase 1 of FEP training, theory development, takes place over an intensive period consisting of 45 hours of training spaced over 3-week or 5-week blocks of time. Trainees have 30 hours of classroom time, during which an experienced FEP therapist teaches the theoretical assumptions; the role of the counselor and counselee; the dynamics of change, and process, methodology, and evaluation. Table 10.2 provides a typical schedule for this initial phase of training.

Trainees spend the remaining 15 hours of Phase 1 training in an FEP therapy group. The groups are led by experienced FEP therapists, and trainees participate like any other group members. In Phase 1 groups, therapy is facilitated by the experienced FEP therapist and follows the FEP format as specified in this manual. Some time may be taken at the end of a specific piece of work or at the end of each 3-hour session to relate the work of the group to the theory taught within the 30 hours of didactic instruction. Group members, whose work is discussed in terms of theory and the application of interventions, are always given the option of staying for the theoretical discussion or of leaving the group temporarily. Some are interested in the discussion and gain additional personal insight, while others do not want to be distracted from the impact of their personal work and therefore choose to leave during the discussion period.

Phase 1 group experience places the emphasis on doing personal work in the FEP model in order to gain "experiential understanding." No one is required to work, but it is rare that someone does not. It is important to note that trainees are advised before taking the course that the therapy group is an integral part of Phase 1 training.

TABLE 10.1. Clinical Training for FEP Therapists

Puposes:
1. To provide theoretical basis for understanding this therapeutic specialty.
2. To develop skills in FEP.
3. To identify counselors who are competent in FEP.

Program:

Phase 1: Preliminary Training Level (45 hours)
   Basic workshop in FEP (or its equivalent)
   Content
   • Lectures on theory.
   • Demonstrations (*in vivo* and video).
   • Group work.
   • Tape cutting and review *à la* FEP Compliance Scale.
   Final exam over theoretical concepts.

Phase 2: First Semester Advanced Training (45 hours)
   Entrance requirements:
   1. Working understanding of Gestalt theory.
   2. Tape of a session from basic workshop.
   3. Statement of personal and professional goals.
   4. Recommendations from other professionals in the field.
   5. Master's degree in helping profession (or its equivalent)—graduate students "in
      progress" may be accepted with training staff approval.
   Content:
   • Personal work using the model.
   • Introduction to supervision.
   • Fifteen 3-hour sessions in a group limited to 12 members co-led by FEP therapists.
   • Supervision/review/criteria by coleaders, by
      Phase 3 advanced trainees, and by Phase 2 trainees in triads.

Phase 3: Second Semester Advanced Training (45 hours)
   Requirements: Completion of Phases 1 and 2.
   Content:
   • Emphasis on clinical supervision.
   • Some supervision of trainees in Phase 2.
   • Required number of taped FEP sessions.
   • Review of required number of tapes using FEP Compliance Scale.
   • Live supervision.
   • Personal work as needed/appropriate.

Phase 2: Skill Training and Experiential Learning

Phase 2 of FEP training is limited to those with advanced degrees in the
helping professions or those in advanced degree programs who are approaching their practicum or externship. This phase of training takes place
in a group format with a limit of 12 participants and 2 FEP trainers in each
group. The group meets once a week for 2½ hours, over the course of four

TABLE 10.2. Phase 1 of FEP Training: Schedule

Day	Content of session
Monday	Overview of course Get acquainted Form groups
Tuesday	Lecture—Introduction to FEP Position of persons/theoretical assumptions
Wednesday	Work group
Thursday	Lecture—Role of the counselor/counselee and dynamics of the model
Friday	Work group
Monday	Lecture—Process of the model *Triads—Bring tape recorder
Tuesday	Lecture—Methods/techniques of the model
Wednesday	Work group
Thursday	Lecture—Evaluation procedures in the model *Triads—Bring tape recorder
Friday	Work group
Monday	Use of model in education, business, probation, marriage, family, etc.
Tuesday	Research and special applications
Wednesday	Group work *Final tape due
Thursday	Catch-up day *and* final exam (2 hours) *Readings due
Friday	Wrap-up and good-bye

Note. The session on each day runs from 9 A.M. to 12 noon. Asterisks indicate special reminders to trainees.

months, with one extended 6-hour meeting relatively close to the beginning of this phase.

The Phase 2 group is a combination therapy group and training group. The members continue to be active in their own self-therapy, as in Phase 1, but additionally assume the role of therapist for others in the group. This concept of training is analogous to the Gestalt position on patient practice, which advocates a "safe emergency" in which the patient can experiment with and experience new behaviors. In the Phase 2 group, the trainee has a safe place to experiment with the practice of FEP therapy. The expertise of the trainers provides the safety necessary for some to assume the role of patient and for others to take the role of therapist in the training sessions. This method of training also provides trainees an opportunity to observe *in vivo* behaviors of the therapists, a need recognized by Matarazzo and Patterson (1986).

FEP trainers have become aware of the need described by Feder (1980) to balance training experiences between therapy and didactic learning. One must ensure that the process does not drift into being simply a therapy group or does not retreat to the "safety" of sterile didactic learning. A balance of training and therapy in the skill training group affords the trainee time to have both personal experience through continued personal therapy, and professional experience through practicing the steps of FEP (Holiman & Engle, in press).

Theory is taught in two ways. First, a portion of the training time is specifically devoted to the didactic presentation of theoretical material. This material gives specific attention to the fine-tuning techniqes found in Chapter 7 of this manual. Second, after a piece of work that is illustrative of a particular FEP concept has been completed, that concept is highlighted and discussed.

The microskills necessary for the identification of unfinished business and the establishment of experiments are often taught in early training sessions where trainees work in triads (therapist, patient, observer). Harman and Tarleton (1983) support the suggestion that triads are an effective method of learning experiential techniques and processes. In our experience, triad training helps trainees avoid pitfalls such as asking too many questions or setting up experiments prematurely, because the third party can observe and give feedback on such issues as they arise.

The Phase 2 group uses the first meeting to identify personal growth goals (to elicit work to be done as a group member) and professional goals (to provide training guidelines for trainers). The second and third sessions focus on training of skills needed to identify the firt two steps of the FEP model (identification of work and establishment of a commitment) and the beginning of the third step (introduction of the experiment). Thereafter, the group runs as an FEP therapy group until the group is ready for skill training in working with emotional arousal and contact boundary interruptions.

Microskills are introduced and practiced as suggested by Greenberg and Sarkissian (1984). Microskills taught in this phase include practice in the identification of the markers for unfinished business, the process of moving the patient into a here-and-now experiment, and the enhancement of emotional arousal.

When the group gathers for the experiential phase of training, the trainers lead a check-in round, which is similar to a regular FEP group except that each person identifies two things: the desire for time to do personal work, and the readiness to act in the role of therapist. Once the round is complete, the trainers announce that the floor is open for work. When someone takes the working chair as a patient, the trainers ask that person to choose a therapist from among those who said they were willing. The trainee therapist does two things before beginning. The first is to choose someone aside from the trainers to be a primary observer, identifying what he or she wants feedback about. The second is to make an agreement with the trainers about how to structure "help" from the trainers. Some choose to stop at predesignated times to talk about their "map," while others simply work out a signal that they want or need help from the trainers.

Experience demonstrates that these interruptions do not interfere with the patient's therapy process, because the patient usually learns from the discussion between trainee and trainer, an observation also reported by Harman and Tarleton (1983).

Feedback is given immediately, because it is found to be most effective if applied in this way (Berger & Dammann, 1982; Doyle, Foreman, & Wales, 1977). Feedback is given to the therapist in sequence, beginning with the patient, followed by the "observer," and concluding with the trainers. Trainees are taught to be specific with the information and feedback (Payne, Winter, & Perry, 1975). For example, instead of "I thought you did well in that session," the trainee is encouraged to identify therapist behaviors or interventions that were productive. Once the feedback is given, group members have time to share personal reactions, and then the floor is again open for a new patient and a new therapist.

Training sessions are audiotaped or videotaped, and a trainee is asked to review the tape of his or her session and to use the FEP Compliance Scale (Appendix 1) to reinforce the steps and assess his or her skill with FEP. Kelley (1971) has also found that self-confrontation through the use of taped sessions results in productive outcomes, and trainees are encouraged to give themselves feedback.

At the end of Phase 2, the members of the training group meet with the trainers for individual evaluation. Those who demonstrate a basic, consistent proficiency in FEP in this training phase are encouraged to enter Phase 3.

Phase 3: Experiential Learning and Supervision

In Phase 3, training evolves into a supervision contract. Trainees use FEP in counseling patients from the community, and contract with experienced trainers to supervise their work. Supervision is done either through the use of audiotapes or videotapes or *in situ*, as suggested by Harman and Tarleton (1983). Once trainees can demonstrate consistent, competent use of FEP in an actual work setting, they have completed the training. Competence is determined by supervisors' and independent observers' ratings on the FEP Compliance Scale (Appendix 1).

Special Training Issues

Harman and Tarleton (1983) speak of the tendency of students of Gestalt therapy to move too quickly into an experiment. Often, a premature experiment results when the therapist has not listened closely to or clarified at the beginning what the patient wants. FEP trainers find the same tendency, and attack this problem by using early skill training to practice getting a clear, mutually agreed-upon task for the session. Trainers will also intervene when it is clear that the therapist is widely off target or is moving too quickly.

Expressive and Gestalt psychotherapies call for the therapist to take a relatively directive stance with the patient, as compared to other therapies (Beutler, 1983; Greenberg, 1980; Greenberg & Sarkissian, 1984). In training, the trainees begin to develop the ability to keep a patient in a successful experiment when they learn to switch from questioning, clarifying, and reflecting to the use of direct activity. Both modeling such directed activity by trainers and using skill training help trainees make the transition. Skill training creates practice opportunities for therapists to guide role-playing "patients" through experiments. FEP trainees quickly learn that there is value in teaching patients what to do once experiments are set up. They also learn that once an experiment is established, the therapist can effectively move from an inquiry mode to a mode of primarily making process suggestions and behavioral observations.

It takes time for trainees to learn to develop tailor-made experiments. FEP trainers are reluctant to do many demonstration counseling sessions because it fosters a tendency for trainees to copy the experiments, rather than to respond to the specific needs of specific patients. Continuing to stress the theoretical basis for FEP, emphasizing the experimental nature of any intervention, and teaching a wide range of possible interventions can minimize this danger somewhat.

Sometimes the "personal work" of a trainee focuses on issues surrounding predicted performance as a therapist. For example, a Phase 2 trainee may identify that he or she is having a difficult time volunteering to be a therapist. If that person takes the "working chair" as patient, he or she can address the conflict split (e.g., "Part of me wants to and part of me is scared") often associated with being a therapist in a live supervision situation. This work often produces a resolution to the struggle and an increased readiness to experiment with being therapist.

Trainees in the experiential training phases often express appreciation for the opportunity to work with "live" as opposed to "role-play" situations. They are in a situation where they know there is backup support from supervisors if they get in over their heads. This allows the freedom to move ahead with issues they might otherwise shy away from in a closed, one-on-one situation. The safety of having a "backup" resource also allows supervisors to observe when a therapist is backing off and to explore with the trainee what intrapersonal issues may be manifested in such patterns.

Finally, it is useful to gather information about patterns of the performance of trainees. Evaluation of 46 sessions, using the FEP Compliance Scale in Appendix 1, revealed that one group of trainees had a tendency to be weak at the beginning of a session in establishing the psychophysical benchmarks. At the end of the session, they often neglected to have the patient complete the session by evaluating the value of the work. Finally, they needed to develop specific homework more adequately with each patient. Understanding these tendencies across a number of sessions greatly aided trainers to know what to stress in both the didactic and experiential phases of the training.

Validation of Training Procedures

Our work has resulted in the compilation of data to suggest that FEP is both a teachable method and one that can be applied in a reliable fashion by trained therapists. The first outline of the present manual was pilot-tested through a procedure that entailed measurement of therapy compliance through role-playing activities following a series of intensive training sessions. The subjects for this pilot investigation were 14 graduate students and professional therapists who participated in a workshop on experiential psychotherapy.

A review of the role-playing exercises and trainee compliance suggested that the procedures were promising. Subsequently, a more systematic pilot investigation was undertaken. For this investigation, five therapists were recruited from the community for training in FEP, and two similarly experienced therapists were chosen for training in a comparison procedure that consisted of a pain education group. All of these therapists were selected on the basis of the following criteria:

1. Prior training and experience in group treatments.
2. A PhD and internship (or its equivalent) in professional psychology, or an MD and residency in psychiatry.
3. A license to practice in one of these two specialty areas.
4. At least 1 year of professional experience.

Work samples in the form of audiotapes or videotapes of each of the therapist applicants' actual therapy were also requested; these were reviewed along with the *curricula vitae*, prior to selection, by two senior-level therapists. This material was used to ensure the presence of acceptable levels of skill in responding to patients with empathic acceptance and concern.

From a list of 11 applicants, 5 psychologist therapists were selected for initial training in FEP. One of these therapists was subsequently unable to participate in the project because of a last-minute scheduling conflict. In view of time constraints, this therapist was not replaced. Similarly, from 5 applicants who initially expressed interest in conducting a pain education group after training was concluded in each treatment model, 2 therapists were selected for participation in the study, on the basis of achieving pre-established cutoff scores of competency on the appropriate compliance scales.

In order to assure that the four therapists who were to do FEP could be trained to perform the procedures of FEP, specific comparisons were made both with the therapists' own pretraining performance and with the other two therapists' performance in the pain education group. A scale was constructed in order to facilitate these comparisons. The FEP Compliance Scale (Appendix 1) is a fully anchored instrument that identifies how well a therapist being rated complies with the requirements of the FEP treatment model.

As a first test of training efficacy, FEP Compliance Scale scores of the four FEP therapists were compared from pre- to posttraining. This was accomplished using indices of performance extracted from the material submitted as work samples during the selection phase as pretest scores. Compliance scores obtained on pretraining work samples were contrasted with compliance scores obtained from three therapy samples observed during the final phase of training. In order to obtain these end-of-training ratings, all subjects were asked to conduct two therapy interviews with patients from a university community who were recruited for this purpose. Requests for volunteers desiring free counseling were circulated to selected graduate classes.

Each therapist was observed during the therapy interviews, and FEP Compliance Scale scores were computed by two trained raters who were experienced in the treatment method. Total pretraining scores ($M = 3.96$, $SD = 2.03$) were compared with posttraining scores ($M = 5.85$, $SD = 1.56$), using nonindependent t tests on each subject. The mean t value that resulted from these four comparisons was 3.31 ($df = 20$), and all but one of the individual comparisons were significant beyond the .01 level of probability.

A second test of the training procedure was undertaken by comparing two FEP trainees and the two pain education group trainees. These assessments were designed to confirm the discriminability of the treatment procedures. A between-groups t test was conducted on each sex-matched therapist pair (one FEP therapist and one pain education therapist in each of the two comparisons). Observations of the fifth session of the two contrasting forms of therapy provided the data for this comparison. Each of the four therapists was rated utilizing each of two compliance questionnaires, the

FEP Compliance Scale and the Educational Therapy Compliance Scale, which were constructed for this project. Independent results ranged from $t (20) = 2.25, p < .01$, to $t (20) = 6.60, p < .01$, for the four comparisons. In all comparisons, differences in scores on the FEP Compliance Scale for the pain education therapists on this scale, $M = 2.24, SD = 1.97$) attained the highest t values. In each case, the therapists in the two treatment conditions performed differently, confirming the discriminative validity of the two treatments.

In a final study, the training procedure was assessed by comparing the FEP Compliance Scale scores of two FEP therapists and those of two therapists who were conducting cognitive therapy as part of another investigation of group treatments. Scores for these two groups of therapists were computed on the basis of videotapes of therapy groups obtained during the treatment phase of the investigation. Independent t tests comparing each therapist on the FEP Compliance Scale measures all achieved significances, mean $t (20) = 6.76, p < 0.01$; this suggested that the therapist in FEP and cognitive therapy performed in a discriminatively different manner. FEP therapists earned consistently higher FEP Compliance Scale scores than did cognitive therapists (for the cognitive therapists, $M = 2.40, SD = 1.83$).

The reader will note that FEP therapists consistently performed higher on the FEP Compliance Scale measures at the end of training than did (1) they themselves before training; (2) therapists conducting pain education groups, who were recruited in a similar way; and (3) cognitive therapists, who had also gone through intensive, criteria-based training.

Summary

The literature on Gestalt therapy training, while sparse, is consistent in calling for training that emphasizes theory development, skill training, and experiential learning.

The first phase of FEP training teaches theory development in an intensive course, which also has experiential learning included. A second phase of the training continues to develop theory, while trainees begin to assume the role of therapist in the combination training–therapy group. Emphasis in this phase is on supervised practice in the model. Theory is taught in minilectures and in reviews of the therapy work done in the training group. Skill training also allows trainees to develop facility with subcomponents of the FEP model.

A specific format has been developed for each of the skill training meetings, in which members alternate between the roles of client and counselor. FEP trainers have found that open discussion between supervisor and therapist of the work being done in the training does not interrupt therapeutic work.

The third and final phase of training offers individual supervision for trainees while they work with clients in a variety of group settings.

Trainers use skill training to keep trainees from premature movement into or out of experiments. The personal therapy work of trainees affords other trainees the opportunity to work with "live" as opposed to "role-play" situations.

APPENDIX 1

FEP Compliance Scale

Therapist: _____   Patient: _____

Date: _____   Rater: _____

Videotape: _____   Audiotape: _____   Live Observation: _____

Directions: You are to rate the therapist on scales of 1–7. Every second item on each scale is anchored. Midpoints are to be used when your rating falls between the anchored items. Use only whole numbers in your ratings.

Please do not leave any item blank, except where rater choices are indicated. For all items, focus on the skill of the *therapist*. Rate only therapist behavior.

Note: The emotion described in this form is anger, which is often constricted. However, the patient may present other constricted emotion. When this happens, use the items to reflect how well the therapist worked with the unfinished sadness, grief, fear, hurt, etc.

Part I. Identification of the Work

1. Focusing:

1 ———— 2 ———— 3 ———— 4 ———— 5 ———— 6 ———— 7

Therapist did not attempt identification of specific piece of unfinished business.	Therapist allowed identification of unfinished business to be vague or incomplete for the session.	Therapist helped patient to identify a specific piece of unfinished business for the session.
		Therapist was extremely clear in developing a specific focus, congruent with the content of the patient's world of experiences.

2. Benchmarks:

1 ———— 2 ———— 3 ———— 4 ———— 5 ———— 6 ———— 7

Therapist did not attend to an assessment of the benchmarks.	Therapist allowed the patient to be vague about benchmarks.	Therapist elicited a report of benchmarks as the patient began to work.
		Therapist elicited a full and complete report of benchmarks at the beginning of the work.

199

Part II. Commitment (Setting the Stage for Work)

3. Collaboration in Task:

1 —— 2 —— 3 —— 4 —— 5 —— 6 —— 7

1	3	5	7
Therapist did not work with the patient to get agreement about the task of the session.	Therapist made a weak attempt to get an agreement about the task for the session.	Therapist worked with the patient to get an agreement about the task for the session.	Therapist was excellent at obtaining a clear agreement about the task for the session.

4. Commitment:

1 —— 2 —— 3 —— 4 —— 5 —— 6 —— 7

1	3	5	7
Therapist did not attempt to obtain a commitment to work from the patient.	Therapist attempted to get a commitment to work on the identified task, but did not attempt to keep the patient focused.	Therapist obtained a commitment to work from the patient.	Therapist very ably obtained a definite, strong, and clear commitment to work from the patient and did not proceed to an experiment without it.

Part III. Doing the Work of the Session

5. Here-and-Now:

1 —— 2 —— 3 —— 4 —— 5 —— 6 —— 7

1	3	5	7
Therapist pulled the patient out of working the here-and-now of the session.	Therapist did not attend to the development of working in the here-and-now of the session.	Therapist brought the patient to working in the here-and-now of the session.	Therapist was especially adept at keeping the patient working in the moment and was immediately aware of when the patient left the moment.

6. What and How:

1 —————— 2 —————— 3 —————— 4 —————— 5 —————— 6 —————— 7

Therapist did not attend to what the patient was doing or how the patient was doing it. Did not bring these phenomena to the patient's awareness.

Therapist made a poor attempt at attending to what the patient was doing and how the patient was doing it.

Therapist attended to what the patient was doing and how the patient was doing it. Therapist helped the patient to become aware of those phenomena.

Therapist very ably attended to what the patient was doing and how the patient was doing it. Adept at bringing those phenomena to the patient's awareness so as to make the patient's process public and clear.

7. Patient's Emotional Configuration:

Rater: Go to the Emotional Configuration Scale (see Appendix 2). From that scale, rank the primary and secondary modes of expression or interruptions on the last below. Rank only two.

A. _____ Primary Anger

Interruptive Behaviors

B. _____ Undifferentiated Anger

C. _____ Retroflected Anger

D. _____ Reflected Anger

E. _____ Projected Anger

F. _____ Defensive Anger

G. _____ Instrumental Anger

Rater: Now go to the scale(s) below that addresses/address the primary mode(s) of expression or interruption and rate the scale(s). Rate no more than the two ranked above.

A. If Primary Anger:

1 ———— 2 ———— 3 ———— 4 ———— 5 ———— 6 ———— 7

Therapist did not recognize and/or attend to the need of the patient to complete the emotional expression.

Therapist was limited in ability to assist patient in the completion of the unfinished primary anger.

Therapist assisted the patient to (1) get a focus for the anger, (2) heighten arousal, (3) move toward expressive release and completion.

Therapist was excellent at recognizing the need of the patient to express unfinished anger and was very skilled in getting the patient to express the primary anger and achieve completion.

B. If Undifferentiated Anger:

1 ———— 2 ———— 3 ———— 4 ———— 5 ———— 6 ———— 7

Therapist did not attempt to bring the mixture of emotions to awareness or to have the patient separate the expression of the mixed emotions.

Therapist was limited in ability to recognize the mixture of emotions and/or ability to have patient separate the expression of the mixed emotions.

Therapist recognized the mixture of simultaneous emotions and created ways for the patient to separate the experience and expression of the different emotions.

Therapist was excellent at bringing the mixed expression of emotions to awareness and very adept at providing experiments that assisted the patient to clearly feel and express each emotion individually, according to the need of the moment.

C. If Retroflected Anger:

1 —— 2 —— 3 —— 4 —— 5 —— 6 —— 7

1	3	5	7
Therapist did not attempt to bring to awareness the constriction of emotion or the turning of anger against the self.	Therapist was limited in ability (1) to bring to awareness either constricted emotion or emotion turned against the self, and (2) to promote the outward expression of anger.	Therapist recognized and brought to awareness the patient's constriction or turning back of emotion. Provided ways to express the anger outward toward appropriate target.	Therapist excellently brought constricting or self-harassing phenomena to awareness. Ably created experiments that allowed focused expression of anger toward appropriate target.

D. If Deflected Anger:

1 —— 2 —— 3 —— 4 —— 5 —— 6 —— 7

1	3	5	7
Therapist did not intervene in deflective behavior of the patient or attempt to get the patient to stay focused on unfinished anger.	Therapist had limited ability to recognize and intervene when the patient deflected away from the experience and expression of unfinished anger.	Therapist brought to awareness the deflective behavior of the patient and encouraged the patient to remain focused on the experience and expression of unfinished anger.	Therapist excellently intervened when the patient moved from the present experience of emotion (anger) and continually brought the patient back to the unfinished emotion, encouraging its experience and expression.

E. If Projected Anger:

1 —— 2 —— 3 —— 4 —— 5 —— 6 —— 7

1	3	5	7
Therapist did not intervene when patient was likely to be projecting his or her anger onto others.	Therapist had limited ability to recognize and intervene when the patient disowned anger and projected it to others.	Therapist created experiments that promoted the ownership of projected anger (emotions).	Therapist excellently separated projected anger from anger at others. Continually helped patient to accept ownership of disowned anger, opening the possibility of honest expression of anger (emotion).

F. If Defensive Anger:

1 —— 2 —— 3 —— 4 —— 5 —— 6 —— 7

1	3	5	7
Therapist did not follow cues that the expressed anger might be masking another, more primary emotion.	Therapist had limited ability to recognize cues of emotions masked by anger. Continued to promote the expression of anger only.	Therapist checked cues that the expressed anger was masking other emotions. Encouraged the expression of the full range of emotions.	Therapist excellently brought to the surface emotions masked by anger and ably assisted the patient to recognize, focus on, and express that masked emotion.

G. If Instrumental Anger:

1 —— 2 —— 3 —— 4 —— 5 —— 6 —— 7

1	3	5	7
Therapist did not recognize that the patient was expressing anger only to blame, change, or punish a significant other, not to finish a troubling emotion.	Therapist had limited ability to bring to awareness the blaming, changing, or punishing behaviors evident in the patient's mode of anger expression.	Therapist brought to awareness the evident intent of the patient to blame, change, or punish another rather than to complete unfinished anger.	Therapist excellently thwarted patient's attempts to use the expression of anger in a manipulative way to blame, change, or punish another. Promoted responsible ownership of anger.

8. Global Assessment of Appropriate Interventions:

1 —— 2 —— 3 —— 4 —— 5 —— 6 —— 7

Therapist's interventions continually missed the patient's emotional configurations.

Therapist's interventions were limited in dealing with the patient's emotional configurations.

Therapist's interventions satisfactorily dealt with the patient's emotional configurations.

Therapist's interventions excellently and continually dealt with the patient's primary emotional configurations.

9. Identification of Introjections against Anger:

1 —— 2 —— 3 —— 4 —— 5 —— 6 —— 7

Therapist did not attend to the beliefs, predictions, and rules of the patient that underlay emotional constriction.

Therapist showed limited ability to bring to awareness the introjected beliefs and rules of the patient.

Therapist brought to awareness the introjected beliefs and rules. Helped patient to resolve conflicts about those introjections.

Therapist excellently and continually probed the introjections of the patient. Ably helped patient know what beliefs and rules were acceptable to the patient. Helped patient see connection between introjections and constrictive behaviors.

10. Heightening Emotional Arousal:

1 —— 2 —— 3 —— 4 —— 5 —— 6 —— 7

Therapist did not attempt to increase the patient's level of emotional arousal.

Therapist made only a weak or occasional attempt to increase the patient's general level of arousal.

Therapist continually attempted to increase the patient's general level of emotional arousal.

Therapist showed excellent and varied skills that continually prompted the patient to stay with and fully experience emerging emotions, bringing them to a full state of arousal.

11. Expressing the Emotion (Releasing):

1 ——— 2 ——— 3 ——— 4 ——— 5 ——— 6 ——— 7

Therapist did not attempt to have patient express the aroused emotions. Promoted talking, not expression.

Therapist made only weak or occasional attempts to have patient express (release) the aroused emotions during the session.

Therapist provided support and methods to express aroused, experienced emotions during the session. Brought the patient to contact and release.

Therapist very ably encouraged the patient to make full contact with a significant other and to find appropriate ways of releasing aroused but constricted emotions during the counseling session.

12. Matching Experiment to Patient:

1 ——— 2 ——— 3 ——— 4 ——— 5 ——— 6 ——— 7

Therapist did not create experiments in line with the patient's present self-support system. That is, experiments either did not heighten experience, or were too strong for the moment.

Therapist inadequately matched the patient and the experiment part of the time.

Therapist adequately matched the patient and the experiment most of the time.

Therapist demonstrated optimal sensitivity to the match between the experiments and the patient's level of self-support.

13. Tracking Emotional Shifts within Work:

1 ——— 2 ——— 3 ——— 4 ——— 5 ——— 6 ——— 7

Therapist did not attend to emotional shifts on the part of the patient.

Therapist superficially attended to the emotional shifts on the part of the patient.

Therapist demonstrated a satisfactory ability to identify and respond to the emotional shifts of the patient.

Therapist demonstrated excellent ability to attend to the emotional shifts on the part of the patient.

14. Tracking Patient's Language:

1 — 2 — 3 — 4 — 5 — 6 — 7

Therapist did not intervene with patient's tentative, blaming, or disowning language.

Therapist made weak interventions with patient's tentative, blaming, or disowning language.

Therapist made adequate interventions with patient's tentative, blaming, or disowning language.

Therapist made excellent interventions with patient's tentative, blaming, or disowning language. Interventions achieved "I" language of ownership.

15. Goodbye:

1 — 2 — 3 — 4 — 5 — 6 — 7

Therapist did not elicit a goodbye to conclude the session's work with a significant other.

Therapist attempted to get a goodbye, but allowed the patient to avoid a conclusion to the work with the significant other.

Therapist obtained an adequate goodbye to conclude the work of the session.

Therapist was very skilled at getting a complete goodbye and attended to any cues that the patient had lingering, unfinished concerns that might block a goodbye.

Part IV. Evaluation of the Work

16. Benchmarks (Psychophysical Sensations):

1 — 2 — 3 — 4 — 5 — 6 — 7

Therapist did not attempt to compare present psychophysical sensations with earlier benchmarks.

Therapist elicited some psychophysical awareness from the patient, but allowed this to be incomplete.

Therapist elicited new psychophysical awareness and compared that awareness with earlier reports.

Therapist was especially able to get a specific, clear, and full report of psychophysical sensations and a specific comparison to earlier reports.

17. Assessment of Work Completed:

1	2	3	4	5	6	7

Therapist did not attempt to elicit the patient's evaluation and understanding of the work completed.

Therapist elicited limited feedback from the patient, but did not ask enough questions to be sure what the patient got or understood from the work.

Therapist elicited feedback from the patient to assess the achievement and understanding of the patient.

Therapist obtained a full assessment of the work, helping to emphasize changes observed during the work.

Part V. Future Planning

18. Homework:

1	2	3	4	5	6	7

Therapist did not work with the patient to devise homework.

Therapist attempted but failed to achieve an agreement with the patient about homework, or the homework was off target.

Therapist and patient achieved an agreement about homework that would enhance the work of the session.

Therapist and patient worked well to develop homework that was either specifically tailored to reinforce, enhance, or celebrate newly completed work, or tailored to keep the patient aware of still unfinished work.

Part VI. Global Ratings

19. Understanding:

1 ———— 2 ———— 3 ———— 4 ———— 5 ———— 6 ———— 7

1–2: Therapist repeatedly failed to understand the patient, and consistently missed the point. Poor empathy skills.

3–4: Therapist was usually able to reflect or rephrase what the patient explicitly said, but failed to respond to more subtle communication. Limited ability to listen and empathize.

5–6: Therapist generally seemed to grasp the patient's "internal reality," as reflected by both what the patient explicitly said and what the patient communicated in more subtle ways. Good ability to listen and empathize.

7: Therapist thoroughly understood the patient's "internal reality" and was adept at communicating this understanding through appropriate verbal responses to the patient. Excellent listening and empathic skills.

20. I–Thou Relationship:

1 ———— 2 ———— 3 ———— 4 ———— 5 ———— 6 ———— 7

1–2: Therapist did not develop an I–thou (horizontal) relationship with the patient—that is, did not enter the world of the patient and accept that world as it is, or was not present to the patient in an authentic way (e.g., the therapist language was vertical).

3–4: Therapist demonstrated a limited ability to evoke an I–thou (horizontal) dialogue.

5–6: Therapist demonstrated satisfactory ability to evoke an I–thou (horizontal) dialogue.

7: Therapist demonstrated an excellent ability to accept the patient's phenomenological world and to reveal himself or herself in authentic ways to the patient, thus opening an authentic I–thou dialogue.

21. Structure:

1 —— 2 —— 3 —— 4 —— 5 —— 6 —— 7

1	3	5	7
Therapist made no attempt to structure the therapy session. Session seemed aimless. Therapist did not appear to have a clear grasp of the steps (map) of the model.	Therapist had significant problems with structure; was unable to differentiate the steps; seemed confused as to what to do next. Time was not used efficiently.	Therapist was successful at using the time well and at following the steps (map) of model.	Therapist was especially good at appropriate use of time, at following the map of the model, and at moving through the steps of the model with smooth transitions.

22. Attending to Process:

1 —— 2 —— 3 —— 4 —— 5 —— 6 —— 7

1	3	5	7
Therapist did not attend to the manner in which the patient expressed himself or herself and did not feed this back.	Therapist attended only in limited times or ways to the patient's process as the patient talked to the therapist.	Therapist attended to the patient's manner of expression, so that both the content and process were addressed.	Therapist frequently and skillfully attended to how the patient expressed himself or herself and ably brought this to awareness, thus enhancing the process and enabling the patient to make informed choices.

Part VII. Additional Considerations

23. Did any special problems arise during the session (e.g., nonadherence to homework, interpersonal issues between therapist and patient, etc.)?

Yes —   No —

24. If yes:

1	2	3	4	5	6	7
Therapist could not deal adequately with problems that arose.		Therapist had limited ability in dealing with the special problems.		Therapist dealt with special problems adequately.		Therapist was very skilled at handling the special problems.

25. Were there any significant or unusual factors in this session that you feel justified the therapist's departure from the FEP approach measured by this scale? If so, explain.

Yes —   No —

26. How would you rate the therapist overall in this session, as one capable of using FEP?

1	2	3	4	5	6	7
Poor	Barely adequate	Mediocre	Satisfactory	Good	Very good	Excellent

27. If you were conducting an outcome study in FEP, do you think you would select this therapist to participate at this time (assuming that this session was typical)?

Definitely not	Probably not	Uncertain borderline	Probably yes	Definitely yes

28. How difficult do you feel this patient was to work with?

1	2	3	4	5	6	7
Not difficult Very receptive			Moderately difficult			Extremely difficult

Emotional Configuration Scale

Directions: The rater is to assess the extent to which the patient presents either the emotional configuration of primary anger or an emotional configuration of an interruption mode (either undifferentiated, retroflected, deflected, projected, defensive, or instrumental anger).

Definitions of each emotional configuration accompany each scale.

Anger is the emotion in key focus, but the rater is to attend to the way in which the patient handles any presenting emotion (hurt, grief, joy, sadness, etc.).

Do not use half numbers.

Answer all items.

You are to work in 10-minute segments. At the end of each segment, stop the tape and make a rating. Enter that rating in the space at the right-hand side. At the end of the session, total the ratings and enter the total score.

At the end of rating all segments, examine your total scores and choose the dominant configuration and the second strongest configuration and enter those on the last page.

Part 1. Unfinished Affect

Primary Anger (Emotion):

Primary emotions are those which rise spontaneously in an uninterrupted cycle of sensation, arousal, expression, contact, and relief. They emerge in the present, rather than being emotions that are chronically "carried around" by the patient. Primary emotions possess sensory and bodily components, and tend to last for relatively short periods of time before they come to completion. The patient clearly owns the emotion as a response to a significant other or another stimulus event.

1	2	3	4	5						
Slight or minimal evidence	Some evidence	Moderate evidence	Fairly strong evidence	Extremely strong evidence						
					Seg 1	Seg 2	Seg 3	Seg 4	Seg 5	Total
					___	___	___	___	___	___

Part 2. Interruptions of the Expression of Affect

The patient may be in a state of unfinished emotional release and may continue in that condition through the unaware use of emotional configurations that prohibit the natural cycle of (1) arousal, (2) expression, and (3) release, recovery, and relief. These interruptions are analogous to the Gestalt "contact boundary interruptions." Each form or configuration is described below.

A. Undifferentiated anger:

This is anger that is mixed with other emotions, often hurt or sadness. The person expresses angry words with a hurt tone of voice or through tears. The person is expressing two emotions simultaneously, by blending them together in a complex emotion expressed as spite, complaining, blaming, or whining.

1	2	3	4	5
Slight or minimal evidence	Some evidence	Moderate evidence	Fairly strong evidence	Extremely strong evidence

B. Retroflected Anger:

In one form, the person squeezes off the expression of emotion. The organism is pushing toward completion, but the person interrupts and constricts the emotional release. Generally the person is unaware of how he or she is constricting and often is unaware of results that have become habituated (e.g., teeth grinding, fixed scowl).

In a second form, the person turns the anger expression against the self rather than directing it to an appropriate target in the environment. Frequent cues are expressions of guilt rather than resentment, expressions of depression rather than anger, or statements of self-harassment. In essence, the person is the "doer" and the "done-to." The retroflection is discernible through contextual cues that make it clear that there is an appropriate target of anger in the person's life.

Seg 1	Seg 2	Seg 3	Seg 4	Seg 5	Total
——	——	——	——	——	——

	Seg 1	Seg 2	Seg 3	Seg 4	Seg 5	Total
	—	—	—	—	—	—

1	2	3	4	5
Slight or minimal evidence	Some evidence	Moderate evidence	Fairly strong evidence	Extremely strong evidence

C. Deflected Anger:

Here the person takes the "heat" off anticipated expression of anger by deflecting in one of two forms: (1) the indiscriminate expression of the anger toward people who are not the primary target; or (2) a shift of focus away from emotional expression. An example of the former is a person who is continually angry, scattering anger on a hit-or-miss basis across situations. An example of the latter is a person who changes the subject, who intellectualizes or rationalizes it away, or who only "talks about" feelings but will not experience the feelings. Deflectors often present themselves as lacking a clear focus, constantly shifting from one subject to another, and/or speaking lots or quickly, so as to avoid the feelings lurking beneath the surface.

1	2	3	4	5
Slight or minimal evidence	Some evidence	Moderate evidence	Fairly strong evidence	Extremely strong evidence

	Seg 1	Seg 2	Seg 3	Seg 4	Seg 5	Total
	—	—	—	—	—	—

D. Defensive Anger:

This is a specific form of deflection in which the person presents anger as a mask for another emotion, such as fear. The patient presents himself or herself as angry at a significant other or at the therapist. But a careful monitoring will reveal verbal or nonverbal signs that another emotion is being masked. Verbal signs often point toward a decision not to allow the self to feel vulnerable again: "I'm not going to let you hurt/scare me again." Nonverbally, the expression of defensive anger often does not fit the context of the life experience described by the person. In context, the expression is out of proportion or does not make sense.

1	2	3	4	5
Slight or minimal evidence	Some evidence	Moderate evidence	Fairly strong evidence	Extremely strong evidence

Seg 1	Seg 2	Seg 3	Seg 4	Seg 5	Total
——	——	——	——	——	——

E. Projected Anger:

The person perceives the anger as being in others in the environment, not in himself or herself. The patient's stance is often one of self-righteousness and/or hypersensitivity to anger in others. The behavior of the patient is reactive rather than active. The language tends to be judgmental and avoids any ownership of anger in the self. Often the context reveals that the reaction of the patient to the significant other is excessive and quickly triggered.

1	2	3	4	5
Slight or minimal evidence	Some evidence	Moderate evidence	Fairly strong evidence	Extremely strong evidence

Seg 1	Seg 2	Seg 3	Seg 4	Seg 5	Total
——	——	——	——	——	——

F. Instrumental Anger:

Here the person expresses anger, but a close listening will reveal that the *goal* is not focused on release so that the organism comes to a state of closure and relaxation. Instead, the person is expressing anger with the intent to blame, change, or punish another. The tone of voice is full of blame. Most statements are prefaced with the word "you" rather than "I" (e.g., "You make me feel . . ."). This anger tends not to come to closure, since the energy is focused on the significant other rather than on the patient's present, moment-to-moment experience. The patient tends not to take responsibility for reactions toward the significant other. The rater will notice that (1) the intent of the patient is not to come to closure, and (2) the focus gets shifted from the patient to the behavior of the significant other.

1	2	3	4	5
Slight or minimal evidence	Some evidence	Moderate evidence	Fairly strong evidence	Extremely strong evidence

Rank the top two configurations here:

— Primary Anger

— Undifferentiated Anger

— Retroflected Anger

— Deflected Anger

— Defensive Anger

— Projected Anger

— Instrumental Anger

	Seg 1	Seg 2	Seg 3	Seg 4	Seg 5	Total
	——	——	——	——	——	——

Name of Rater ——————

Session Rated —————— Patient Name or Number ——————

Session Number ——————

Date of Rating ——————

References

Achterberg-Lawlis, J. (1982). The psychological dimensions of arthritis. *Journal of Consulting and Clinical Psychology, 50*, 984–992.

Adler, A. (1930). *The education of children*. South Bend, IN: Galeway.

Arkowitz, H., & Messer, S. B. (Eds.). (1984). *Psychoanalytic and behavior therapy: Is integration possible?* New York: Plenum.

Bach, G. R., & Wyden, P. (1968). *The intimate enemy*. New York: William Morrow.

Beck, A. T., Rush, A. J., Shaw, B. F., & Emery, G. (1979). *Cognitive therapy of depression*. New York: Guilford Press.

Berger, M., & Dammann, C. (1982). Live supervision as context, treatment and training. *Family Process, 21*(3), 337–344.

Beutler, L. E. (1983). *Eclectic psychotherapy: A systematic approach*. New York: Pergamon Press.

Beutler, L. E. (1986). Systematic eclectic psychotherapy: Growing into separation. In J. C. Norcross (Ed.), *Casebook of eclectic psychotherapy* (pp. 53–90). New York:

Beutler, L. E., Crago, M., & Arizmendi, T. G. (1986). Research on therapist variables in psychotherapy. In S. L. Garfield & A. E. Bergin (Eds.), *Handbook of psychotherapy and behavior change* (3rd ed., pp. 257–310). New York: Wiley.

Beutler, L. E., Engle, D., Oró-Beutler, M. E., Daldrup, R., & Meredith, K. (1986). Inability to express intense affect: A common link between depression and pain? *Journal of Consulting and Clinical Psychology, 54*, 752–759.

Beutler, L. E., Frank, M., Scheiber, S. C., Calvert, S., & Gaines, J. (1984). Comparative effects of group psychotherapies in a short-term inpatient setting: An experience with deterioration effects. *Psychiatry, 47*, 66–76.

Beutler, L. E., & Mitchell, R. (1981). Differential psychotherapy outcome in depressed and impulsive patients as a function of analytic and experiential treatment procedures. *Psychiatry, 44*, 279–306.

Bohart, A. C. (1977). Role playing and interpersonal conflict resolution. *Journal of Counseling Psychology, 24*, 15–24.

Calvert, S. C., Beutler, L. E., & Crago, M. (in press). Psychotherapy outcome as a function of therapist–patient matching on selected variables. *Journal of Social and Clinical Psychology*.

Childress, R., & Gillis, J. S. (1977). A study of pretherapy role induction as an influence process. *Journal of Clinical Psychology, 33*, 540–544.

Corsini, R. J. (1981). *Handbook of innovative psychotherapy*. New York: Wiley.

Daldrup, R. J., & Gust, D. (1988). *Freedom from anger: The Daldrup method*. Aptos, CA: Living Business Press.

Dahlstrom, W. G., Welsh, G. S., & Dahlstrom, L. E. (1972). *An MMPI handbook; Vol. 1 Clinical interpretation*. Minneapolis: University of Minnesota Press.

Dollard, J., & Miller, N. E. (1950). *Personality and psychotherapy: An analysis in terms of learning, thinking and culture.* New York: McGraw-Hill.

Doyle, W. E., Foreman, M. E., & Wales, E. (1977). Effects of supervision in the training of non-professional crisis intervention counselors. *Journal of Counseling Psychology, 24,* 72–78.

Enright, J. (1970). An introduction to Gestalt techniques. In J. Fagan & I. L. Shepherd (Eds.), *Gestalt therapy now* (pp. 40–68). Palo Alto, CA: Science & Behavior Books.

Fagan, J., & Shepherd, I. L. (1970). *Life techniques in Gestalt therapy.* New York: Harper & Row.

Falloon, I. R. H. (Ed.). (1985). *Family management of schizophrenia.* Baltimore: Johns Hopkins University Press.

Feder, B. (1980). Gestalt therapy training in group. In B. Feder & R. Ronall (Eds.), *Beyond the hot seat: Gestalt Approaches to group* (pp. 167–175). New York: Brunner/Mazel.

Feder, B., & Ronall, R. (Eds.). (1980). *Beyond the hot seat: Gestalt approaches to group.* New York: Brunner/Mazel.

Frances, A., Clarkin, J., & Perry, S. (1984). *Differential therapeutics in psychiatry.* New York: Brunner/Mazel.

Frew, J. E. (1983). Clarity of boundary condition in interpersonal contact. *The Gestalt Journal, 6,* 117–123.

Garfield, S. L. (1978). Research on client variables in psychotherapy. In S. L. Garfield & A. E. Bergin (Eds.), *Handbook of psychotherapy and behavior change: An empirical analysis* (2nd ed., pp. 191–232). New York: Wiley.

Garfield, S. L. (1980). *Psychotherapy: An eclectic approach.* New York: Wiley.

Garfield, S. L. (1986). Research on client variables in psychotherapy. In S. L. Garfield & A. E. Bergin (Eds.), *Handbook of psychotherapy and behavior change* (3rd ed., pp. 213–256). New York: Wiley.

Garfield, S. L., & Kurtz, R. (1977). A study of eclectic views. *Journal of Consulting and Clinical Psychology, 45,* 78–73.

Gendlin, E. T. (1968). Client-centered: The experiential response. In E. F. Hammer (Ed.), *Use of interpretation in treatment* (pp. 208–227). New York: Grune & Stratton.

Gendlin, E. T. (1978). *Focusing.* New York: Everest House.

Goulding, M., & Goulding, R. (1979). *Changing lives through redecision therapy.* New York: Brunner/Mazel.

Greenberg, L. S. (1979). Resolving splits: Use of the two-chair technique. *Psychotherapy: Theory, Research, and Practice, 16,* 310–318.

Greenberg, L. S. (1980). Training counselors in Gestalt methods. *Canadian Counselor, 14*(3), 174–180.

Greenberg, L. S., & Clarke, K. M. (1979). Differential effects of the two-chair experiment and empathic reflections at a conflict marker. *Journal of Counseling Psychology, 26,* 1–8.

Greenberg, L. S., & Dompierre, L. (1981). The specific effects of Gestalt two-chair dialogue on intrapsychic conflict in counselling. *Journal of Counseling Psychology, 28,* 288–294.

Greenberg, L. S., & Rice, L. N. (1981). The specific effects of a Gestalt intervention. *Psychotherapy: Theory, Research, and Practice, 18,* 31–37.

Greenberg, L. S., & Safran, J. D. (1981). Encoding and cognitive therapy: Changing what clients attend to. *Psychotherapy: Theory, Research, and Practice, 18,* 163–169.

Greenberg, L. S., & Safran, J. D. (1984). Integrating affect and cognition: A perspective on the process of therapeutic change. *Cognitive Therapy and Research, 8*(6), 559–578.

Greenberg, L. S., & Safran, J. D. (1987). *Emotion in psychotherapy: Affect, cognition, and the process of change.* New York: Guilford Press.

Greenberg, L. S., & Sarkissian, M. G. (1984). Evaluation of counselor training in Gestalt methods. *Counselor Education and Supervision, 24,* 328–340.

Harman, R. L. (1977). Gestalt awareness training for graduate students. *Counselor Education and Supervision. 15,* 140–144.

Harman, R. L., & Tarleton, K. B. (1983). Gestalt therapy supervision. *The Gestalt Journal*, *6*(1), 29–37.

Heimelstein, P. (1982). A comprehensive bibliography of Gestalt therapy (Ms. 2421). *JSAS Catalogue of Selected Documents in Psychology*, *12*(1), 9.

Hill, D. C. (1986). *The relationship of process to outcome in brief expressive psychotherapy.*

Hoehn-Saric, R., Frank, J. D., Imber, S. D., Nash, E. H., Stone, A. R., & Battle, C. C. (1964). Systematic preparation of patients for psychotherapy: I. Effects on therapy, behavior and outcome. *Journal of Psychiatric Research, 2,* 267–281.

Hoehn-Saric, R., Liberman, B., Imber, S. D., Stone, A. R., Pande, S. K., & Frank, J. D. (1972). Arousal and attitude change in neurotic patients. *Archives of General Psychiatry, 26,* 51–56.

Holiman, M., & Engle, D. (in press). Guidelines for training in advanced Gestalt therapy skills. *Journal for Specialists in Group Work.*

Kaplan, A. G., Brooks, B., McComb, A. L., Shapiro, E. R., & Sodano, A. (1983). Women and anger in psychotherapy. *Women and Therapy, 2,* 29–40.

Kaplan, M. L., & Kaplan, N. R. (1985). The linearity issue and Gestalt therapy's theory of experiential organization. *Psychotherapy: Theory, Research, and Practice, 22,* 5–15.

Kaszniak, A. W., & Allender, J. (1985). Psychological assessment of depression in older adults. In G. M. Chaisson-Stewart (Ed.), *Depression in the elderly: An interdisciplinary approach* (pp. 107–160). New York: Wiley.

Kaszniak, A. W., Sadeh, M., & Stern, L. Z. (1985). Differentiating depression from organic brain syndromes in older age. In G. M. Chaisson-Stewart (Ed.), *Depression in the elderly: An interdisciplinary approach* (pp. 161–192). New York: Wiley.

Kelley, M. D. (1971). Reinforcement in microcounseling. *Journal of Counseling Psychology, 13,* 268–272.

Lambert, M. J., & DeJulio, S. S. (1978, March). *The relative importance of client, therapist, and technique variables as predictors of psychotherapy outcome: The place of therapist "non-specific" factors.* Paper presented at the annual midwinter meeting of the Division of Psychotherapy, American Psychological Association, Scottsale, AZ.

Lambert, M. J., Shapiro, D. A., & Bergin, A. E. (1986). The effectiveness of psychotherapy. In S. L. Garfield & A. E. Bergin (Eds.), *Handbook of psychotherapy and behavior change* (3rd ed., pp. 157–212). New York: Wiley.

Lauver, P. J., Holiman, M. A., & Kazama, S. W. (1982). Counseling as battleground: Client as enemy. *Personnel and Guidance Journal, 61,* 99–101.

Lazarus, A. A. (1981). *The practice of multi-modal therapy.* New York: McGraw-Hill.

Leventhal, H., & Everhart, D. (1979). Emotions, pain and physical illness. In C. E. Izard (Ed.), *Emotions in personality and psychopathology* (pp. 261–299). New York: Plenum Press.

Levitsky, A., & Perls, F. S. (1970). The rules and games of Gestalt therapy. In J. Fagan & I. L. Shepherd (Eds.), *Life techniques in Gestalt therapy* (pp. 93–107). New York: Harper & Row.

Lieberman, M. A., Yalom, I. D., & Miles, M. B. (1973). *Encounter groups: First facts.* New York: Basic Books.

Mahrer, A. R. (1980). The treatment of cancer through experiential psychotherapy. *Psychotherapy: Theory, Research, and Practice, 17,* 335–342.

Mahrer, A. R. (1983). *Experiential psychotherapy: Basic practices.* New York: Brunner/Mazel.

Mahrer, A. R. (1986). *Therapeutic experiencing: The process of change.* New York: Norton.

Mahrer, A. R. (in press). Existential psychology and psychotherapy. In R. J. Hunter (Ed.), *Dictionary of pastoral care and counseling.* Nashville, TN: Abingdon.

Mahrer, A. R., & Gervaize, P. A. (1984). An integrative review of strong laughter in psychotherapy: What it is and how it works. *Psychotherapy: Theory, Research, and Practice, 21,* 510–516.

Mahrer, A. R., Nifakis, D. J., Abhukara, L., & Sterner, I. (1984). Microstrategies in psychotherapy: The patterning of sequential therapist statements. *Psychotherapy: Theory, Research, and Practice, 21,* 465–472.

Matarazzo, R. G., & Patterson, D. R. (1986). Methods of teaching therapeutic skill. In S. L. Garfield & A. E. Bergin (Eds.), *Handbook of psychotherapy and behavior change* (3rd ed., pp. 821–843). New York: Wiley.

Megargee, E. I., Cook, P. E., & Mendelsohn, G. A. (1967). Development and validation of an MMPI scale of assaultiveness in overcontrolled individuals. *Journal of Abnormal Psychology, 72,* 519–528.

Megargee, E. L., & Hokanson, J. E. (1979). *The dynamics of aggression.* New York: Harper & Row.

Mintz, E. E. (1983). Gestalt approaches to supervision. *The Gestalt Journal, 6,* 17–27.

Nichols, M. P. (1974). Outcome of brief cathartic psychotherapy. *Journal of Consulting and Clinical Psychology, 42,* 403–410.

Nichols, M. P., & Bierenbaum, H. (1978). Success of cathartic therapy as a function of patient variables. *Journal of Clinical Psychology, 34,* 726–728.

Norcross, J. C. (1986). Eclectic psychotherapy: an introduction and overview. In J. C. Norcross (Ed.), *Handbook of eclectic psychotherapy* (pp. 3–24). New York: Brunner/Mazel.

Oaklander, V. (1978). *Windows to our children.* Moab, UT: Real People Press.

Orlinsky, D. E., & Howard, K. I. (1986). Process and outcome in psychotherapy. In S. L. Garfield & A. E. Bergin (Eds.), *Handbook of psychotherapy and behavior change* (3rd ed., pp. 311–384). New York: Wiley.

Payne, P., Winter, D., & Perry, M. A. (1975). Modeling and instructions in training for counselor empathy. *Journal of Consulting Psychology, 22,* 173–179.

Perls, F. S. (1947). *Ego, hunger and aggression.* London: Allen & Unwin.

Perls, F. S. (1973). *The Gestalt approach and eyewitness to therapy.* Palo Alto, CA: Science & Behavior Books.

Perls, F. S. (1969). *Gestalt therapy verbatim.* New York: Bantam Books.

Perls. F. S., Hefferline, R., & Goodman, P. (1951). *Gestalt therapy.* New York: Julian Press.

Plutchick, R. (1980). *Emotion: A psychoevolutionary synthesis.* New York: Harper & Row.

Polster, E. A. (1985). Imprisoned in the present. *The Gestalt Journal, 8*(1), 5–22.

Polster, E. A., & Polster, M. (1973). *Gestalt therapy integrated.* New York: Brunner/Mazel.

Polster, E. A., & Polster, M. (1976). Therapy without resistance: Gestalt therapy. In A. Burton (Eds.), *What makes behavior change possible?* (pp. 259–277). New York: Brunner/Mazel.

Prochaska, J. O., & Norcross, J. C. (1983). Contemporary psychotherapists: A national survey of characteristics, practices, orientations, and attitudes. *Psychotherapy: Theory, Research, and Practice, 20,* 161–173.

Rhyne, J. (1984). *The Gestalt art experience: Creative process and expressive therapy.* Chicago: Magnolia Street.

Rice, L. N., & Greenberg, L. S. (1984). *Patterns of change.* New York: Guilford Press.

Roden, R. B. (1985). *Two techniques for eliciting emotional arousal: An analog study of catharsis.* Unpublished doctoral dissertation, University of Arizona.

Rogers, R. (1983). The role of retroflection in psychogenic pain: A treatment perspective. *Psychotherapy: Theory, Research, and Practice, 20,* 435–440.

Rubin, T. I. (1969). *The angry book.* New York: Collier Books.

Satir, V. (1967). *Conjoint family therapy.* Palo Alto, CA: Science & Behavior Books.

Satir, V. (1972). *Peoplemaking.* Palo Alto, CA: Science & Behavior Books.

Scheff, T. J. (1979). *Catharsis in healing, ritual, and drama.* Berkeley: University of California Press.

Schramski, T. G., Feldman, C. A., Harvey, D. R., & Holiman, M. (1984). A comparative evaluation of group treatments in an adult correctional facility. *Journal of Group Psychotherapy, Psychodrama and Sociometry*, *36*(4), 133–147.

Seltzer, L. F. (1984). Role of paradox in Gestalt therapy and techniques. *The Gestalt Journal*, *7*(2), 31–42.

Seltzer, L. F. (1986). *Paradoxical strategies in pscyhotherapy: A comprehensive overview and guidebook*. New York: Wiley.

Simonton, O. C., Simonton, S., & Creighton, J. (1978). *Getting well again*. Los Angeles: J. P. Tarcher.

Smith, E. W. L. (1986). Retroflection: The forms of nonenactment. *The Gestalt Journal*, *9*, 36–54.

Stevens, J. O. (1971). *Awareness: Exploring, experimenting, experiencing*. Moab, UT: Real People Press.

Strupp, H. H. (1981). Toward the refinement of time-limited psychotherapy. In S. H. Budman (Ed.), *Forms of brief psychotherapy* (pp. 219–242). New York: Guilford Press.

Strupp, H. H., & Binder, J. L. (1984). *Psychotherapy in a new key: A guide to time limited dynamic therapy*. New York: Basic Books.

Strupp, H. H., & Bloxon, A. L. (1973). Preparing lower-class patients for group psychotherapy: Development and evaluation of a role-induction film. *Journal of Consulting and Clinical Psychology*, *41*, 373–384.

Swanson, J. L. (1982). The paradox of the safe emergency. *The Gestalt Journal*, *5*, 57–64.

Tobin, S. A., (1975). Saying goodbye in Gestalt therapy. In J. O. Stevens (Ed.), *Gestalt is* (pp. 117–128). Moab, UT: Real People Press.

Van de Riet, V., Korb, M., & Gorrell, J. J. (1980). *Gestalt therapy: An introduction*. New York: Pergamon Press.

Wachtel, P. L. (1977). *Psychoanalysis and behavior therapy: Towards an integration*. New York: Basic Books.

Weeks, G. R., & L'Abate, L. (1982). *Paradoxical psychotherapy: Theory and practice with individuals, couples, and families*. New York: Brunner/Mazel.

Weissman, M. M., Prusoff, B. A., Thompson, W. D., Harding, P. S., & Meyers, J. K. (1978). Social adjustment by self-report in a community sample and in psychiatric outpatients. *Journal of Nervous and Mental Disease*, *166*, 317–326.

Welsh, G. S. (1952). An anxiety index and an internalization ratio for the MMPI. *Journal of Consulting Psychology*, *16*, 65–72.

Woollams, S., & Brown, M. (1978). *Transactional analysis*. Dexter, MI: Herron Valley Institute Press.

Yalom, I. D., Houts, P. S., Newell, G., & Rank, K. H. (1967). Preparation of patients for group therapy. *Archives of General Psychiatry*, *17*, 416–427.

Yalom, I. D. (1975). *The theory and practice of group psychotherapy*. New York: Basic Books.

Yost, E., Beutler, L. E., Corbishley, A., & Allender, J. (1986). *Group cognitive therapy: A treatment approach for depressed older adults*. New York: Pergamon Press.

Zajonc, R. (1980). Feeling and thinking: Preferences need no inferences. *American Psychologist*, *35*, 151–175.

Zinker, J. (1977). *Creative process in Gestalt therapy*. New York: Brunner/Mazel.

Index